Where Does the Parent Stand?

Where Does the Parent STAND?

Tolerance Lamar

WHERE DOES THE PARENT STAND?

iUniverse books may be ordered through booksellers or by contacting:

iUniverse
1663 Liberty Drive
Bloomington, IN 47403
www.iuniverse.com
1-800-Authors (1-800-288-4677)

ISBN: 978-1-4759-8086-8 (sc)
ISBN: 978-1-4759-8085-1 (hc)
ISBN: 978-1-4759-8138-4 (e)

Library of Congress Control Number: 2013904261

Print information available on the last page.

iUniverse rev. date: 07/17/2015

CONTENTS

ACKNOWLEDGMENT

In 1996 I started writing this memoir. It has been a pleasure to see that by the age of 49, year 2014, my long-term goal of publishing this book is finally a reality. To be honest, on some occasions, I felt like I wasn't going to see such a day. It has been a long journey, indeed.

First, I want to thank Jehovah the Almighty God for giving me the strength to get up every morning. I'm truly grateful because when I started this project, I was a ninth grade drop-out who wrote in big, bulky letters. Throughout the years, God has given me the ambition to learn to write, edit, and revise this book during my small amount of free time. Now, I am proud to say that I can now read and write proficiently.

I want to give thanks to my wife Sybil Tillman. When I was incarcerated in 1998, she supported me by supplying me with pens and erasers that were prohibited in the prison compound. She encouraged me to resume writing this biography and she found a way to help me. I thank you Sybil, for your devotion.

Likewise, I want to thank at the time my girl friend Tonita Williams. Although we gave each other hell from time to time and didn't tolerate much from one another; she managed to not argue with me when I was writing.

I also want to thank Tonita's daughters, Carrisa Barnes and Jasmine Williams. Carrisa is now sixteen and smarter than ever. She has periodically helped me spell words I wasn't sure of, and helped me text and navigate the computer when asked. Jasmine seventeen would see me on the computer working on this book for hours; she'd come and kiss me on the jaw followed by a hug, asking how the book was coming along. That alone motivated me to keep going. Thank you.

I would like to give a special thanks to my younger sister Keitha and to Ginger Carlson. Keitha heard me stressing about getting up the money to have this book professionally edited. Without me asking, nor acknowledging what was in her heart, she provided the funds. That was grand, and I thank you dearly. Ginger Carlson proofread the manuscript for this book. She pointed out grammatical as well as spelling errors the Elite Proofreader had missed. I wished I had known of you earlier Ms. Carlson, a fine Proofreader indeed.

I also appreciate my friends Robert Clarke, Antonio Livingston, and Anthony Terlizzi. Both Robert and Antonio gave me editing advice for the front cover of this book. For eight years, my Italian friend and ex-boss Anthony had financially helped me by providing me daily work. You and your family have certainly seen me through. I thank all of you.

I also want to thank my children, my flesh and blood, especially Toler and Tina for helping me to realize the importance to write this book.

I want to thank my parents for creating 'the need' to write this book. Unfortunately, my great grandparents couldn't, or just didn't, take the time to raise my parents properly so that they could be a good example for their children. I really can't explain way my parents were so chaotic and selfish, but I do know that their behavior negatively affected the lives of my two sisters' and I. I just thank God that Keitha and Rena and I had enough willpower to shake off the terrible things that our parents took us through, so that we could become law-abiding citizens.

Finally, I want to thank my haters, whom likes to sit around and talk negative about me lets me know I'm doing something right, and I thank you.

I hope that all my readers find their own inspiration to achieve their long and short term goals and dreams. Enjoy.

PREFACE

My name is Tolerance Lamar and I hope that my story will help you realize how important it is to read and apply what you have learned in which will help you with the different aspects of your life. There is one powerful phrase you can read and apply and will help you do well in life is called The Golden Rule: Do unto others as you would have them do unto you. However, one would have to be taught, or treated well to exude good treatment to others. Unfortunately, the world today is lacking goodness. There are too many ignorant people becoming parents. I just don't know how else to say it.

When it comes to parenting, I truly believe that a child's upbringing plays a large part in the reason why the world is so dangerous and corrupt. Each year babies are being born to people who are not fit to raise chickens, much less human beings.

There were times when I've felt a little uncomfortable writing because of some of the bad circumstances and vulgar language that was said. It all seemed okay back when it was happening, but now, as an adult, I recognize how crazy parts of my life were. I faced a decision when writing this: either sugarcoat this book and make it a fictional story full of partial truths and partial lies or I could tell it like it happened and ensure that this book remains a nonfiction account of truth and facts. I chose to tell it like it was said and done, and I hope that someone is able to learn from my mistakes and not become a statistic.

I hope this book leaves you with the realization that children of all races should be raised with the utmost care and that disciplining our children is tantamount to the structure of a peaceful society, as well as healthy relationships between spouses.

The primary reason I wrote this novel is to help my children understand who their father is and what I stand for. I pray that my children forgive me for the pain I may have caused them, and that I love them. I pray they make better decisions in life, and not ever, experience the painful ride and setbacks that I endured.

CHAPTER 1

AUGUST 17, 1980
TAMPA FLORIDA

On a hot, sunny day, seven days after my 15th birthday, I officially became a father to a beautiful baby boy. Ms. Bennett, Roxann's mother smiled as she announced that I was a daddy. I was excited by the news as I headed out the front door. As I walked through the hot sand and made my way home, I couldn't help but notice that this was not the place for a child to live. As a young teen, it was hard to see my little 3-year-old sister, Keitha playing outside. The dirty hot projects, what we called Central Park, were a chokehold on my pride. The thought of my baby sister playing with my son in the backyard of a fifteen by fifteen foot area in hot sand, peppered with patches of dead grass surrounded by five foot of concrete blocks made me wish that I was rich instead of poor. The crack heads and drug dealers walked about as if they were content.

As I entered my mom's apartment, I grimaced at the dirty kitchen that was infested with roaches. It was always humid and I felt swallowed by the dirty walls and worn furniture. My mother's home was not like my father's apartment. He too was poor and lived in a low income apartment across town, but his apartment was clean, comfortable and well-furnished.

I called for Rena, my 17-year-old sister from the staircase, but there was no answer. I climbed the stairs and went into the bathroom. As I splashed water onto my face, I could hear my mother calling hogs, *snoring*, from her bedroom. There was no need to wake her and tell her that Roxann had a boy. She was too drunk off of her cheap gin to give a sincere response. So, I left the house and headed for the bus stop. When I got there, I lit my celebration cigar and waited anxiously for a ride to the hospital so I could welcome my son to the world. While traveling on the bus, I had a strange feeling of importance that I, Tolerance Lamar, at the age of 15, was now the youngest father in Tampa Bay. That day I named my son after myself, and as I held him, I was suddenly struck with an overwhelming feeling of the need to make sure that my son had the best of everything that life had to offer. However, my son's mother Roxann and I had to live with my mother. In order to get our own place, I had to find a job somewhere, somehow, even if it meant quitting school. I began to feel the pressure knowing Roxann and my son depended on me.

I vowed to myself that I would go looking for a job that following day and if I didn't find one, I would keep looking until I did. Even if I couldn't find one, I knew that I had darker alternatives. At the tender age of 8, I learned from my father how to be a thief. I know that may sound strange, but when I was a kid, my dad would yell for my sister and me to get in the car. He would then drive us to a store of his choice, which was usually a small grocery market or convenience store. My sister and I would go into the aisle and stuff canned goods and other food items into our clothes and walk out. We would hit two to three stores, until the backseat of the car and its floor was full.

I remember one day we were out stealing and we stopped at a convenient store. We parked in front of the door that you go in at. Dad told my sister and me to stay in the car. He went inside to steal a case of beer. On his way out the cashier hit the electronic locks, locking him inside. I remember hearing the click sound as the door locked. I just stared at the door with my mouth open. I was like, oh boy, this is not good. Suddenly the door flew open and out came our Dad with blood on his clothes and his open pocket knife in hand. He was limping as he dashed into the car and fled the scene. He said nothing to my sister and I, it was a silent ride back. Right to this day I still don't know what happened inside that store. I do know one thing, I'm glad my sister and I weren't in the store to see it.

During that time, we were actually living with my father's mother, our Grandma Stacey. She was down to earth, but very stern. When she told us to do something, she expected it done promptly. Grandma reminded me of the dark skinned lady that played in *Beloved*; the movie with Oprah Winfrey and Danny Glover. Oprah played as a slave named Sethe, whom escaped from a cruel Kentucky plantation. Sethe recalled this elderly dark skinned woman who would preach in the woods to her slave friends and family; she would have them dancing and singing in the woods. Grandma Stacey looked just like that old woman.

I recall one night my dad's television blew out on him.

He must have been complaining to his mother about it because she yelled, "Go steal you a TV!"

I was smart enough to comprehend that Grandma Stacey was the root behind the stealing, which back in the day, everyone called it hustling or hit a lick. Although I was more than willing to work to support my family, I knew that if push came to shove, I would hustle or hit a lick, if you will.

Months passed and nothing was going as planned. I could not find a job because I was an underage dropout. I did end up stealing to get by, but even that had decreased because the stores were tightening up their security. I had been caught twice and was sent to W.T. Edwards Juvenile Detention Center for twenty one days on each charge. At that time, W.T. Edwards was easy time because the girls that were locked up could go to the meetings with the boys. Although the girls were fun, that place wasn't for me and I didn't want to wind up there again. I couldn't fathom the thought of not being around to look after my son and Roxann. They meant the world to me.

Roxann and I were in it together and we did our best to make it work. When our son was born, she was seventeen, almost two years older than me. She stood about 5 foot 4 inches and 110 pounds soak and wet; her skin tone was smooth brown. What she lacked in height and weight, she more than made up for in feistiness and frankness.

I was bright skin in complexion an only stood 5 foot 5 inches and 158 pounds. We both are short in stature and I was also short in temper as well. Roxann's feistiness and frankness to talk crap to me would sometimes result to her running across the field in full speed like a Grey Hound; and I was right in her tracks like a Rhodesian Ridgeback snapping at her buttocks. I didn't like when my woman got too mouthy with me and she knew it. Anyway, we both attended Monroe Junior High together. Many times, we would skip school and play cards, gambling from dusk till dawn. We pretty much did what we wanted to do, which eventually led to our predicament.

While we were a good pair, our relationship was turbulent. I was Roxann's first and only, and I wanted to keep it that way. Yet I was promiscuous during our relationship. One day, she got back at me by having an affair with my blood brother Jensen. Jensen was also a couple of years older than I. The fact that I had only sisters and no brothers, I thought Jensen would be a good friend; a pair of brothers if you will. With that in mind, we performed a ritual to become blood brothers. We sliced a thin incision into our index finger and then tightly held our hands together, allowing our blood to merge. I was the doctor who couldn't take his own medicine. In a jealous rage, I attacked Jensen when I learned he had relations with my Roxann, and that's when I discovered something about fighting and that the knee is powerful, because I got my ass whipped with a capital W.

The first thing Jensen did was grab my hair, which was lengthy at that time. When he got a good grip onto my hair, he repeatedly drove his knee into my stomach and upper torso while holding down my head. I was good and dizzy by the time he let me go. Embarrassed, I stumbled away looking like a drunken Don King. From that experience, I promised myself that I would never pursue a fight with a head full of hair and, not to mention, trust a blood brother again.

Such was the nature of my relationship with Roxann, but my problems didn't end with joblessness and girlfriend issues. Not long after getting my ass whipped, my 21-year-old sister on my father side named Angela, suddenly fell ill and was admitted in the hospital. Within a few hours, she was pronounced dead. That was another big pill for me to swallow. Life seems to be unfair, and it is, but it is something we should not take for granted.

When I turned 16, my life seemed to go down a more destructive path. I didn't finish school, but I graduated from stealing food, diapers and clothes to breaking and entering and auto theft. Things got so bad and desperate that I even tried to snatch a purse and failed. The little old lady held a surprisingly tight hold on her purse as I dragged her, and the look that was on her face made me let go and flee the scene. I vowed to never do that again. Even today, years and years later, the look of shock and sadness on that old lady's face is something I will never forget.

Along with my increasing desperation, my juvenile criminal record was increasing as well. Eventually, I found myself partying with the boys in the hood and the consequences of this led to numerous street fights. I got into fights to earn respect from both the guys and gals. Most of the girls in the hood admired how I stood my ground. However, some girls would flirt with me, telling me that I was a pretty boy with hands. The girls that admired me were pretty much the ones that dropped their panties. It was this type of temptation that made it easy for me to sometimes forget how bad things really were.

Before I knew it I started getting violence charges against me such as concealed firearm and assault charges. These charges came about because the thugs were growing bigger and stronger and would sometimes pick fights with me. Consequently, at the age of 16, with a little juggling by the States Attorney, I was certified and bound over as an adult and thrown in jail with some of the stinkiest, greasiest and most ruthless drug-crazed adults I have ever seen. This was enough to scare me straight, at least for a while. I needed to get out of there, and I knew that my mom and Roxann didn't have money to bond me out. Their little welfare checks would be almost gone by the time they hit the mailbox. Thanks to my Dad, I was eventually bonded out. Upon walking outside the jail house, my father greeted me with a pat on the back as if he had my back.

I was put on probation and yet, my stealing did not stop. In fact, my experience in the county jail ultimately didn't deter me from a life of crime; it inspired me to be more cautious and find more clever ways to get over. Furthermore, shortly after my release, I found out that the mother of my partner-in-crime, Larry, was trying to convince him that I was bad news and that he should stay away from me. This left me feeling hurt and angry. It stung knowing that his mom thought badly of me; I was getting the bad rap when she did not see that her son was not the little angel that she thought him to be. Hell, to be honest, Larry was the master mind of most of what I did. He was the one who knew what crime to commit and where. And, on top of that, he did not care what it took to get what he wanted. That's why we made such good partners-in-crime; I was bold and he was cold. However, Larry preferred stealing cars and breaking into stuff, while I felt more comfortable shoplifting. I remember walking through the projects to Larry's house; and I called out Larry's name to let him know that I was outside. His mother came to the door and confronted me about leading her son down the wrong path.

"It's not me! It's your badass son!" I said angrily before walking off.

Shortly thereafter, I was arrested on a grand theft charge that violated my probation. Again, I was reinstated. It was this situation that convinced me that my five-finger discounts had to stop. There had to be a better way to make it in this concrete jungle.

Days passed and in the midst of my struggles, I was informed of some shocking news. Marshall, a girl I once dated, was murdered by her estranged boyfriend. She had beautiful brown skin with unusually long natural hair, and was now dead from a bullet to her head. A couple of days before that, a woman was found in the park naked and dead with a soda bottle stuck up into her vagina. This, along with a string of other brutal murders that were committed, made me realize how cruel people can be. Black on black violent crimes had become a norm and I knew that I didn't want to grow old in this neighborhood. I began to try to figure out how to escape.

Finally, I landed a job at Morrison Cafeteria. Later, I landed a second job at a local bar as a DJ. I was pretty proud of myself; things were looking up. As for Rena, who was now 19, she had become a mom to a baby boy, by a young man named Don. Don and I befriended each other shortly after meeting. He agreed to open and DJ until I got off work from Morrison.

Disc jockeying at the age of 17 was beyond exciting and even though I was underage, my boss didn't mind. All he wanted was a DJ who could bring in a crowd and I most certainly did that. My DJ name was T.T., better known as Terribly Terrific. On occasions, my mom and dad would come out to drink and dance the night away. My paycheck didn't amount to much, due to my bar tabs, but we all had big fun.

The good time came to an end one night when Don forcibly lifted me up off the ground by my collar and threatened to kick my ass for no apparent reason. The crowd had been good that night. Everyone was jamming off of the latest song by Barbara Mason, *Another Man Is Beating My Time*. Next thing I knew Don jacked me up; my hand hit the turntable and the music stopped to a scratching halt, everybody turned toward the disturbance. Don was well over 6 foot tall and was very muscular, so I had to think fast. I tried to reason with him.

"Don! What is wrong with you? Put me down and tell me what I did!"

Don proceeded to drag me out the back door of the club by my collar. As he was pulling me, I was pleading for him to let me go, while at the same time, I was easing my pocketknife out of my back pocket.

Click! *His ass was mine*!

I sliced Don across the chest and he let me go turning to get away from me; when he turned I tried to slice his ear off. I was so mad that I was crying, and slung a couple of pool balls at him as he dashed around the pool table and out the front door. Finally I cooled down and started packing up my equipment when Don returned with the cops. He was wrapped with ace bandages like a mummy from Egypt.

I grimaced as he pointed his finger toward me to be seized. In a flash, I was arrested and charged with a violent crime. My probation had been violated; therefore, there would be no bond.

After three weeks sitting in jail, I finally went to court. My father was there to speak on my behalf. Thankfully, my probation was extended with a written order to stay out of bars. Morrison Café was my hope to have something positive going for me. My request to resume work was denied, I was terminated. So there I was, right back in the same old ball game, a game that I was getting tired of playing. I was frustrated and I knew that

I was walking on thin ice. A judge had already become tired of Larry's behavior and sentenced him to prison. I knew I had to stay out of trouble or I could easily be next. I didn't know what else to do but daydream and hope for a miracle.

Nineteen eighty three was a busy year. I was 17 when Roxann gave birth to a baby daughter, whom we named Tina. In addition to that, in the same year, I fathered another daughter by another woman, whom I named Theresa. Theresa's mother was Roxann's next door neighbor, Elizabeth.

Elizabeth was a 15-year-old girl from the Carolinas. She was a dark, gorgeous girl about 5 foot 7 inches, was big-boned, had a curvy frame, weighed about 140 pounds, and was crowned with shiny, thick, shoulder length hair. Hell, I didn't even know of her until she started whistling at me from her bedroom window; which was fifteen foot from Roxann's window. It seemed as though Elizabeth staked out and watched to see when she would have an opportunity to seduce me with bold whistles. A whistle is usually something a man would give a good looking woman. I wasn't expecting a girl to do that to me. Needless to say, her bird calls landed me in her bed.

How could I resist?

She would often exude a smile that I found to be irresistible. She would flash the same smile whether she was giggling or fuming. When it came to Roxann, however, she had only one setting on her dial of emotions: pissed. Whenever she spotted Roxann, she'd never hesitate to fix a fiery stare on her to make it clear that she wanted her head on a platter. And yet, Roxann never blinked. The two inevitably started fighting one another. I remember Elizabeth, fueled by jealousy, started the first fight and lost as Roxann got the best of her. Elizabeth was a girl who ran on pure emotions. Her anger and false pride fueled her to attack Roxann on many occasions. These scraps were no little cat fights either; those girls battled like gladiators, scratching each other's eyes and bruising each other's faces. During one fight Elizabeth swung on Roxann who quickly ducked causing Elizabeth's fist to land right smack in Roxann's mother's eye. From that day on, Ms. Bennett made sure to yell *stop it* from a distance. A lot of neighbors were impressed with how Roxann handled Elizabeth, who was much bigger and meaner. The fight between the two young mothers was ceaseless; they scrapped before their pregnancies, during, and after. It got so common to see them going at it that I started betting on who would win. To be honest, to see the girls fighting over me made me feel like I had it going on.

I wasn't spared from any altercations. Elizabeth's 18-year-old brother, Bubba, whom stood 6 foot 3 inches and had a size 14 shoe wanted to start a fighting spree with me. Bubba and three other dudes ran up on me as I was leaving the Red Top bar. They hit and kicked me as I blocked for cover in the dirt. Luckily, I survived the brutal attack. Dazed, I managed to stagger to a pay phone and call my sister Rena, who was now living in her own apartment with our great Grandma Alma, my mom's mother's mother. Rena was there in a matter of minutes with Grandma's 9mm revolver. I grabbed the gun and furiously took off on foot towards Bubba and Elizabeth's house. I walked up on Bubba and, at close range, opened fire. Bubba turned around running, and I was right in his tracks, shooting at him. The neighbors who were out at the time yelled "Don't shoot that boy!"

What was strange about that particular incident was the fact that I was less than 20 feet away aiming directly at him and I didn't hit him once. I know I'm a skillful shooter because I used to hunt. I've shot many wild rabbits that were on the run and yet, I still missed Big Bubba. I must say that fate intervened that night.

The police arrived and began the process of arresting me. My mother and Rena were irate. Bubba was much bigger than I was, yet ganged up on me and I was the one being arrested. The cop got me in the car and drove off with me, but then released me away from the scene. He explained that he felt that I was a victim of circumstances because my face was bruised from being kicked and there was no proof of a gun. He went on to explain that I needed to show up in court and if Bubba didn't appear, the assault charges would be dropped. Bubba never pursued the prosecution, nor did he and his goons attempt to bother me again.

Shortly thereafter, my dear Grandma Alma passed away, leaving behind her words of wisdom.

Roxann, the kids and I finally moved out of Central Park Village when I was 17. We moved into our own project home in College Hill Homes, which was just a subtle name for projects. Roxann and I were glad that we finally had our own place. A week or so after moving from out of my mother's home, I was blessed with a job as a mason attendee for a retired man named Mr. Williams. The job meant that I was finally providing for my family and that made me feel really good. I knew that another arrest would destroy the good feeling that was within me, so I tried my best to avoid the temptation of a quick hustle. Working for the old man seemed promising, especially after giving me a dollar raise shortly after being hired, which brought me up to six dollars an hour. In 1984, with my record and job history, I considered that to be a pretty good blessing for an uneducated, young, black man like me. Moreover, my hustling came to an almost complete stop. I felt good and held on to my dreams like a life preserver.

One day, without any prior warning signs or inclinations that something was wrong, I got news that the old man died. The job, no doubt, was a great loss, but losing the old man was even worse. He not only paid me well, but he had also given me words of wisdom along the way. He had the ability to motivate me to work harder than hard, to be independent and to do well in life. He helped me see that I did not have to steal for a living. Because of the impact of Mr. William's lectures, I still had the fight in me to rebuke the urge to steal that was instilled in me by my father. His death didn't change anything. Even though I was really hurt by his passing, it seemed like he was still helping me, beyond the grave. Thanks to everything the old man had taught me, I was able to land a job with one of the largest concrete companies in Florida. I was now making a little more money per week, but still not quite enough to move us out of the projects.

As time passed I was fortunate enough to buy an old Ford Catalina for three hundred dollars from a woman in the neighborhood whom I called Ms. Audrey. Thumbs up to her, she was a single parent who had the guts to change people, places and things. Unlike a lot of us who get comfortable with our lot in life, she never settled for less when she felt her and her daughter deserved better.

Ms. Audrey and her daughter, Hafeezah, a 17-year-old girl I used to play house with when we were kids, were moving to Los Angeles. That day, I drove them to the airport to see them off. From the terminal, I didn't take my eyes off their plane until it had disappeared into the clouds. I'd hoped for a kiss by Hafeezah, but I never got one. I was somewhat disappointed. As I was leaving the airport, a sinking feeling came over me. I realized that I was in way over my head. I had three children, a son and two beautiful daughters, and I began to wonder how I was going to keep them safe and secure. I knew that the projects were the wrong place to raise children, especially girls. I wanted out, but I just didn't know how to escape. I already could not afford the court ordered child support HRS demanded for my daughter Theresa. The pressure led me to some serious thinking and drinking. Before I realized what I was doing, I was introduced to crack cocaine.

It was just beginning to turn dark when Rena and her boyfriend, Johnny, pulled up in his purple van. They entered our apartment with big, beefy smiles. It wasn't unusual for Johnny to light up a joint and pass it around; smoking marijuana wasn't new to me. This particular evening, Rena asked me if I wanted to smoke. The joint she held was different; it was laced with crack cocaine. I had heard of this drug several times before, but had never tried it.

"You want to try it? Rena asked.

"Yeah," I replied, and so I did.

I took a big pull from this joint. There was a quick rush to my brain and it felt as if I was floating off the ground. My ears began to softly hum as a high came about me like I never felt before. I handed the joint back to Rena, she hit it and a serious look formed on her face as she held the smoke. Johnny reached for the joint and grinned at me.

I could only murmur, "Wow, that shit is good!"

"That ain't nothing," Rena said. "You got some ashes?"

Johnny pulled out of his pocket a yellowish white substance and sat it on my table. It was the size of a French fry, but not as long.

"What's that," I asked.

"A slab, this that butter," Johnny said.

"That's the shit," Rena interjected.

Johnny took out a razor blade and start slicing on the crack that he called butter. He put a piece on a small glass pipe and lit it with his lighter. Johnny's face, too, suddenly formed a serious look.

"I want mine on a can," Rena said.

Johnny handed me the pipe and put a small piece of crack in it. I looked over at Rena who was punching holes in a beer can. I hit the pipe as Johnny did. First, I heard a crackling sound coming from the cocaine as it melted.

I inhaled.

"Hold it in bro," he said.

I felt pressure build up in my head as I held the smoke. I exhaled, and whoa, it was on and popping. My jaw went to twitching and I wanted to thank the maker of that creation. The rush gave a high that I needed more of and the three of us stayed up all night long.

A few days passed, I was giving a friend's brother, Charlie, a ride to work. Out of nowhere, I had a head-on collision with another car. Everyone, including the other driver, screamed in shock. When it became apparent that no one was seriously injured, the other driver began screaming in anger. I wasn't hurt, but my chest mildly aching from slamming into the steering wheel. I shook out the cobwebs and looked over at the driver. It was a white woman who was yelling so hard that her face was red. When I was finally able to think clearly again, I realized that I did not have a driver's license and that I was most likely going to jail. The thought of leaving Roxann and my kids in the projects made my heart drop and I began to panic. I knew I needed to get out of there. I looked and saw that my car was smashed pretty badly, but the engine was still running. Without a second thought, I slammed the transmission into reverse and burned rubber out of there. Charlie wanted me to stop the car, so when I was far enough away, I let him out.

The following day, a detective left a message with my mother for me to call him. Needless to say, Charlie had dropped a dime on me. My choices were limited: turn myself in or else, and I didn't want to choose *else*. So, once again, I found myself standing before a judge. The judge informed me that this would certainly be my last chance before her and she sentenced me to two years of house arrest for leaving the scene of an accident and for failure to pay child support.

CHAPTER 2

THE CRACK ATTACK

By 1984, at age 19, I had been smoking crack for about a year or so. I remember going out after dark to sell my .22 riffle that I once used to go hunting, so I could buy more crack. The rifle was unloaded and wrapped in a towel. The dude I was looking to sell it to wanted to see the gun, so I unwrapped it and handed it to him.

"How much?" he asked.

"Sixty dollars," I said.

With that, he took off running sixty miles an hour, leaving me to just stand there looking like a deer caught up in head lights. I walked my dumb ass back home empty handed.

I recall one night I scraped up my last bit of money to buy a dime rock, which is ten dollars worth of crack cocaine. It is a small piece of crack about the size of a kernel of corn. The dealer spotted me as I approached the dope hole, which is what we called a street or alley to purchase crack.

"What'cha need?" he asked.

"A dime," I replied.

"Here you go, I got that good shit" he said, as he dropped his product in my hand.

I gave him my ten and walked back home. After walking a mile and a half, I was eager to see how good the crack was. I put the rock on the table and got my can and ashes ready to use as a pipe, I got out my razor blade and proceeded to slice off a piece to smoke and my razor blade broke. I picked up my ten dollar piece to discover that it was the real thing, it was a real rock.

That Motherfucker!

A couple of months prior to that, I bought a twenty dollar piece. It looked and tasted like the real cocaine rock, but when I lit it up to smoke it; my mouth started smelling like zest. I discovered it was soap, damn soap powdered with baking soda, which helped pass the taste test. What really got my attention was on one evening, after I got my paycheck, I went and bought my kids some clothes, and later that night, I started smoking crack. I ran out of money and wanted more. I was on it so bad that I sold the meat out the freezer and sold my kids' new clothes that I bought. I tried to sell anything of value and it all went up in smoke. I looked like an owl and I would have had my teeth pulled and sold if they were of any value.

Roxann came to mind, she was upstairs asleep in bed. I had seen Roxann put the money I gave her in her shirt pocket and I knew that she wouldn't give me anything but a lip battle. I headed up the stairs and she was still in her clothes. I lay next to her close to our bedroom window, which was open and didn't have a screen. I lay there waiting for her to fall back to sleep. I then eased my hand into her pocket and slipped the money out. I laid there for a minute or so, and then rolled toward the window. I began to climb out and onto the ledge and Roxann suddenly grabbed me by the seat of my pants and pulled me back onto the bed.

"I don't want no rock head," she growled.

Her eyes burned into mine and at that moment, I was tired of it all. Sometimes, when I wasn't high, I'd sit and daydream that I was a super hero who would catch and lock up all the dope dealers. Free the world of drugs. I was tired of the drugs and its ruthless dealers, and tired of seeing my kids playing in the hot sand of the projects. Tired of the dirty, bleak outlook that life in the projects was giving me. I was tired of Roxann looking at me and shaking her head in disgust, knowing that the rock cocaine was the reason why my jaw was twitching; teeth were gritting and wide eyed. I felt her eyes following me, but honestly, I was tired of myself, really tired. I knew that I had it in me to improve and that I was a better man than this. I just couldn't seem to shake the turmoil that was stirring within my soul. I was stuck and crack had me by the throat. The desire for drugs was still taunting me and then, the kicker: I realized that my children's mother was pregnant again. I sank into a deep depression, as I knew that I was nowhere near prepared to raise another child in this society. I was struggling with the desire to smoke crack. The concrete jungle, or what some people refer to as the ghetto, had certainly got the best of me.

My life had become a real mess. One night, Roxann and my kids were upstairs away from me as I finished smoking my last bit of crack; I sat in the dark of the house, taking stock of what was left of my life. There were no more steaks in the freezer, nor clothes, jewelry, weapons, or paychecks; it had all gone up in smoke. I remember how much I hated myself as I peeped out the windows and scanned the floors. I got down on my hands and knees and rubbed through the carpet with my fingers hoping to find a crumb. As I crawled around, there was a voice inside me that ridiculed me and called me embarrassing names that I hated and despised.

You are disgusting. Look at you, nothing but a rock monster. You will die like a stinking rat!

I tried to ignore the scolding voice that was within me, but I couldn't. My inner voice spoke the truth. Having little Tolerance (who we called Lil' Toler, for short) and his sister Tina to take care of, as well as my other baby, Theresa, whom I had with Elizabeth was hard enough, and now, another child was on the way. And here I was, smoking crack and crawling around on the floor for crumbs. The realization that I had become a rock monster made my insides churn. I got so angry and disgusted with whom I had become that I called the police on myself and for the first time, they wouldn't arrest me.

"Look, look," I said. "Here is the can that I smoked the crack with."

"I don't see any crack. Show me some crack. Where is it?" one of officers asked sarcastically. That got me really upset. I couldn't even get myself arrested! After the officers left, I took a pair of scissors and started cutting off my hair. When I was done, I slinked back in the bedroom like a dog. I crawled into the bed beside Roxann and like always, she cuddled under me. Her hand moved up my back and toward the base of my neck. When she got to my head, I felt her hand stop, then quickly move around, as if she was trying to make sense of something that wasn't right. She quickly sat up in bed.

"What is wrong with your head?" she asked frantically, as she felt the patches. She jumped up and turned on the light. She studied my head for a moment and started to snicker. "Man you're losing it," she said.

I got back up and cleaned up the mess I had made of my head. I had no other choice but to shave it down, completely. I ended up looking like Uncle Fester from the Addams Family. My family and friends laughed at me. I laughed with them, but, on the inside, I didn't find it amusing at all. I was caught in Satan's grip and was crying out for help. I knew that cocaine was one of his crafty ways to corrupt the nation and I had fallen for it. I felt that there was only one way out for me. So I called my probation officer and told her I wanted to go to prison. She granted my request that same day, which was on a Friday. Since I only had less than a year left on house arrest, she got me a year and a day in Florida State Prison. The following Monday, I simply kissed Roxann and my kids goodbye and walked to my probation officer's office. I was asked to be seated and wait for the police to come and take me away.

I can remember the long, silent ride as I stared out the window of the prison transport van. During the ride, I thought back on all of the things that the boys in the hood had told me about prison. For instance, keep to yourself and if an inmate tries to give you candy or something, don't accept it. Don't be friendly and never shower alone. Exercise and fight like a madman if challenged. The odds that I would face in prison would be against me. Weighing less than 200 pounds, short and with a baby face, I knew that I had to toughen up fast and avoid making friends.

I arrived at a prison called Lancastle. It was a prison that incarcerated young men under 21. The first thing I noticed was that the majority of the inmates were black, peppered with Hispanics. I'm not saying that there weren't any whites, but there were so few I could count them on one hand. The one thing I hated from the first day of my arrival was the yelling officers telling me what to do, when to sleep, when to eat, when to shut up and when to speak, and there was nothing I could do about it. I just did what I was told and stayed to myself. Until one cold morning, I got into a rumble with a bully about my own coat. The big Latino must have felt that my coat would fit him better, so he tried to convince me to give it up. I may have been small, but my pride was big. Besides, it was cold outside and it wasn't going to go down like that. I earned an extra two months for fighting for what was mine. That was a wake-up call and the following day, I started doing curls on the weight pile.

My mother and Roxann would send me money for the canteen. I would stand in line to buy cigarettes and oatmeal pies. I never cracked a smile and I looked at my fellow inmates like I would fight them at any moment. All they did was talk about sex, drugs and stealing. I had been there and done that. I remained stand-offish because I knew that there was more to life than that crap.

Finally, after serving four and a half months, I was released from prison, and I was ready to fly right. Lil' Toler, Tina and Terran, my new 2-month-old son, were a sight for sore eyes when I returned home. I had seen and experienced enough crap to make me realize that my kids and their mother needed me. I didn't want them to be disappointed in me ever again. I made an oath to never go back to drugs or return to stealing. I wanted to have a normal, productive life for them, as well as myself, so I enrolled in United College Trade School for AC and Refrigeration repair. I began attending classes and I never missed a day. I was focused and eager to learn my new trade.

In 1985, Roxann became pregnant with our fourth child, whom we named Terrance. I decided after this child, I was not making another one. Roxann needed to get her tubes tied, cut, clipped or something! Anything to stop her from blowing out babies; I was trying to establish some marketable skills to give my family a better living situation. I couldn't take the stress of having more children, so I spoke to Roxann about getting her tubes tied and she did.

Months passed and one evening, we were sitting around watching television when a commercial came on advertising a school that trained people to become professional semi-tractor trailer drivers.

The commercial caught my attention when it said in bold words, be *your own boss*. The commercial went on to say that there would be a growing demand for drivers in the coming years. I discontinued my studies at United College and traveled by bus to Bridgeport, Connecticut to attend a six-week training camp for future drivers.

In 1986, at age 20, I flew back to Tampa with a diploma in my hand, designating me as a professional truck driver. After returning home, I quickly landed a job at West Coast Transportation. The job, indeed, provided a better income for my family, but my career had not progressed to the point where I could afford a house. I tried to get Roxann to help me out by signing up for section eight or getting a job.

"I'm happy in the projects. My momma always lived in the projects," she said.

So, there she remained, sitting square on her ass in the projects. Nevertheless, I was proud of myself and took solace in the fact I had finally become a law-abiding citizen. Roxann and I couldn't come to an agreement on where we wanted our lives to go and we began to drift apart. It wasn't long until I found myself getting more involved with other women. Black, white, and yellow, race didn't matter. Every chance I got I had an affair, even with Roxann's friend, Marlene. Marlene stood about 5 foot 9, she held a reddish complexion, like my self, and had a shape that would make an old man wish he was young again. Besides Marlene, it wasn't necessarily the physical intimacy I was looking for; I was searching for a woman who wanted something more out of life, someone who would appreciate a hard working man and would help provide a decent living for my kids and me. Roxann, no doubt, was attractive to me, she had a sexy, petite figure, good hygiene and she was a good housekeeper (or should I say project keeper), but I wanted more.

Time passed and during one eventful evening, Roxann, her friend Marlene, my co-worker Mike, and I downed a half bottle of Seagram's gin with some juice. We later decided to do a little shopping at Pack N' Save

Grocery. During shopping, I was eating a green Granny Smith apple and I forgot to pay for it at the checkout counter. An officer in the store saw me and accosted me about it. The way he stepped to me about an apple, no less, pissed me off. I tried to defend myself, but my evening of drinking gin-n- juice didn't help matters.

"That's why your momma had three black babies in the supermarket!" I growled to the officer as he was escorting me to jail for petty theft.

When we arrived, the angry cop got out, opened the door and pulled me out of the car by my hair, I was still talking shit and this resulted in me getting a beat-down by three officers. At my court hearing, I pleaded not guilty because the granny apple only cost 40 cents and I had a pocketful of money. I had truly forgotten to pay for the apple after I had eaten it, so I took it to a jury trial.

The jury trial ended in one day with a guilty verdict. I was then sentenced to jail for 30 days. Roxann and Marlene walked off, shaking their heads in disbelief while Mike giggled his ass off as he escorted my women out of the courtroom.

In jail, I couldn't help but think about how quickly my law-abiding status that I tried so hard to keep was destroyed over a 40 cent granny apple. At that point, I didn't know whether to laugh or cry, and the mischievous grin Mike had left me with didn't help any either.

I served my sentence quietly and was fortunate enough to get reinstated with my former employer.

Things didn't improve in my relationship, though. By 1989, Roxann still didn't care to go any further in life than the ghetto. It's sad to say, but I only thought of how I felt, so I left Roxann and the kids in the projects.

CHAPTER 3

THE STEP MOM

In 1991, I married a young lady by the name of Harriet Smith, a 22-year-old divorcee; she was one year younger than me. I had met her a year prior when Roxann and I were trying to save our dying relationship. Harriet had a medium build and a crown of thick, shoulder length hair. We were both the same height, and bright skinned. We wanted the same things in life. Harriet was also a mother of two; she had an 8-year-old girl named Amy and a 6-year-old boy named Junior.

Harriet quickly became the light of my life. She taught me many important life skills that I had never been taught, such as banking, how to use a checkbook and how to manage an ATM card. Her cooking was superb and her wide, bedroom eyes, smooth, titillating hands and full, curvy lips made me want to do back flips! Harriet made me feel like I was truly blessed. I'm not trying to paint a perfect picture of her because she was far from perfect. She had an ironing board ass, a flabby stomach and big feet. I used to joke with her that if she wanted to water ski, all she had to do is jump off the boat and hang onto the rope. She wasn't a beauty queen, but she was beautiful to me and I thanked God for her. I'd hoped she felt the same way because I had no room to talk.

One of the most important things Harriet did for me was introducing me to the Jehovah Witnesses. I was curious about who they were, so I examined the King James Bible and, after reading *Exodus 6:3*; I confirmed that God's name is Jehovah and his people bare witness to him. I dove into the Bible and did more studying. *Isaiah 43:10* and *Acts 20:20* told me about how Jehovah's people went knocking from door to door, preaching the good news. It all made sense and I wanted to learn more. Soon, we started attending a nearby Kingdom Hall and started our own Bible study in our brand new apartment. I had a strong desire to get custody of my kids and teach them what I was learning and create a big happy family. As I was trying to figure out a way to make that a reality, I stumbled upon a rumor that Roxann was smoking crack cocaine. This jolted my heart.

"No, not my Roxann," I moaned as I went to investigate.

Tears slid down my face as I kept telling myself that it was a lie. Sadly, the rumor about my children's mother turned out to be true. There was another rumor that her live in lover, Terry, who happened to be my old neighbor and a friend of my family, was the one feeding her the crack. Terry was old enough to be her daddy and, on top of that, he was supposed to be my friend. Friends don't mess with each other's exes. Most of all, I was scared of the impact that she was having on my children. I immediately called Human Resource Services and had them raid Roxann's apartment for drugs. My intention to stop the drug trafficking among my youngsters was successful, but unfortunately, my kids were placed in HRS custody and this was not my intention. Therefore, I had to take a stand to get my kids out of the hands of the state and with a lot of effort; I was able to get them back and move them into a four bedroom house.

With our six kids, Harriet's two kids and my four, the two of us had a serious challenge, indeed. Nevertheless, all were attending school and, though the kids could be pretty noisy, they got along well. Unfortunately, this lasted only a short time because, before I knew it, my marriage started to crumble. The kids started fighting because Harriet began taking sides. She would buy new shoes only for her two kids, while giving my kids the more worn clothes to wear. I didn't stand for that at all, so we began to argue like hell. In addition to that, I started complaining about how poorly she kept the house together. Harriet seemed to have an excuse for everything, so I decided that I would be the one to work.

"Stay home, take care the kids and keep the house up," I said. "I will work and foot the bills."

That was like music to her ears. Thereafter, I would always beat her home from work. When I arrived home dirty clothes were always piled up higher than our washer and dryer. When I asked what was going on, I would be greeted with an attitude, as she would claim that she had been visiting her sick grandmother. So, our home continued to go neglected.

Harriet eventually confessed that she didn't believe in cleaning because her parents never made her clean when she was growing up. I questioned her about her past relationships, regarding cleaning and I learned that when I first met Harriet, the reason why her apartment was empty as if someone had cleaned her out was because someone did clean her out. The man took back his furniture because she was too nasty. As if I needed more evidence of her lack of cleanliness, I recall a letter I found in her closet. It was from her ex-boyfriend who called Harriet filthy and her grandmother evil. As much as I hate to admit it, my first instinct when I read the letter was to ignore it and other such signs and pursue building a relationship with her. I ended up paying the consequences for that. As for my kids, they completed all of their chores, leaving Amy and Junior to dodge theirs. We ended up having so many pointless arguments about the same issues that I had a nervous breakdown. Harriet called the paramedics to revive my breathing and nurse my hands and lips that were now looking deformed. I lay on the floor while the paramedics tended to me as tears ran from my eyes.

"Why, why me," I wept.

It seemed as if I was the only man whose family was being torn apart because of something as simple as keeping a clean house, or at least halfway clean. It seemed like it should have come naturally with being married. But, Harriet didn't see it that way.

"You got five fingers, you clean!" she would yell.

On occasions I would go get my younger sister Keitha, who was now 11- years-old to help me clean, which allowed her to earn some money. Harriet and I still had cleaning issues and our problems festered. The next thing I knew, Harriet went to her grandmother's and filed a restraining order on me to not go there.

I loved Harriet and I wanted her and her kids back home, so I visited Harriet at her grandmother's place. Funny enough, when I got there, Harriet's grandmother was fine and not sick at all. The old woman loved every minute of seeing me plead and beg Harriet to return. The two had no sympathy for me and they called the police, and, just like that, I was arrested for violating Harriet's restraining order.

After I bonded out, I went to go pick up my kids from their grandmothers. When we got home, I discovered that my television was missing. I later found out that it had been carried out of the house by Harriet and her first husband, who was the father of her children, the ex who was supposed to be in Georgia. *Hmm… no wonder she was at her sick grandmother's house everyday.*

My role as a parent doubled. Meanwhile, I continued to try to save my marriage. Days followed and periodically, my driving career forced me to pick up my kids late from day care. I assured the people at the day care that the lateness wouldn't continue.

Needless to say, I really needed Harriet to step in and help, especially when it came down to giving my daughter, Tina, a good hair combing. Tina complained many mornings about how the kids at school picked at her hairdo. I felt helpless. There was only so much I could do. Reality finally set in to where I had to accept the fact that I just wasn't good at Mr. Mom.

One evening, due to heavy traffic, I was again late picking up my kids from day care. When I arrived, I found out, to my horror that my kids were in the custody of HRS. It took all that I had not to get violent with the agent who had my youngsters locked up in his cruiser. Evidently, I was late a little too often because they were eventually placed in the care of their grandmother. Within a month or so, I regained custody. Harriet had discovered my weakness and she had me looking like a pure idiot running behind her. She became quick to abandon me and my children. Still, I would go to Harriet's grandmother's house and beg and plead for her to return home.

No, I wasn't pussy whipped; I just needed help with my children. Harriet and her two were part of my family now. Well, maybe I was a little whipped. To be honest, sometimes I felt like I couldn't live without her. My emotions were running wild and I didn't like rejection. Harriet kept telling me that it was over, perhaps I kept pleading because I was no longer in control. I was a man who was used to having his way. I became stupid and fell out of character. I went as far as trying to get Roxann to take on some of our responsibility. I dropped my kids off with their grandmother with a message to get Roxann's attention. The outcome was that Roxann never came for her children. I was told that Dell, Roxann's older sister, was pursuing legal custody and my chance to regain custody was slim to none. I was restricted from getting my kids back until there was a court hearing. As I write this, my stomach churns. It is still painful, and makes me angry realizing what I had done. All I had to do was to be strong, but no, I grew weak under the pressure and dropped my kids off, so I could go and run behind this woman. To add insult to injury, Harriet eventually came back, then later abandoned my dumb ass again!

I was in a bad way. I'd already lost Hafeezah and my old partner-in-crime, Larry, who had recently been sentenced to 20 years in prison from a drug case, and now, my kids. I was angry at the world. Things just didn't seem fair anymore. Resentment toward my parents began to build. I began to feel that it was my parents fault as to why I was going through so much turmoil and misery. I felt that if it wasn't for their poor parenting, like my mother allowing me to sleep with Roxann at the young age of thirteen, and my father teaching me to be a thief, I wouldn't be going through this shit! I would've been childless and perhaps, in college. The burden became so overwhelming that people would ask me why I was looking so sad.

One gloomy evening, I was sitting at home alone, staring at the same old walls, when the phone rang. The voice on the other end belonged to my father. He had picked up on my depression and decided to drive over. My father's visit turned out to be very informative.

First, he helped me decide a name for the chow puppy I had bought from my neighbor; Mrs. Smokey is the name we came up with. Second, Pop gave me some insight on how women can get when angered.

"It's a thin line between love and hate, and the heart ache that comes with it is a mother!"

He went on to say that I should always keep a spare tire, even if it meant giving money to keep the second relationship because women change overnight.

I didn't want my father to learn about my weaknesses, so I quickly changed the subject and asked him what happened between him and my mother. What a stunning story that turned out to be.

CHAPTER 4

STUNNING STORIES

P op had no problem explaining how it all started in Detroit, Michigan. He claimed that my mother had become lazy and that all she did every day was drink wine and sit on her fat ass. He went on to say that when he returned from work, my mother would be on the couch, slobbering like a mule with empty MD 20/20 bottles thrown under the couch. Pop confessed that this, along with her rapid weight gain, led him to start dating other women. Pop added that my mother used to make him mad as hell when he took her out for fried chicken.

"I'm gonna need two buckets," he told the cashier, chuckling and nodding towards Mom.

He admitted that Mom's face was still bright and pretty and that all she had to do is lay off the wine and stop eating so much. She started rapidly gaining weight; we're talking three hundred pounds and climbing, he emphasized. Pop said that because he was a light-skinned, handsome, freckle-faced man, my mother became extremely jealous over his interactions with other women.

As a result, their marriage was crumbling slowly, but surely until it finally ended on the night he arrived home early.

Pop took a drink from his beer, and then wiped his mouth. I watched him gather his thoughts and how he squeezed his eyes shut for a moment as he remembered what he was about to tell me.

He said that it had been a slow night at work, so he returned home early. When he arrived and was walking onto the porch, he heard a moaning and groaning sound from the bedroom window. He thought his ears were playing tricks on him, so he stopped to listen more closely. He went to the window to investigate. It turned out that there was nothing wrong with his ears. Pop said he left the window and crept inside to discover that there was a naked man on top of my mother. In an instant, he realized that the mystery man was his best friend, Leslie.

"Give me this pussy!" Pops said he heard Leslie grunting.

"All I saw was asshole and swinging nuts," he said intensely.

After hearing his blunt and open descriptions, I didn't know how to respond. The way he shared it made part of me want to burst out laughing, but the other part felt embarrassed and disappointed. I could feel my face flush with emotions as I pictured what he was saying. He said that when his friend heard him, he bounced off my mother, grabbed his clothes and fled, leaving my mother scrambling to cover herself. Pop went on to say that my mother tried to explain that she was drunk and to please forgive her. Pop took another swig from his Old Milwaukee and looked at me, his eyes were red.

Suddenly, my mind began to rewind back when I was 7-years-old. At that moment, there was no need for my father to go any further. I'd remember my parent's last encounter.

That horrifying night, my sister and I heard the screams from my mother begging my father to stop hitting her. The blows from my father's fists filled the air like raw meat being punched by a mad man. The following day, my mother was in a body cast, and here it was 18 years after my parents' separation, I finally learned the cause of it.

After hearing my father's marriage experience and thinking about the experience that I was going through myself, I realized that a marriage can be devastating if not nursed and handled with love and compassion.

A couple of days after Pop's confession, Harriet and I got back together, and soon after we had sex, my heart was at ease. After a few more hugs and kisses, followed by a fine dinner, I was ready for the world.

In the midst of making the proper arrangements to regain custody of my kids, I couldn't help but notice that with my kids gone Harriet and her kids still wouldn't clean behind themselves. I was irate because of this and voiced it openly.

Two weeks later, Harriet must have woken up realizing that I was going to stand firm on the cleaning tip because that morning, I'll never forget, Harriet had on my Pittsburgh Steelers football cap cocked back on the side of her head. We laughed and talked while she drove me to work. The kids kissed me goodbye and when I got out and started walking towards the warehouse I worked, the kids yelled from the car.

"I love you Dad!"

"I love y'all too," I yelled back.

I felt really good as I headed into the warehouse. At the end of the day I waited for Harriet to come pick me up, but she never showed.

I caught a ride home with another co-worker. When I arrived home, the new car Harriet was driving wasn't there. I entered our home and was shocked to find the entire three-bedroom house was empty. All the furniture that I had worked so hard for was gone. I dragged myself out the door in a daze and suddenly, by impulse, punched the door of Harriet's broken down car, practically breaking my hand. Dave, the guy who drove me home was now getting out of his truck.

"Are you alright, Toler?"

"She done cleaned me out!

This woman even took my personal property like my fishing rods, my jewelry, everything I had, even my new pack of boxers. She could have at least left me a mattress to sleep on.

When I pulled myself together, I called the Sheriff's department and reported my new Daihatsu Sedan stolen. The officer informed me that the fact that Harriet and I were married, the furniture and other belongings were a loss.

"What's hers is yours and what's yours is hers," the officer concluded.

My neighbor, Jake, came over to give me the scoop on what happened while I was at work. I listened as he recalled how Harriet came with her aunt and cousins and bum rushed the house, leaving me nothing but my stereo, which seemed to only play *End of the Road* by Boyz II Men. I remember a couple of nights after Harriet had run out on me, my father came by to console me. That very song led me to ask my father if he thought Harriet loved me.

"Love you? Hell, she don't even like ya!"

My parents and Jake offered me a place to stay until I got myself together, but I declined their offers. I wanted to remain strong and stay at my house. It was hard, especially when I heard that got damn song. Things weren't necessarily easy at my workplace either. Every day at work, as soon as I entered the warehouse, a group of co-workers would gather and start singing, *When a Man Loves a Woman* then burst out laughing. They constantly picked at me. Although my heart was aching, I managed to smile.

A couple of weeks went by after I had been robbed by Harriet, a Sheriff called me when I was at work. He left a message for me to call him and so I did. He informed me that my car had been found in Georgia and that the driver was my wife, in accompaniment with her ex-husband. Harriet was arrested and my car was to be towed back to Florida to its dealership, so if I wanted the car back, I would have to pay for the tow and the postponed monthly installments. My financial status was pretty rocky, so I was no longer interested in the vehicle. My emotions were pulling me in every which direction and I ended up making a lot of ill-advised decisions.

A day or two later, I'd finally had enough of my co-workers taunting me, so I quit.

Luckily, my commercial license landed me a job at a major recycling plant hauling rubbish to a local dump. The job paid well, but I wasn't on the job for a week before I heard that my Aunt Bill had died, my dad's mother's sister. My mindset was so screwed up at that point that I didn't even make it to her funeral. Regretfully, I should have because I ended up losing the job anyway when I flipped my trailer during a dump.

My commercial license came through for me again when I landed a job with a freight carrier called Southern Freight. The job was definitely helpful, but coming back home every day was torture. I could no longer stand living in that empty house. I decided that I needed to stay with someone if I was going to stay sane. I then took up my neighbor on his offer to rent out his younger sister's old room.

Jake and his brother showed good hospitality and we got along well, though my stay was temporary. Fortunately, I had saved up enough money to buy a used car and made arrangements to move in with my sister Rena.

One evening, while driving down the blistering pavement, I started thinking about Harriet, I came to realize I needed someone to talk to, someone who shared my plight. I immediately refused the thought of visiting my father; I didn't want to discuss anything with him after that last visit when he sarcastically made fun of my situation. I really tried not to think about what my dad had said, but I couldn't help it.

He had been sitting on his couch, sipping on an Old Milwaukee. I was sitting across from him, expressing my dilemmas when he suddenly blurted: "Man, Harriet is probably somewhere with nine inches of dick stuck up in her!"

He gestured the length of nine inches with his hands and burst out laughing. I glared at him as he held his chest and almost rolled off the couch in laughter. I got up and dismissed myself. After that experience, I decided to go talk with my mother about my troubles. When I got to my mother's place, I ended up telling her about the conversation pop and I had concerning their separation. My mother listened intently with her mouth open as I told her what my father had told me.

My mother's face formed a disgusted look. She took a deep breath before yelling: "That motherfucker is telling a got damn lie!"

She adjusted herself in her seat, and then plunged her face toward me, looking me directly into my eyes. Her voice was cold and harsh.

"That nasty motherfucker was screwing his own daughter! That stinking son of a bitch!"

Her eyes were now red.

"I wasn't no drunk! He was the got dam drunk!" she yelled. "And what friend, that bitch didn't have any friends! He was too got damn mean and nasty! He'll fuck anything! Hell, I even caught him in bed with another man!"

I was already stunned at what my mom had said about my dad screwing his daughter, I was wondering which daughter, he had two of them. When my mom made accusations that my father was sleeping with men, my mouth went dry. My mind refused to process all that she was saying and I just couldn't believe her.

Not my dad! He wouldn't do any shit like that. My father wouldn't mess with his daughters and lay with men, I told myself.

I looked deep into my mother's squinted red eyes, looking for any signs of envy of some sort. I was snapped out my silent investigation by the flicker of my mother's cigarette lighter.

"Let me get a cigarette," I said, as I took a deep breath.

My mother handed me one and, as I smoked to gather my thoughts, she began to mumble to herself. I continued to reassure myself that my mother was only saying those bad things about my dad because she was still bitter, holding resentment toward my father for the simple reason that he didn't want her.

I remembered at that moment, a time when I was young, when my mom went into the bathroom and tried to kill herself by slicing her wrist several times with a razor. She wanted to bleed to death because my father would always curse her and flee to other women. I recall the many bottles of wine that she drank called MD 20/20, most people called the wine Mad Dog due to one would end up fighting after consuming it. I've seen my mom with my own eyes drink this wine. Even today, she drinks cheap gin out of the bottle, yet she says she isn't a drunk. If she wasn't a drunk back then, she sure is one now. I scanned her wrist for the tracks of scars to confirm my silent protest, and there they were.

Hell, she's just miserable and angry because she still loves my dad. She's mad because dad never returned, so now, she would rather sit around and lie on him because her life was a mess. This is why after 18 years of separation, she still hadn't divorced him.

With that, I was convinced that mom was lying. I ended our conversation with a goodbye peck on her jaw and headed for the door when my mom said aloud, "Yo dad is nothing but a freak!"

31

I knew that such accusations would really hurt my father's feelings, so I decided not to mention the awful things mom had said. My dad was more than a dad to me; he was like a brother. He was my best friend, therefore, not only did I not mention it, but I dismissed it from my mind.

During the days that followed, I tried everything I could to convince Roxann that we should try to get our children back and become a family again. After a lot of talking, my wish was granted and Roxann was reunited with me. My father and Viola, my father's live-in girlfriend of 18 years, supported our efforts by letting us live with them so that we could prepare to regain custody of our kids.

The following week after returning from work, Viola informed me that Roxann had once again fled back to Terry and his drugs. Despite Terry, I continued to try to get my Roxann back.

One morning, I saw Roxann leave the crack shack, where she and Terry resided and I proceeded to follow her. I picked her up and bought her some new clothes, had her hair professionally groomed, bought her some jewelry and gave her some spending money. Roxann felt pretty again and she deserved to. She again took a good look at herself and agreed to stop the drugs. I took her to get signed up at DACCO drug center. Unfortunately, she failed to attend treatment.

I returned to the crack shack, where Terry repeatedly told me that Roxann was not there when I knew she was. Determined, I came back a couple of days later. Roxann was sitting on the porch and I called her to my car pleading with her to leave the drug scene. I said that I loved her and that our children needed us. She agreed and signed up at ACTS drug treatment facility. There, she would have to admit herself for a number of weeks, which she did. I was so happy to see that finally my kid's mother was taking a stand against the addictive drug. I was there every day to give Roxann my support and encouragement to complete the treatment. It all came to a head when Terry paid her a visit. Roxann left with him and never returned. I was fuming when I learned this. I had thoughts of killing Terry.

Deep down inside I knew that I was to blame. If I had never left home, Roxann would have never gotten hooked on drugs. I've had many years to consider this and while I don't feel that way anymore, I still wonder what kind of role I had in her descent into drugs.

I learned that when you make a drastic decision, when others are involved, it is essential to ask yourself how your decision will affect them. I came to the conclusion that shooting Terry wasn't the solution. I am a family man and it was obvious that I needed love; I needed to be a source relied on. The fatherly image that I once possessed with my kids was severely damaged and I hated that feeling. As a result, I fell into a depression so deep that I no longer had the desire to drink.

I was like a fish out of water.

Desperate to find some place in the world, I was suddenly overwhelmed with the desire to try and pick up the pieces with Elizabeth, my other daughter's mother.

Well, Elizabeth frowned at the sight of me.

"What you want?" she barked.

When I inquired about my daughter, I was called every name in the book except *child of God*. I didn't think any of the ugly names were called for, but I kept my mouth shut and took it. Within minutes, it was clear that creating a family with my daughter Theresa and her mom was out of the question.

After Elizabeth's rejection, instead of going through the proper channels to be the father I wanted to be for my child, I folded. I let her drive me away and, in turn, I felt like no one in the world wanted me and I got lonely. I called Harriet's grandparents, hoping Harriet had returned from Georgia. Harriet answered the phone; and we started talking. I learned that Harriet had moved back to Tampa and had moved into her own apartment. She said that she missed me and that she wanted to see me. I took down her address and hung up feeling somewhat relieved. My car needed repairs, so I caught the bus to her place. Harriet claimed that her family had talked her into cleaning me out like she did; and that she was later arrested in Georgia for driving with a suspended license. Tears ran down her face as she begged me to forgive her. She was sincere. I was then invited to live with her in her apartment that was furnished with all of the furniture that she had taken from me. In addition, my personal items were given back to me from a local storage facility.

As the months followed, Harriet and I got more involved in attending meetings at a local Kingdom Hall. Because of my mother's alcohol problem, as well as the cruel treatment she frequently displayed toward my little sister, I moved Keitha in with Harriet and me. My sister was very happy with my decision, and I was too. The last time I was over at my moms, she slung a beer bottle at Keitha, just because she was mad with her man. It would have put me in a real bad position if that bottle would have hit my sister in my presence. I also hated to see my mother abuse my teenage sisters just because she was getting old and fatter. That was no reason for my mother to call her daughters 'bitches' and 'whores'. It's not the daughter's fault when the mother's man starts looking at them the wrong way.

So, I got my sister out of there. After that, I was blessed to be able to buy a Dodge convertible and later, I paid cash for a 15 foot boat. My driving pay increased to where I was fortunate enough to pay off my white leather furniture that I had previously placed on layaway a year before. We were also able to place all of this nice furniture in an elegant apartment. I worked hard to furnish that apartment with luxurious items, such as a 6 foot wall aquarium, exotic birds, life-sized ceramic animals and plants. It made me feel good to see the actual manifestations of my hard work. I remember my mother's reaction when she saw the new apartment for the first time.

"Toler and Harriet's apartment is fit for a president!" she said.

But, some things never change. My repenting wife wasn't too sincere about making our marriage work because I had to actually put up signs in neglected areas of the house that read, "A clean house is a happy house".

This sign was first written and hung in our huge laundry room. I had built shelves to store the linen, but all were ignored. Dirty clothes piled as high as the washer and dryer themselves. The white leather furniture that had taken me a year to pay for began to look gray and began to match the dirty, finger-smudged walls. In hope for a solution, I added an everyday chore for Amy and Junior to abide by. In addition, mostly because of Junior's junky bedroom and rebellious behavior, I put up a Booty Board. This board had a big booty drawn on it. I designed it for Harriet to write down any unwanted behaviors that Amy or Junior displayed. Upon my return from work, I would read the board and then verbally discipline the child and decide whether or not to conclude with a spanking or punishment. Harriet approved of this board because it got Junior's attention, so she had no problem charting down his mischievous conduct. My persistence to keep Junior in check pretty much kept him from having his name charted, so the Booty Board ended up working. Still I couldn't find a solution to get Harriet's attention on keeping up her duties as a wife. She probably just didn't give a damn because slowly but surely, everything I really enjoyed having was being demolished before my eyes. I continued to brainstorm, in hopes to finding a solution, but this problem kept raising its ugly head.

It suddenly dawned on me that since Keitha, who was now 15-years-old and was living with us; I could offer her the job of keeping the house clean and I would pay her weekly.

Keitha had no problem filling in for Harriet's shortcomings.

We had a saying in my old neighborhood, *Money talks, bullshit walks!*

You can solve almost anything with money. But, this ended up pissing Harriet off because now, her money was being cut short. I tried to defuse my situation by buying Harriet a used car. Still, Harriet had an attitude and turned her nose up. At this point, she had gotten on my last nerve. I felt like splitting her wig.

Apparently, Harriet's feelings were mutual because a couple of days later, I had returned from work, and was informed by a brother from our Kingdom Hall that Harriet and her kids had walked. Just up and left for San Francisco. Needless to say, Harriet again had abandoned me.

I sat in the quiet, emptiness of my home and stared at one of the beautiful angelfish gliding through the waters of my aquarium. I noticed on the bottom of the tank, sitting on top of a rock, sat my little buddy, a crawfish. It seemed that he too was going through something because he sat there with his claws extended out and open, with a mean look on its face. As I sat staring at it, I realized that we hadn't been in the apartment for a good four months and she had left already. I did all I could do to salvage the marriage. The crawfish now had a goldfish in its claws. In an instant, the crawfish cleaved the fish in two and I watched the two halves of the beautiful fish float down to the bottom of the tank. At that moment, I'd wished I was the crawfish and that Harriet was the fish. I quickly dismissed the thought of my deceitful wife. In my mind I replaced her with Roxann and my kids. I jumped up, locked up my house and took off into the car that I'd bought Harriet. Within minutes, I was parked in front of the crack shack, blowing the horn for Roxann, but she never answered.

The following day, after returning from a delivery in Miami, I dropped off my trailer and headed straight to the crack shack. Apparently, Roxann still did not want to face me. Again, I was alone and I didn't know what to do with myself. I had to do something that would satisfy my soul. I didn't want to fall back into a rut of loneliness and start thinking about Harriet. I went home, and after I showered, I tried to enjoy my apartment alone. I psyched myself out by thinking that I had it going on, I was a free man and was going to have fun playing the field.

I started going to bars more often than usual and even got laid on some occasions. I kept telling myself that I was only 27-years-old, well-established and made a decent living. But I knew deep down that the man I was trying to portray just wasn't me. *I was miserable.*

One evening, after dragging myself home from a frustrating work assignment, I showered and proceeded to relax. I poured a drink of spiced rum and coke and grabbed the CD remote to allow Sade's smooth voice to fill the room. After about thirty to forty minutes of relaxing, I was suddenly disturbed by a sharp knock on the door. Harriet's face immediately popped in my mind. I opened the door and to my surprise, there stood Hafeezah, my first girlfriend who had left to go to Atlanta with her mother years ago.

The woman's beautiful smile immediately cheered me up. My arms automatically opened to embrace her. I couldn't believe how tall she had gotten. I had to practically tiptoe to hug her. Beside her stood a handsome little boy and an investigating little girl, and when Hafeezah introduced them, I immediately sensed that they were well-mannered. Hafeezah went on to say that she had another daughter who was with her father. No doubt, Hafeezah was no longer the same young girl I had discovered 18-years ago. She was now almost 6 foot tall, a beautiful woman with milk chocolate skin that gave a distinguishing glow. Her black silky thick hair fell just above her shoulders and complemented her skin. Her jeans clung tightly against her curvy hips as she gracefully entered the house.

That evening, Hafeezah and I sat and exchanged our past experiences while we sipped on some rum and coke. The stories weren't pleasant on either side. I listened intently to how cruel her husband had become toward her. Listening to Hafeezah and hearing about other relationships that had gone bad, not to mention my own, I knew that there are two sides to every story. For some reason, most females have a tendency to blame the man. As if, the man is supposed to succumb to whatever she says or had done.

I knew, almost better than anyone, that most married couples don't know how to control their emotions like anger, bitterness and resentment. I wanted to let her know how important it is for one to learn how to deal with these unwanted feelings. Trust me, one doesn't have to cheat to create these feelings; it can take only a couple of nasty, hurtful words to tear down a good relationship. But, I didn't want to make Hafeezah feel defensive and leave me looking dumb, so I said nothing about the part she may have played. I must say, despite whatever mess had gone on in Hafeezah's household, somebody other than herself had instilled obedience and respect in her children. I was very impressed by how quiet and respectful they were.

I'm not saying that a woman can't achieve this alone, quite the contrary. Hafeezah seemed capable, along with thousands of other amazing women. It's just that there seemed to be a difference in a child's demeanor when they are raised in a balanced household with both parents.

I offered Hafeezah kids something to eat, which they declined, but did agree to go in a spare bedroom and watch television while their mom and I sit and talked. Hafeezah explained she wanted to see me, so she called Rena and learned of my dilemma and where I lived. She went on to say how impressed she was to see how mature and independent I had become. We started reminiscing about our childhood and our sexual encounters together, like the day I got my first orgasm. Man, I was grinning from ear to ear. I thought I had made a baby! We laughed and recalled back when she was mad at me over some girl and how she had tried to beat my head in with a plastic bat. Good thing it was plastic, I thought, as I rubbed my head. The girl had a temper.

I recalled when she was mad at me about another girl. I was leaving the house when she had sweetly called me over as she stood at her mom's back door. I turned and went to see what she wanted. When I got about 12 feet in front of her, the screen door slung open and she threw a knife at me, narrowly missing me. I chuckled and briefly thought about the seriousness of it as she smiled sheepishly. I looked into her sexy, penetrating eyes, then down to her full glossy red lips. Hafeezah exhaled as she reminisced ten years before when I had taken her and her mother to the airport. She recalled the look I had on my face when I waved her goodbye. We again gazed into each other's eyes, searching for unspoken words.

Hafeezah changed the subject by telling me that her mother had moved back in the area, only a few miles down the street and that her two brothers were still living with their grandmother. That night, I invited Hafeezah and her kids to stay over. She cooked a delicious meal and later, during the wee hours of the morning, we made love.

Before she dozed off, she softly murmured, "I love you Tolerance."

At dawn, Hafeezah and her kids left to fulfill her daily plans. I laid there, ambivalently trying to sort out my thoughts. However, the more I thought about Hafeezah returning, the more perplexed I became. Deep down I knew what I had to do.

After a week or so, Hafeezah started inquiring about a future relationship. I knew where she was heading and I sincerely expressed the way I felt. She listened intently as I explained that I had once let my children down by leaving them, and ran off to support and take care of somebody else's kids. I told her that my conscience wouldn't let me rest if I did the same thing again. I reminded her that my kids were under HRS and that Roxann and I were going to work things out and raise our children. Hafeezah sighed with disappointment, but understood my situation. She decided to go on with her previous plans and leave for Atlanta Georgia. A few days later, she was off to seek and create a better life for her and her children.

CHAPTER 5

BAD DECISIONS

The following day, as I was driving home from work, I continued my quest to get my family back together. Having four children by Roxann during a twelve-year relationship, I felt that she was who I needed to be with. I wistfully hoped that Roxann would get tired of the drug scene and reunite with me. The more I thought about her and my kids, the harder I pressed down on the gas pedal. I realized I was speeding, so I let up off the gas. I headed to the crack shack and when I got there, I laid on the horn. Much to my surprise Roxann rushed out of the old run-down wooden shack she called home and greeted me with a peck on the jaw.

"What's up?' she asked.

"Get in the car."

Roxann got in the car and went home with me. The thought of restoring my family gave me a feeling that I couldn't totally describe, but I can say the feeling was powerful, profound and ambitious. I was ready to move mountains if I had too. Again, I sat Roxann down and had a long talk about our future.

Roxann agreed to stop the drugs and restore us as a family. I told her that I would get a divorce and marry her as soon as she showed me that she was serious. I started leaving cash on the dresser and I would come home to find the money untouched. My hope was strengthening by the day. I worked hard to keep Roxann comfortable and pleased. Roxann seemed to remain positive.

A few days later, she was back at that crack shack. I was stabbed by disappointment and her inconsiderate decision. I knew I couldn't continue to let her set me up for such painful crash landings. Moreover, I found it disgusting that she knew of the HRS requirements to get the kids back, and yet she still failed to comply.

I'm sure you have heard what people on crack are like and that the addiction is hard to break. That is very true. But, a person can only fail so much. I believe that people who love themselves and their children will not let crack, heroin or any other drug put them in a position they can't get out of. True, one may struggle to kick the nasty habit, but he or she will prevail because they'll refuse to go out like a diseased dog. The person will care too much about their life.

I say that to say this: one who cares about themselves and their family will find a way to stop the addiction. When you hear a person say *I can't stop my drug habit*, well, I think that's bullshit. I don't think that the person truly wants to stop. Again, if a person loves themselves or someone else, like their children, that person will do whatever it takes to stop using the drug so to regain custody of their kids. Like I mentioned earlier, the fallen father or mother might struggle to kick the habit, but it shouldn't take a lifetime. The love they have for themselves or their children should be greater than the drug. Furthermore, if a person hates what is going on in their life, he or she will find a way to put an end to it. In Roxann's case, it was clear where she, as a parent stood. Apparently, Roxann loved crack cocaine more than she loved her children, not to mention herself. Therefore, she stood for crack.

I remember one day, when I was on Roxann's side of town, I happened to see her crossing the street. She was walking aimlessly toward an open field as she held a small Church's chicken box. The dirty clothes she had on were far too big for her skeletal body. Her head looked a mess. The fragile patch of hair on top of her head wasn't long enough to hold a barrette. As I

40

sat there at the stoplight, I couldn't take my eyes off her. My heart screamed for her. Tears blurred my vision as I drifted off into a lovely image I had of her and me at a picnic with our kids. The light changed for me to go, and that is exactly what I had to do, is go.

As I got further down the street, my daughter Theresa, came to mind. This urged me to try to befriend Elizabeth again, in hopes of being able to honor my visitation rights with my daughter. I decided to head to her house. As soon as I parked and was about to get out, Elizabeth stormed out of her house with a pad and pen. I sat in my car, somewhat shocked as she marched around the back of my car and started writing down my license plate, murmuring to herself. I revved my engine and burned rubber out of there. I never returned.

To help me feel better about myself and my unhappy life, I decided to buy a tractor from this trucking company. I made an agreement with the seller that I would use the rig to haul rock material to and from the Florida sand mines. The company automatically deducted truck and fuel payments from my pay until the old Mack truck was paid off. Gradually, the type of living I desired started to diminish due to the jacked up payment plan. I had already totally lost my convertible due to a wreck by a careless driver. My birds had died after I spray painted their cage for a new look and didn't let the cage completely dry before putting them back into it. They died the following day. My plants withered and even my fish tank crashed to the floor during a cleaning. On top of that, my new girlfriend Fay, who quickly moved in with me, told me that she preferred being with a woman and that my sister, Rena, was a fine candidate.

That did it; I was about cross-eyed with all of the drama.

Man, if it would have been raining Cokes, I would've gotten hit by a Sprite! I was about to holler, "Man down!"

The following day I returned that freak I had staying with me back to the ghetto. Days passed and I was still cursing like the miserable man I was. Like before, I fell into a rut of being lonely and depressed. Fed up with it all, I parked that fuel-drinking tractor in front of K-Mart and called Silver Sand, its seller, to come get it and slammed down the phone. I caught a ride to a local U-haul to purchase a rental truck and called a brother from the Jehovah Witnesses congregation to help move me. Within an hour, a couple of witnesses were at my house. Wearily, my bad experiences and decisions had indeed gotten the best of me because I didn't want to hear anything about God's standards; all I wanted was to get away from it all.

The Jehovah Witnesses wished me well and concluded that I must seek Jehovah for guidance. I concurred. Now that I had all my property in storage, I had Keitha go back to live with her mother and I went into the woods. I wanted to get away from the world and I decided to make the woods my new home. Don't get me wrong, I still had mom or dad to go to, but I had too much pride to go crawling back to my parents. So, living out of the trunk of my car in the woods overlooking the Hillsborough River seemed like the next best option.

It wasn't long before I landed a job working for a temporary service hauling freight in and out of state when needed. On the relationship front, I got involved with an older woman name Vicky.

Vicky was 37 years of age, nine years my senior; a petite red-boned woman whose marriage had also gone bad. She resided with her mother, who had custody of her three children. Besides our regrettable pasts, we shared a number of things in common. The biggest thing we both wanted was a mate to help cope with living in this dog eat dog world.

Vicky and I fit together like two peas in a pod. Vicky would sometimes travel with me on my job assignments and she even started living with me in the woods. If I'd fart, she could tell me what I had eaten that day. Vicky and I would visit my parents, eat, drink and dance our ass off. When the hour would grow late, we would return back to the woods and walk onto the old boardwalk that extended over the Hillsborough River. We would sit and laugh, strip and drink and screw. Sometimes, I would run through the bushes naked, just to make Vicky laugh her ass off. I must admit, we had some fun times together.

I remember one night, there was a half-moon out, but it was pitch black, as the sky was shrouded in clouds. Vicky and I were parked in our usual spot in the woods. We sat on the 20-foot dock that extended out above the river. We downed a couple of quarts of Colt 45 and then we started making love on the pier. We later headed for the Seville Cadillac that I recently purchased and used as our sleeping quarters.

As I drifted off to sleep, I was attacked by three wicked spirits. I've heard that evil spirits or demons, if you will, would enter into one's subconscious mind during sleep and try to scare the person by chasing them in hopes of causing a heart attack. I didn't know, however that their blows could actually cause physical pain. These spirits were hitting me and I was literally feeling the pain. I'll never forget it. They were shaped in a cloudy image of a man. I could see no facial features; only the figure of men. Their grayish-white hands were hitting me and I did my best to run away. When I knew that I wasn't going to get away, I stopped and turned around to face them.

"What are you doing here?" I screamed. "You don't belong here! In the name of the Lord, get out!" The spirit on the far right fell to its knees like I had injured it by the words I spoke. And every time I repeated those words, it blinked off and on until it finally vanished. I ran and was chased by the other two spirits. I stopped and faced them.

"What are you doing here?" I repeated. "You don't belong here! In the name of the Lord, get out!"

This time, the demon on the left fell to the ground, blinking from the words my Grandmother had always told my sister and me to say if we ever encountered evil spirits. The demon fell and got back up, running and swinging more violently than before. The pain roared through my shoulders, I tried to flee but it seemed like I was running in slow motion. My heart was pounding and pounding. I turned and again repeated my mantra until the demons again started falling and blinking until they vanished. I gasped and my eyes suddenly snapped open. I looked around and found that my entire car was surrounded by a thick rolling fog. I couldn't see anything but the movement of that fog. Vicky was lying in the front passenger seat with the car running the AC.

"Vicky Vicky! Get up!"

"Wha… What's wrong?" she asked, wiping her eyes. "What's wrong? Why are you crying?"

I touched the wetness on my face. "Look!" I said, pointing toward the window.

Vicky looked and her face confirmed that something was strange about that fog. "Let's get…"

Before she could get the words out of her mouth, I had already jumped across into the driver's seat and got the hell out of there.

Nightmare my ass!

The pain in my shoulders was still aching and it was a pain that I couldn't describe. After that experience, I had no more pride. I drove Vicky to her mother's place and I went to mine.

I stayed with my mother for about a week or so. I want to thank my mother for being there for me, but waking up in the hot ass projects depressed the hell out of me even more. I was almost ready to go back out into the woods and take my chances with the boogie man. Instead, Vicky and I hooked up and went to stay with my father.

Vicky and my father got along well because she kept telling him how good he looked, Plus, they both drank like fish. My father went from wearing old button up shirts and slacks to Hawaiian shirts with pleated pants and glittering jewelry. I knew I had to get my own place soon before I ended up kicking somebody's ass or become a serious alcoholic. Periodically, during our stay, despite listening to music and drinking every day, Vicky and I found the time to attend her church. You see, I had developed an attitude that if the Jehovah's Witnesses were like Harriet, I didn't want to have anything to do with them, so I figured I'd try Vicky's church.

The first thing I noticed was the preacher, who happened to resemble Eddie Murphy. He had a salt and pepper afro and a beard. When he saw me, he beamed like some pimp spotting his next whore. The preacher periodically stared at me and I began to feel somewhat uncomfortable. An hour or so later into the service, he startled me by suddenly yelling.

"It's somebody in here that is going to get a lot of money! You, young man," he shouted, pointing at me. "I can feeeeel it! God has something in store for you!"

God must had lied and told him I was sitting on money because he started passing out collection trays. When the tray got to me, I put one dollar in the tray and when the tray circled back the second time, I balled my empty hand up and faked a move like I tossed in money.

That preacher, I can't even remember his name, drove a white Cadillac and had a gold ring almost on every finger was a trip. His sermons were becoming more and more predictable. Every visit, he would call Vicky to the pulpit and grab her by the head and start speaking in tongues. Then, Vicky would start slobbering like a white-mouthed mule, jumping and kicking like she lost her damn mind, until Wham! She would hit the floor, dead weight. I wanted to yell, *Get your ass up off that damn floor!* But I knew better, so I just remained silent and watched the other ladies follow suit. It was evident that church hadn't changed much since my Grandma Alma's days. It was common to hear gossip about deacons and preachers having sex with members of the church. This is one of the reasons why Jehovah Witnesses don't call their place of worship church.

I personally know a lady who got pregnant by her deacon at a very similar church. What got me was this same lady swore that she was saved! One day at her church, she started shouting and screaming for Jesus as she dashed toward the pulpit. She was just jumping and jiggling her booty all over the stage and she ended up busting her head wide open. There was blood gushing down her face and she was slinging blood all over the place. Right then, I knew her spirit was not of God. I knew that Jehovah's spirit is of humbleness and love, not of some raving, slobbering bloody wolf. Although this type of bloody scene didn't occur every week, the theatrics did.

If I wanted to be entertained, I would have gone to a concert. I've seen it time and time again when a member of such a church would go roaring toward the preacher and fall to the floor. She would create such a spectacle of herself that the ushers would throw a sheet over her open legs to prevent people from staring at the woman's fat monkey.

In some of these churches, the women could win Oscars as they shivered and jerked as if they were going into a holy convulsion. This would go on and on until the woman on the floor starts peeping out of one eye, waiting for the usherette's assistance.

I stopped attending Vickie's church because one Sunday, the preacher called me up to the pulpit. I was aware that the few men who attended the church were never called upon and if he thought I was going to act for him, he had another thing coming.

"Me?" I mouthed, pointing to my chest.

"Yeah, you," the preacher shouted. "God is telling me that you are deeply troubled."

The preacher was now looking up at the ceiling. I looked at him and thought for a moment. *Damn, I'm sure in trouble.* I was getting deeper and deeper involved with an alcoholic that would wake up in the morning looking like the Crypt Keeper himself.

I looked at Vicky's dark, circled eyes looking back at me.

"Go – he's calling you," Vicky encouraged.

Oh, what the hell. I got up and approached him. When I reached the preacher's pulpit, he suddenly gripped my forehead. The shock from the sudden impact of his wet, premeditated clench caused me to become submissive while he repeatedly jerked my head back and forth, as if he wanted me to fall to the floor. He spoke this weird language as he continued to jerk my bobbing head, but I refused to fall. The preacher suddenly started shouting louder, jerking my head more viciously and shoved me down on the floor as my head landed into a waiting woman's lap. When I regained my composure and walked back to my seat, I had an overwhelming feeling that I had just been hypnotized. The preacher was now prancing around like he had just raised Lazarus from the dead. At the same time, he ordered his ushers to pass the money trays. Unfortunately, because of Vicky, my father and my excessive drinking, I only had a five dollar bill. When the pan got to me, I gave it up. When the pan made its rounds back up to the pulpit, the preacher stopped and counted it.

"This is not enough," he yelled.

He passed the pans again. I couldn't believe his ungratefulness. Here there were poor single mothers trying to raise their kids and support him and his church and he was standing there with two fistfuls of money and no appreciation. I tell ya, that day, I should have patted myself on the back because I held my peace by keeping my mouth shut when I really wanted to shout, *why are you so ungrateful?*

I left the church that day and never returned.

Sometimes, I didn't know whether I was coming or going and the stunts that Vicky sometimes pulled made me want to stop dealing with her entirely.

One evening, Vicky, my father and I were over my mother's house, celebrating Easter with my kids when Roxann decided to show up.

Roxann's skinny, 30-year-old body was dressed poorly and looked weak as she took a seat near the front porch where I stood. I tried to ignore her, but I couldn't help but notice the silver hair bow that dangled on top of her head by the threads of her remaining hair. Her face was sunken in like a poorly fed racehorse and her skin was ashy colored with just a hint of light brown on her cheeks. She was hard to look at, so I turned to go inside where the others were, and Roxann stormed in behind me.

"Why are you treating me like this?" Roxann growled.

Before I could respond, Vicky was up and in Roxann's face. They both furiously started fighting toward the door onto the porch, and that is when Roxann tore into Vicky.

Scrap Iron. That was one of Roxann's nicknames, given to her because of her ability to defeat much larger opponents and as messed up as she was, that nickname still applied. She fought like a monkey from hell. Roxann now had Vicky in a headlock and Vicky couldn't go on anymore. She was exhausted. She managed to look at me as I stood a few feet away watching, and she looked into my eyes as if she was telling me to stop the fight. So I did. At some point, someone had called the police. When they arrived, Roxann was still cursing and carrying on.

"Go dig a hole and bury yourself!" I yelled to Roxann as she was being escorted to the police car just so to remove her from the scene.

I'll never forget that look she gave me as she was being pushed into that cruiser. It was a look of intense pain. Although Scrap Iron had defeated Vicky, we both had lost.

I wonder if she saw the pain in my eyes.

We returned back home with my father and, as soon as we got there, Vicky headed straight to our bedroom and humbly lay in bed for three days. No drinking, no partying, nothing, just a nibble of food here and there. Pop and I teased Vicky, saying that she needed an ass whipping like that more often - Pop and I burst out laughing.

CHAPTER 6

SHE LOVES ME SHE LOVES ME NOT

June 1995, Orenthal J. Simpson had television newscasters in a running uproar! It was near June 14th, which was Harriet's and my third year anniversary. This particular day, I was visiting my mother when the phone rang and I answered it. The silence from the other end immediately told me that it was Harriet. My heart started pounding when I heard her voice.

"I want you to come home," she whispered.

As bad as I wanted to get my life together, this was like music to my ears. Not only was I overjoyed, but I was deeply relieved. Actually, I felt like I had been rescued. A few minutes later, a local florist delivered a dozen roses to me with a note reading:

Happy Anniversary
Love always,
You're Wife

I must admit, I hadn't felt that good in months. And the thought of going back to the Kingdom Hall and working for an elder in a congregation in California sounded promising. So, just like that, I was California bound.

The following week, I purchased a rental truck and hitch to pull my boat, got my things out of storage, loaded up a few items and gave my mother the rest of my furniture. In addition, I gave Keitha my car for her and my mother to get around in and I left Florida with flying colors.

Four and a half days of traveling, I finally arrived in Hayward, California, a small city that was only a short distance from the extraordinary city of San Francisco.

I was so excited for the new change that I immediately chucked my remaining cigarettes out of the vehicle. I was through smoking. I was ready to serve Jehovah and be the best husband and father I could be. My dream was to create a home that was fit for summer visits for my children and perhaps, in the future, regain their custody. Unfortunately, I had to work harder than I realized because when I arrived, I discovered that Harriet was living in one of Hayward's worst areas. If you closed your eyes and imagined the ghetto, you'd be picturing Harriet's neighborhood.

She done tricked you again you DUMMY! She called you to come up here *to work and help her get out of this hellhole* I mumbled to myself.

I just sat in the car for a while and just looked at the trashy, dirty streets and apartments. The people that stood on the corners looked as if they had seen a ghost. Some roamed aimlessly, looking like they were searching for that mighty rock. I was very disappointed, as I had no idea that my new life was going to start amongst crack heads. I'd seen enough of that back home. Nonetheless, I decided to make the best of it. I greeted Harriet with open arms and said nothing about the appearance of her neighborhood.

Harriet and I immediately started attending the Kingdom Hall. I was hired to drive for Maxi Transportation, which was a trucking company owned by an elder of her congregation. It went just as she planned. As time progressed, I felt really good working for this elder because he paid well and gave me the proper spiritual food that I needed. Furthermore, members of the congregation started commending me on how I stepped in and got Junior's unacceptable behavior in check. Mrs. Peters, my boss's wife, told me how glad she was that I came because Junior really needed a father figure. She went as far as to say that Junior is only 10-years-old, has a bad habit of taking advantage of women, and that he could be a real

49

menace. This wasn't new news to me. When I first came into the picture I had my fair share of dealing with Junior's manipulating behavior. I immediately became his attitude adjuster. I just thanked God that his sister Amy was the total opposite.

I was back and after all had been said and done, I still loved my ready-made family and I worked hard to provide generously for them. Harriet later landed a job driving a short school bus chauffeuring the elderly. In between time, I had advanced biblically to the point where I was allowed to give 5 minute talks at the Kingdom Hall service meetings.

My 29th birthday came in August, 1995 and things seemed to be promising for Harriet and me. That was until I started noticing how filthy our apartment was becoming again. Apparently, I was working late, not realizing that my wife's poor housekeeping had again reared its ugly head. I spoke with Harriet in an effort to encourage her to not let this become a problem like before.

"I'm not planning to stay here much longer anyways," Harriet said.

"That shouldn't be the reason to not keep things presentable," I explained.

Harriet didn't budge. I suppose she felt that since I didn't have family there, I would have no choice but to accept her and her kids' filthiness. She was mistaken. I called Brother Peters from the hall to pull a house call for Harriet and me. A house call is when qualified elders visit your home to discuss your dilemma in hopes of solving it. We definitely needed a mediator.

A couple of hours later after I called, my boss and another elder were at our door knocking to assist us. When the elders listened to both our sides, they immediately referred us to the Bible, where it states that God's people are clean people, which they are not of filth. However, Harriet was in denial, as if I was only exaggerating. For this reason, I showed them every junky room in the apartment, even the trashy soured refrigerator. I pointed out that although I worked, I still maintained a well-groomed yard that was once only dirt and this was done despite of our future view. I also informed them that I try to encourage the kids to clean by giving them a weekly allowance, the amount of which would vary according to their achievement. Finally, Harriet confessed that maybe she was letting the apartment get a little too far out of hand and that things would get better. I concluded the house call by agreeing to pitch in with Harriet for a thorough cleaning. When the elders left, Harriet wanted me to leave right behind them.

"You didn't have to do that Tolerance Lamar," Harriet yelled.

I smirked, as I picked up her inside-out stained panties from the bedroom floor.

"You came way down here just to make me look bad!" she said.

"No I didn't!"

"You're a liar!" she exclaimed. "You didn't have to go tell them about our business in Florida. You're still living in the past!" Harriet eyes were fixed on me as a baboon would at its intruder.

"And you're repeating the same old shit," I shouted. "I've told you over and over again that I'm not going to be living like a pig!"

So, it turned out that calling the elders didn't help our situation. Contention escalated. A day or so later, Harriet placed a restraining order on me.

"I need some space," she replied icily.

Harriet wanted me to get to packing and find somewhere else to live. I again called the elders to intervene. When it was all said and done, I had to abide by the law of the order. Therefore, I had to prepare to leave until we worked out our problems. The elders promptness made things a little easier to handle.

"I'll get my things and sleep in the truck" I muttered.

"Brother Smith lives alone and I think he has a vacant room. I'll call him to see if you can stay with him for a while," Brother Peter offered.

"That's ok, the truck has a sleeper I'll be fine, thank you."

And with that, I packed up my things and left.

The cold breeze from San Francisco Bay was torture because the semi heater wasn't working. When nighttime rolled around, the cab over engine tractor was like an icebox. After that experience, I took up Brother Peter's offer.

I had been staying with Brother Smith for about a month when Harriet pulled up in front of the house. Brother Smith exited the vehicle and thanked her for the ride. Instead of leaving, she opened the hood of her car as if she had a problem. I did as she expected. I came out to assist her, and a few days later I was back with Harriet. I wasn't back in the house a good two weeks when she reinforced the restraining order and had me kicked out again because I had sneered at her kids' room and complained.

Man, it was too embarrassing! Brother Smith's roommate was back at home, so staying with him wasn't an option. Again, Brother Peter intervened and offered a heating pad for my truck. The pad helped, but Jack Frost was biting with big teeth!

One morning while I was on duty during my job assignment, I went off route and purchased a dozen roses on a whim. I swung by Harriet's apartment, in hopes that she would be in a forgiving mood, but she wasn't home, so I neatly placed the roses in her mailbox that was mounted beside her door and left. I drove two miles up the road and parked to eat my lunch while studying biblical literature until lunch was over. While I was reading, a sharp knock on my door interrupted me. I opened the driver's door and looked down into the eyes of an officer, who ordered me to step down out of my truck. The officer then asked where I had gone earlier. As I was explaining myself, another patrol car was pulling up. This is when I noticed Harriet sitting in the passenger seat and when the car came to a complete stop, the cop stepped out of his car and Harriet followed suit. The look of her stone face gave me a sinking feeling of fear. Harriet walked up to me and stopped.

"Tolerance Lamar, you are under arrest."

I looked at her, then back at the officer in disbelief. The officer briefly explained that my wife had a right by choice to a citizen arrest. I then looked back at Harriet.

"Why?" I exclaimed.

"Didn't you come by my apartment, leaving a note and flowers, knowing you have a restraining order not to come there? Did you not, Tolerance Lamar?"

I was speechless as the officer was now placing handcuffs on my wrists. Just like that, I was taken to Santa Rosa County Jail.

The following day, I was standing in front of a judge who was notoriously hard on domestic violence. The recent and sensational murder of Nicole Simpson certainly didn't help matters. Luckily, I didn't have a criminal record there in California, so I was sentenced to three years of unsupervised probation, followed by 300 hours community service. The community service consisted of cleaning the streets, alleys and highways on weekends. Later, that evening I was released along with a few others; among the few stood a female who kept looking at me. Actually, we kept looking at each other.

The female stood about 5 foot 7 inches and she had a slim figure. Her lengthy black hair partnered well with her sexy squinted eyes and yellow skin. Yet as a whole, her ruby luscious lips were the thing that really got my attention. Eye contact led us to start talking and that is when I learned that her name was Cynthia, she was 28-years-old and she was in jail for bank robbery. She had been released when all the charges were dropped and placed on her boyfriend who had actually committed the crime alone. She continued that her boyfriend was a white man whom she was greatly fond of.

"He would do anything for me," confessed Cynthia. I looked into her brown eyes for tears, yet there were none. Cynthia and I left the jail walking and talking, all the way to the bus stop. Finally, the last 10:00 pm bus arrived and we boarded. To make the long story short, we ended up at a hotel. The conversation didn't stop when we got there.

"I'll go to the bar and be talking to a dude," Cynthia said, "and I'll say, 'I will bet you twenty dollars I could show you something you have never seen.'

The guy would bet and that's when I would pull up my skirt. That's how I make my money."

"Damn," I said as she showed me a sample. I couldn't help but touch it. It was so sexy.

I took a moment to admire her. It's funny because I don't like body piercing. I think most piercings are ugly, especially hoop earrings in the eyebrows and nipples. But when she removed her pants and showed me her gold hoop on her clit. I was amazed and ready to find out how it worked.

Half nude, Cynthia was standing at the foot of the bed, rambling through her bag. While she was busy, I placed my Lifestyles tuxedo in my reach and quickly checked to see if the hotel offered a music channel. I found one but it was terrible, so I turned the television back off, kicked off my boxers, pulled her to me and kissed her. Just as we really started getting into it, she pulled away.

"You are a good kisser" she said, then slammed her open mouth back onto mine. I didn't feel like talking, my hormones were in full gear and Tarzan was anxious to meet that curious metal ring down below.

The next day, after departing from my amazing encounter, I was knocked back down to reality when I realized that Harriet had moved. Fortunately, I still had my job and was blessed to be able to move in with another member of my church who was also enduring a marital separation. This was good for the both of us because we could converse about related issues.

I saw Harriet around town, but she did her best to keep me from knowing where she lived. A month or so passed and I was still attending the Christian meetings at the Kingdom Hall that Harriet and I had once attended as a couple. Harriet too was there at every meeting, with her nose up at me, acting stuck-up if you will. Then, one week, she was different. When I looked over at her, I was surprised to see her giving me the, I want you stare.

It turned out that Harriet's application for a brand-spanking-new HUD apartment had come through for her. Unlike the other low-income housing, this state-of-the-art project carried a decent monthly bill. The apartment came equipped with top-notch security, a washer and dryer, a balcony in the master bedroom and an elevator near her front door.

Would it be safe to assume that, perhaps, she needed my assistance? I recall once, when I asked Harriet, in front of the elders, if she loved me, her reply was, "Yes, I'm a good provider." It was clear that she had me around for one reason. And my dumb ass keep running back like the puppy my sister Keitha, once quoted.

True, I knew this woman could be cold as ice, but I loved her and hoped for the best. I knew God hated a divorce and so did I. I believed that things would get better as long as I kept seeking first the Kingdom without letting up. This was easier said than done of course. As time went on, resentment set in and my intuition told me that I was sleeping with the enemy. Before I knew it, I started going to a local bar to relieve tension.

One night, when I returned home, Harriet was in the mood for sex. I'm talking oral sex.

Don't get me wrong, I've been there and done that. The problem was that we both confessed to be Christians, and oral sex was said to be unnatural, as if God didn't make our mouths for those purposes. I know everybody has their own opinion, but at that time, our biblical leaders admonished the congregation regarding oral sex. Therefore, Harriet and I tried to refrain from that type of activity.

Well, you know the old saying, The flesh is weak. Within minutes, I had Harriet squirming against the headboard. I finally rose up, my lips glazed like a fresh Krispy Kreme donut. My turn! I flipped on my back, but Harriet regained her composure and started quoting scriptures.

"Oh, don't get holy on me now!" I told her. Harriet politely got up and left me in the bed holding my erection.

She done beat me for my head, I angrily thought.

I was downright mad and the drinking didn't help any. I couldn't hold it in any longer, I told Harriet about her deceitful, no good ass!

That night, my sleeping quarters again went from a warm room to a cold vehicle. Finally, I was fed up with Harriet's back and forth nature. I called my boss and told him that I was going back to Florida and he said that he didn't blame me. He gave me the notion that he believed Harriet wasn't what she made herself out to be. The elder went on to say that the congregation would be taking a closer look at her and that they wanted me to resume my creed in Florida. That morning, I turned in the company truck, received my pay and rented a U-haul and trailer. I loaded my boat, car, stereo and other personal items in and hauled my butt back to Florida.

CHAPTER 7

HOME SWEET HOME

By May 10, 1995, after five days of traveling, I was back in Tampa. Thanks to my father and his friend Carl Warren, who worked in Public Assistance, I had my own apartment within 30 days. My apartment was off of 48th Street and Busch, which was eight blocks down from Tampa Bay's beautiful theme park, Busch Gardens. As the days passed, my main focus was to quickly find a job and maintain my blissful start. In the midst of my mission, Keitha came back to live with me; not because she loved and missed her brother, but to beat the heat from them hot ass projects! I was delighted to see her cheesy grin; it was a sight for sore eyes.

In no time at all, I had landed a driving job for a company called King Provision. My duties were to deliver food products to Florida's Burger King Corporation. Around forty days after leaving California, the peace in my life evaporated when Harriet began to accuse me of fondling her son.

Man, I had never been so upset in my life until I heard of that disgusting lie. Not only did she call my mother with that bullshit, she even called Hafeezah and my other friends. Although I didn't have to prove anything, as my character spoke for itself, I was still tempted to go back to California and file charges against her for defaming my character. Unfortunately, I didn't have the money to do so. By the grace of God, I was able to block out what my wife was trying to do to me and carry on with my life.

Again, I was filled with a longing to rescue my kids and their mother from her addiction. After my latest attempt, I was able to get Roxann safe and sound in my bed. To keep a close eye on her, I started taking Roxann to work with me, but she found hauling freight boring. However, Roxann seemed auspicious, which gave me joyous hope that our family relationship might be restored. Moreover, every evening when I returned from work, I would make sure Roxann had used her face cream so she could regain her brown complexion that had turned an ashy black, due to lack of nutrition. I would cook potatoes and other starchy foods to help Roxann regain the weight she had once held. In addition, some evenings I would comb her hair with African oils to restore a healthy look. Roxann's natural beauty was returning and I was so happy and proud to see such a change in her.

Finally, I called Roxann's older sister Dell, who had legal custody of our four kids and told her that Roxann and I were ready to get our children back. I set a date for her to come over and visit us to discuss the matter. Dell must have gotten comfortable living off the monthly income that the HRS and SSI provided for the kids because her response to me was as though I was a nuisance, but I kept my cool. She agreed to meet at my apartment.

When Dell arrived, along with her was her other sister Rein. Rein was older than Roxann, somewhere in her late thirties, and was a year or so younger than Dell. I could easily tell the two apart because Rein had more of a reddish complexion. Rein greeted Roxann and me with a genuine, bright smile, whereas Dell's smile was missing. She gave us a tight *hey* and hastily walked in scanning the place. Rein immediately noticed Roxann's weight gain and marveled at her recovery, Dell was practically sneering.

After we were all settled, we proceeded to discuss the matter concerning my children. Dell was stone-faced as I explained to her that Roxann and I were preparing for a court hearing and that our determination to do so was serious. Rein smiled at me when I showed proof of what I proclaimed. Dell became so alienated and threatened by my ambition that she got up and left with an attitude. I was saddened to see Dell act in such a selfish, hostile manner by completely disregarding the fact that Roxann and I were only doing what loving parent's would attempt to do.

Even though I was upset by Dell's attitude, and not to mention the fact that my kids were being neglected while living with her, I still wanted to hug her and thank her because I was grateful that my four kids were together, living in the same household. HRS would have split them up and that would have mentally killed me, but thanks to Dell, they were all together.

As days followed, the tension that Dell created made me forget about my compassion and feel only resentment towards her. It was disturbing to see that Dell allowed the almighty dollar to turn her away from supporting our efforts. It was obvious that she wished we would go away.

I remember when Dell first got custody of my children. There was little hope that Roxann would escape her meaningless drug addiction. One evening, I approached Dell and humbly asked her to allow me to move in with her and my kids so we could both raise my children together. She looked me dead in my eyes to witness and remained silent for a moment.

"No, that's okay," she finally said. "I'll manage, but thanks for asking."

Sure enough she managed and managed quite well because the government checks she was receiving for my kids turned into a large house and nice car, unlike the hot projects and bus line she was used to. Greed took strong root in my sister-in-law. Not only did she belittle Roxann and me in front of our children, she also wanted me to stop all communication with them. She essentially wanted me to just disappear. Dell would actually raise holy hell with my kids if they tried to hang out with Roxann and me. She was mean and very strict toward my children, always making them clean the house like they were work horses and yelling at them endlessly. Their hair was always poorly groomed, and they wore hand me down clothes. Spending time with my kids was almost impossible. And then, the next thing I knew, Dell got married to a man who was unemployed. The two were building a better life for themselves off of the expense of my children.

I know they say that money is the root of all evil, but damn, what happened to morals and the love for family?

If you need money, go hustle, but don't hustle your family. Hell, I was about ready to go fight them. I had actually paid Dell's husband a visit after a heated phone conversation. I remember I was gripping a .357 hand gun as I knocked on their door. He never answered, thank God. I knew that killing the man or getting killed wasn't the solution, I don't know what would have happened if the door had opened. Taking a stand as responsible parents was what Roxanne and I needed to do. I was saddened to see what the almighty dollar brought out of them, so I started writing instead of fighting.

A couple of days after the meeting with Dell, I had a talk with my 13-year old-daughter Tina, at her grandmother's house while waiting for Dell to pick her up. I happily told Tina about her mother's and my plans. Tina frowned, saying that her mother wasn't going to do nothing but leave and go back to Terry, like she always did. I tried to convince my daughter that mom was serious this time. A few days after talking with my daughter, I returned home, only to be greeted by my sister.

"Roxann left again," Keitha fumed.

As I seated myself, all of my energy suddenly drained from my body. I knew where to find her, but I felt it wouldn't be wise going there, since I knew that Terry would probably be there with her. Things could get ugly, besides, I felt weak. I kept telling myself that Roxann wasn't worth it, to just go on with my life. I suppressed my emotions about two days or so until I just couldn't hold them anymore. I found myself parked in front of the crack shack, blowing the horn for Roxann once again.

Terry appeared at the screen door, and then stepped onto the porch. He stood 6 foot tall with broad shoulders and a healthy beer gut. He was in his mid-forties, 15-years-older than me. I had heard people say that Terry and I looked a bit alike because of our red skin tone and beefy smile, but I like to think that any other comparisons between the two of us stops there. Terry was a prime example of a grown man afraid to grow old. Everything about him from his clownish jewelry down to his baseball cap that he wore turned sideways on his head screamed man-child.

Terry glared at me as he walked to the far end of the porch, his shoulders arched higher than normal.

"What you want?" he asked in a intimating voice.

I stared at him for a moment.

"Roxann in there?"

"Yeah, she's here, but she don't want to talk" he answered coldly.

I felt a wave of heat rush through my body. I got out of the car.

"Tell Roxann I need to see her about our kids."

I was walking onto his lawn when unexpectedly Terry's younger brother Frank appeared at the door. He was taller than Terry, had a pot belly like his brother, and he was also heavier and posed more of a threat than Terry. Frank walked out to the other end of the porch and folded his arms, sneering at me. I disregarded the disadvantage that I faced and I again demanded to see Roxann.

"She don't want to see you," Frank intervened.

I suddenly was overwhelmed with the feeling that Roxann was being held against her own free will.

"Why can't she tell me that?" I shouted in anger.

Frank only shrugged his shoulders. Terry was now looking at me like The Rock would at Stone Cold, yet this situation was far beyond wrestling. I felt that they were holding Roxann hostage, so I quickly got into my car and sped off. I was overcome with anger and ready for war. I needed a gun, as well as someone to watch my back. I dashed into a fueling station to gas up and gather my thoughts. Then, to my surprise, my Aunt Ducky's son, Michael, a thug who would fight at a drop of a hat, pulled up beside me. He even had two of his thug buddies in the car with him. I jumped out of my car, greeted him and frantically told him that my baby mama had been abducted at Terry's house and I needed help. Michael was a dark-skinned cat who was in his late teens and he always seemed to be overflowing with energy. His two buddies seemed to be around the same age as Michael and perhaps a couple of inches taller and a few pounds heavier. But Michael was cockier and meaner. As he stood before me shirtless, showing off his rippling muscular build, he immediately got amped up after hearing my situation.

"What!" Michael and his goons asked. "Where they at?"

Michael ducked in the car and pulled out a revolver from his seat and cocked it with an ominous *click click* sound. Michael's driver followed suit and asked me if I was strapped, and I said that I was.

"Let's go. We'll follow you," said Michael.

I jumped in my car. *It's on*, I thought to myself.

We skidded out of the parking lot like Miami Vice and in a matter of three minutes we were slamming the brakes and the tires screamed to a halt in front of the crack shack.

Terry and Frank were still on the porch when we startled them. We jumped out of our cars and approached the two men. I could see the blood drain from their faces. The sneers and browbeating no longer existed as the three thugs stood off about 25 feet from them, each positioned with one hand along the back of their thighs, their faces were cold and deadly. I approached Terry and Frank like a gangster, fueled by the fear in their eyes. I demanded to see Roxann once again. My hands were in the same position as the three jits behind me. The only difference was that I held a pack of Salem cigarettes in a balled-up paper bag, bluffing as if I had a gun.

"Toler, I told you that Roxann didn't want to talk. I don't know why!" Terry said softly.

Michael intervened and demanded to know where she was.

"She's in there," Terry said, motioning with his arm toward the front door.

"I'll go in and get her," Michael said.

"Go ahead, we got your back," the other thug said.

Michael looked my way and I nodded my head confidently as the leader, knowing, that if Terry and Frank pulled out a gun and started shooting, all I could do is throw a pack of cigarettes at them and run like hell.

After my nod to proceed, Michael walked up on the porch and into the house while the other two goons kept their eyes on Terry and Frank. I could hear Michael ask Roxann what was up. Roxann said nothing was up.

Come on, baby, come on, I whispered to myself.

A couple more words that I couldn't clearly understand were passed between the two, followed by a moment of silence. Suddenly, Michael stormed out the door.

"She don't want to come. Fuck her let's go!"

And just like that, we got into our cars and left.

I'd hoped that Roxann was being held against her will because that would have said that there was still hope for the two of us and our children.

Obviously, that wasn't the case. Roxann had made me look like a fool for the last time. Whatever she was looking for in life, I hoped that she would find it because I threw in the towel. Somehow, someway, I would find other means to help my children.

In the coming weeks I kept myself busy on the job but little did I know, Keitha was staying pretty busy herself. She was dating a 25-year-old man. Our mom approved of this because, even though, Keitha was 17, the guy looked just as young as her. Actually, Keitha looked like his big sister because he was so short. He looked like a grinning little buck-toothed monkey. One couldn't help but like him because he was always grinning. Still, I wasn't down with her playing wife in my apartment, so I sent her back to our mother's place. The following month I lived alone and it was hard. I tried so hard not to feel lonely and vulnerable because I really didn't want to make any more regretful decisions.

As much as I tried to deny it, Harriet still had her claws in me because there were many nights where I laid in my bed thinking about our sensational encounters. I missed her witty sense of humor and not to mention, her superb cooking. Sometimes I would prepare my meals and eat feeling sorry for myself because I didn't have anyone to share it with.

CHAPTER 8

RON'S RECALL

August 9, 1995, a day before my 30th birthday, I was sitting, watching television. A love story was on and I remember watching some man kissing a lady. A sudden wave of loneliness struck me as I sat there. Tears began to run down my face and I muttered to myself that I wanted a girlfriend. I wanted somebody who wanted me for me and I began to feel overwhelmed. I got up from my chair and turned off the television. When all was quiet, I got on my knees and started to pray. I asked God through His precious Son Jesus Christ, to bring a good wife into my life. I was tired of dealing with no good women, and I just wanted God to bless me with a good lady. As I was praying, my words grew louder and louder and my tears began to flow more heavily. This gut prayer lasted about ten minutes until I raised my head and saw that the chair I was leaning on was soaked with my tears. I was amazed; I had never prayed like that before.

The next day, Jake, my friend who worked for Jones Cable Company, the same guy who had given me a place to stay when Harriet cleaned me out offered to hook up my cable. When he was finished, he handed me a phone number with the name Sybil written on it.

"This is a good woman for you," Jake said.

I stuffed the number in my pocket and forgot about it. That night I went to visit my father and when I got there, I remembered the number Jake had given me. So I dug in my pocket and called her. The phone rang three times before a voice answered.

"Is this Sybil?"

"Who is this?" she demanded.

"Your husband," I said humbly.

"My husband, I don't know you! How did you get my number?"

I made up some story that her sister gave it to me, and then I confessed that I was searching for a good companion. Sybil began to sound excited, as if God had answered her prayers. That night we agreed to talk more in person. Sybil and I decided to meet on 40th and Yukon. I told her to look for the King Provision tractor and trailer and that I would be parked waiting. I sat with my hazard lights flashing and soon enough, Sybil pulled up and parked next to me. I climbed out of the truck and politely greeted her. Sybil was a petite little lady. Her brown skin tone was flawless. She stood about 5 foot 4 and had the most gorgeous bow legs; I couldn't help but notice them as we walked across the street to a 7- Eleven to grab a soda and then headed back to my semi. I hoisted Sybil up into the tractor for a brief conversation and I realized that God was giving me what I had prayed for.

During our conversation, I learned that Sybil was 35-years of age, five years and seven months older than I. She was also a mother of two sons, Keeven her 10-year-old; and Kevis a 17-year-old. She worked as a nursing assistant at a local retirement home. Our spark was immediate and Sybil and I started dating the day after we met. At my place, I would prepare dinner for Sybil and Keeven. The two would just marvel at the dishes I prepared for them.

The first night at the table Keeven gave his approval by saying, "This is cool!" Keeven was a good respectful lad, whom actually called me Dad the very first day he met me. He was the type of child that would straighten right up when you talked to him. I only had to spank him once for lying to his mother and I. Months passed, finally I told Sybil that she could move in with me. The reason I procrastinated was because of Kevis, Sybil's oldest son.

Kevis was totally the opposite of Keeven. He had dropped out in the 8th grade and preferred doing as he pleased.

One morning, I had to literally jack him up. It was a cold early morning. I was dispatched to take my assigned tractor and trailer home with me and resume delivery later that evening, so I drove home. Sybil and Keevan were sound asleep, whereas Kevis was lying on the couch talking on the phone. I told Kevis to come and spot me, meaning, to make sure I didn't back up onto a parked car. He said ok as I headed back out the door and back into the tractor. I also wanted to park my trailer flush against the wall of our apartment to keep the thieves out. The semi gave a beeping sound as I was proceeded slowly backing up the trailer. I looked into the side rearview mirrors for Kevis but he hadn't come out yet. I stopped the truck, looked at my front door, waited another minute or so and still no Kevis. I was now becoming heated as I attempted to park without him but the end of the trailer was on my blind side. I slammed the truck in park and jumped out heading for my front door. I slung the door open, Kevis was just getting off the couch when I rushed and grabbed him by his neck jacking him up against the wall.

"Who in the hell you think you are?" I yelled looking up into his face. "You think you grown"?

"No" he said softly.

Sybil was now up asking what was going on. I loosened him and expressed my anger. Sybil helped me get parked and gave me no fuss about my decision. The young man was just straight hard headed. He wouldn't go to school and he wouldn't work; he just wanted to hang out with his friends come home and eat, shit and sleep, followed by giving his mother lip. Well, needless to say, a man will only allow so much to go on in his household before he takes a stand. That very morning, I told Kevis to get out of my apartment before I end up splitting his wig. Child, my ass! I wasn't going to take any more of his shit.

So, Sybil took Kevis to his uncle's to live.

Sybil was a good supportive woman indeed; and she had an endearing eagerness to learn about Jehovah and why He put us on this earth. Sybil started attending the Kingdom Hall with me. My father even started accepting bible study by a qualified Jehovah witness, in hopes of learning accurate knowledge of God's word not from false prophets or the philosophy of men.

Sybil was far different from the other women I've known. She was very home-bodied and she didn't mind working to make sure the home was taken care of. She didn't smoke nor drink and she always carried a serious look on her face. Sometimes, I would have to ask her to loosen up a little. I loved listening to music and drinking and I would often try to entertain Sybil, but I just couldn't get her to laugh; she would only stare at me as if I was from another planet. Before getting bored, I would join Keevan in playing video games. This was enough to keep me going on most occasions, but eventually, boredom set in. I had a live-in companion and I was still lonely. Consequently, I lost interest and started going to clubs to enjoy myself.

After all was said and done, Sybil and I got along because she let me do what I wanted without any complaints. For the first time in my life, I was able to slow down and not work so hard. Actually, I ended up not working at all. I would just lie around and let Sybil work and pay the bills. This went on for about four months. Although she made it easy for me, I found myself not happy.

Days passed, a long lost family member named Sheryl Jean had passed. I remember standing there during the procession, thinking about everything that had been bothering me. That evening, I confessed to my dad how I was feeling.

"Living with Sybil is like living with Grandma," I told him.

Dad listened to me, but he didn't say much. Days passed, I couldn't shake my negative feelings and I kept telling myself that I was going to have nothing but a boring life with Sybil. With that, I decided to find another woman, someone with a sense of humor and who liked to have fun.

Was this rational thinking or was I just fooling myself?

You know, the Bible speaks on matters like this, namely, the taunt of fleshly desires; at this time of my life, biblical counseling was going in one ear and coming out the other. It got to where I just completely stopped going to the Hall. I started drinking heavily to medicate the pain of not having my children around. After four months of not working, lying around and partying; thanks to Jehovah's mercy, I was able to get a grip of myself and resume studying God's word. In addition, Nation's Bank granted me a loan to renovate a corner house in West Tampa.

In February of 1996, my divorce was finalized and I was convinced that I would never find a woman who was capable of satisfying me like Harriet. I felt cheerless.

One day, I went to visit my sister, Rena, who had recently served a three-year prison term for trying to support her ugly crack habit. She was bless to get out unharmed and within a few weeks, she was able to get her own apartment. Thereafter, she was granted custody of her four boys, Ron 16, Leon 14, Jonteral 11, and Lil' Johnnie 10. My nephews were fortunate to have a mother who took a stand to get them back. In no time, Rena had everything up and running.

Out of nowhere, an ugly rumor surfaced. It was said that Rena was visiting Roxann and that the two were smoking crack together. This rumor made me irate. I mean, my sister went through all the trouble to regain custody of her kids, and allow crack back into her life knowing how that drug can make you get. Really!

One evening, I decided to pay Sister Rena a visit. When I arrived at her apartment, I knocked and after a minute or so, she opened the door.

"What's up, baser!" I said sarcastically as I walked toward the living room.

Rena stood 5 foot 11 and around 230 pounds. Her size, coupled with her notoriously quick temper, made me make sure that my peripheral vision was working at its best. Her mouth was open, as her eyes stay fixed on me. The look like on her was like, *No he didn't.*

"I'm just joking" I said before she decided to kick me out or hurl something at me.

Rena went into her room with a huff and I chuckled. Moments later my 16-year-old nephew Ron, came out of his bedroom.

"What's up, Unc?" he greeted.

We started talking and to my surprise, he told me that Keitha was six months pregnant. It suddenly dawned on me.

"That's why she always grinned at me when I would tell her that she was gaining weight," I said to Ron.

Ron found this amusing, but I didn't. I actually found it to be quite deceitful, a person you can't trust.

Ron's mood changed and his eyes started to turn red. I sensed that something was deeply bothering him. I asked him what was wrong and after a few minutes of silence, he let it out. What he told me not only turned my eyes red, it blurred my vision.

Out of all of the time that I have spent writing this book, this section was one of the most painful, disturbing things I had to endure. As I write this, I can say that I will be glad to get past this part and turn the page.

Ron recalled back when his mother was in prison and my father and his ole lady Vi had legal custody of him and his brother Leon. One night, Ron got up to use the bathroom. When he headed back to bed, my father met him, pinned him against the wall and started trying to kiss him. I watched as tears ran down Ron's face as he told me how hard he had to fight to keep my father from tonguing him.

"I felt his whiskers pressing onto my face." "His breath smelled like old beer."

As Ron continued to fight off my father's sexual attack, Vi yelled from their bedroom, "What's going on out there?" My father then let Ron go and left the room without a word. At that point my vision was blurred with tears. My heart felt like it was in the pit of my stomach, curled up in pain and anger. For Christ's sake, this was my father this boy was talking about! That alone sickened me. I immediately wanted my father punished for his sick, disgusting act.

"Rena!" I exclaimed. "Did you hear what Pop did to Ron?"

From Rena's bed room she yells back that he had told her.

I was stunned. Here I was ready to warn the neighbors; and yet Rena lay in her bed undisturbed as though she had accepted it. Ron concluded that he was drunk.

I knew that there was no fitting excuse for what my father had done.

"That's bullshit! There's no amount of drinking that will make a man do something like that unless he had already wanted to. Pop positioned himself to be a father to Ron, a grandfather, a male figure and he took advantage of the boy. There is no excuse for that! Me and Ron are going to go to pops neighborhood and knock on doors, we are going to put out fliers to warn the neighbors that Mr. Lamar, my father, was a sick and perverted man." I ranted.

I wanted him to feel the embarrassment and pain that he had caused Ron and me.

I noticed that Ron's body language was telling me that he wasn't willing to go to those extremes.

As I wiped the tears from my face and came to grips with the fact that maybe I was a little too angry and overreacting, I forced my anger to subside a little. I then asked Ron to write a letter to my father expressing how he felt about the awful thing he tried to do. Ron agreed and went into his room then returned to the kitchen table with a pen and paper. As I sat waiting for Ron's letter, I thought about what my mother had once said, *your dad ain't nothing but a freak! He will try to screw anybody!*

At that moment, I resented that I was named after my father.

And one thing I knew for sure, as long as his ass hole was toward this ground, he better not ever, and I mean ever, try to put his filthy paws on one of my children nor my little sister. After Ron gave me his letter, I headed home thinking about when I would pay that dad of mine a visit. I told no one about this; it was too embarrassing for me to bear. The Lord knew that I loved my father, but this type of behavior was totally unacceptable. I would have had him locked up, and that's after I would have mopped the floor with his ass!

The following week, I visited my father. After thirty minutes or so of sitting across from him, I handed him Ron's letter. I didn't know what he was thinking about to be smiling, but when he started reading it, his smiled turned upside down.

"Ron done lost his mind," my father said, his face frozen in innocence.

He tried to make me believe that Ron was becoming mentally ill and that his accusations were only lies.

"He is losing his mind cause of what his mother has taken him through," he said.

He went on to say how jealous Ron would get when a man would kiss his mother.

"He hates to see Rena with another man. He is obsessed with his mom. The boy is sick can't you see that?" he grimaced.

My dad was gazing into my eyes, hoping to see some kind of agreement. I acted like what he was saying was confusing and may have some truth to it. The love I had for my dad made me want to believe him, but deep down in the pit of my soul, I knew Ron wouldn't just make up something like that. Yet, I couldn't stand to see my dad's dispirited composure. I struck up a different issue so that we could get off the subject. Once again, I suppressed the accusations against my father.

By August 10th, my 31st birthday, Sybil, Keevan and I had settled in our remodeled home in West Tampa, along with our new Rottweiler puppy that we named Boneshaker. I remember that we were sitting outside, looking at our freshly landscaped yard. Sybil glanced my way and gave me a smile. We both had worked hard, sometimes even from dusk till dawn. We would be painting and cleaning our new home. Even Boneshaker seemed happy and content as he flopped down in the cool grass.

Things looked good for Sybil and me except for one thing: Sybil was just not my type. I felt bored with her. I wanted somebody who did some of the things I liked to do, like party and clown a little. Actually, I seemed to crave everything except the right thing. Now don't get me wrong, I did make an honest effort to strengthen our relationship. I tried spending quality time with her by going to the movies, boating and biblical gatherings, still I found life with her to be boring.

You are going to have a boring life if you stay with her, I kept telling myself.

That pessimistic feeling followed me, as though it was a curse. What was so troubling was that I knew, without a shadow of a doubt, that Sybil was indeed marriage material. She was a good, loyal, devoted woman that a man doesn't find every day. Something was wrong and I couldn't put my finger on it. As I sat on my porch pondering, my eyes caught site of my red, 15-foot boat that I had named The Red Snapper; then, that father of mine came to mind.

Father's Day was a few months after Ron's egregious accusations about my dad. Still I honored that day by taking him fishing. That day, my father and I loaded up our fishing gear and headed to the gulf. Along the way, I said nothing about what Ron had said. Once we were out into the bay, we dropped our anchor directly under the Sky Way Bridge and started catching small grouper. From a distance, I could see dark clouds hovering over whatever city was below. I didn't think much of it because it was so far away so we continued fishing. The next thing we knew, we looked up and those black clouds were right over us. Bolts of lightning started shooting from it then heavy rain and loud thunder. The Red Snapper started rocking violently as the wind and waves grew stronger. I pulled up the anchor. A sea of rain blurred my vision making it difficult to see ahead of me as my boat's 90-horse out-board motor hummed its way to safety. Once we were back on land, we realized that 30 minutes of trying to escape a severe storm seemed like hours. We went straight to ABC Liquor, bought a half gallon of Hennessey Cognac, and started celebrating for surviving the storm's ruthless waves and cracking lightning. That evening, Pop ended Father's day by standing next to the Red Snapper and praising about how the old boat saved his life. I recorded his celebration with my new camcorder that I had recently gotten. Actually, since I got my little toy, I went camcorder crazy! I just hate that the monstrous storm didn't allow me to record my dad trying to stuff himself into the bow of the boat. He was scared shitless! He jumped every time lightning cracked and thunder roared. Indeed, it was a day of remembrance.

CHAPTER 9

LOVE, LUST AND INFATUATION

Time went on. Sybil still worked on decorating our remodeled home, but I had stopped working on it weeks ago for one, simple reason: I had lost interest. I was bored. I wanted someone who could fill up the empty feeling that I felt inside, someone who could make me laugh. The next thing I knew, I started going to bars again.

One night, I went to this bar called The Interstate Lounge on a karaoke night. As I was sipping on rum and coke, I struck up a conversation with a woman named Tangy. We hit it off pretty good and she quickly became my buddy. We started hanging out every chance we got. The sex was good; her company was good; good enough to where she started going to work with me. We would ride up and down the highways talking and laughing. Tangy began to open up more about her past. She told me that she used to be a prostitute. I learned that she had a rough upbringing and that led her to do what she had to do. She recalled her three beautiful children, all from different men, two boys and one girl. The two boys were mixed, and they had the most beautiful skin and hair I had ever seen on a child. My heart shifted as I thought about men bragging about how they used to screw my girlfriend for money. I would be embarrassed and ashamed. So I asked Tangy what city she was prostituting in. My heart was crushed when she said Tampa. I began to really like Tangy, but I wanted a wife to be proud of as well. I still saw Tangy but yet was very skeptical about her.

One night, I pulled up in her grandmother's driveway, her place of stay. Grandma said Tangy wasn't there. She had walked down the street somewhere. I got back into my car and waited for her. An hour or so later, out of the dark, she walked up. I noticed all she had on was a big, long, white tee shirt and panties. No shoes, no bra. To make the long story short, I felt Tangy had just left some man's house that stayed down the street. We got into an argument about this. I got back into my car and was going to back up and leave. Tangy stood outside my car still talking crap to me about Sybil. I said something sarcastic back to her. Out of anger, and she thumbed her lit cigarette into my shirt. I jumped out of the car trying to shake the cigarette out of my shirt because it was burning my skin. The cigarette fell out and in anger, I charged at Tangy to only grab her shirt ripping it as she dashed into the house. She yelled she was calling the police as I was leaving. As karma would have it, Tangy later came to me saying that she was pregnant with my baby. After her tee shirt and panties stunt and confession about her promiscuous behaviors, I didn't think so but I thanked her for sharing!

A week or so later, Keitha informed me that my ex-wife had called and left her number for me to return her call. As I wrote down the number, an anxious feeling came over me, followed by a big beefy smile. I grabbed the phone and called the number. When she answered, I immediately noticed how soft and apologetic Harriet's voice was as she told me how much she had missed me. I must admit the feeling was mutual, but resentment was still within me, especially after she accused me of fondling her son. Before I realized what was happening, I was going in on her, telling her how big of an atrocious liar she was. Harriet suddenly broke my verbal attack.

"Tolerance, I have changed. You have to forgive me or God won't forgive you," she said, softly.

She went on to say that she had been disfellowshipped by the congregation because of her wrong-doings and that, for the past year, she had been taking inventory on herself so that she could become a better person. She seemed like she was sincere and, again, my love for her began to raise its head. I apologized to her for our past confrontations, that maybe I was a little too hard on her and that I should had been more patient. We both concurred that Satan was out to destroy people and their families. She then put Amy and Junior on the phone and, in unison, they both apologized for the sex charges that they had fabricated, lies that could have caused me serious prison time. I learned that the investigator closed the case when Amy slipped and said that Junior had been playing with himself. Amy age 13, two years older than her brother apologized and confessed that she had been against it from the start. Nevertheless, I loved Amy and Junior like my own and after I got off the phone with them, the resentment was lifted.

Five minutes later, my home phone rang.

Sybil, I thought.

"Hello?"

"Is this the Tolerance Lamar residence?" a deep, manly voice asked.

"Yes it is," I replied.

"This is Clarence – what's up, dude?"

I caught the voice, it was Harriet and I cracked up laughing. Man, she was hilarious! That was one of the things I loved about her: her buffoonery. She didn't mind clowning and she could have you laughing and crying at the same time.

Harriet's voice returned back to normal and she confirmed that she would be in Tampa the coming weekend to see me. The following evening, Harriet called again. Sybil handed me the phone, saying that some guy named Clarence wanted me. Harriet and I cracked up together. Every day, my ex-wife would call pretending to be this Clarence character until the day she boarded her flight to Tampa. That particular day, while packing my things, I suddenly had a thought that I should leave Harriet stranded at the airport and tell her that I changed my mind. The voice told me to tell her that I didn't want to have anything to do with her and hang up. I ignored my inner voice. I packed my tote bag like I had to go on a delivery out of state. This gave me a few days away from home without Sybil becoming suspicious. My cell phone rang and when I saw that it was Harriet, I kissed Sybil goodbye and left.

I arrived at the airport terminal, scanning the scene for Harriet. There she stood, about a hundred or so yards in front of me. Our eyes met and I was pleased to see that Harriet was as beautiful as ever. Somehow, I had forgotten about her bright complexion and how it glowed softly against her silky, black hair. I forgot about her wide bedroom eyes and those Whoopi Goldberg lips. We rushed to each other and kissed. I happened to be wearing hazel-green contacts and Harriet warmly complimented them, lustfully telling me how they increased my sex appeal. Not long after, Harriet and I were at the Economy Inn, reconnecting. Later, we left to find something to eat while reminiscing about the good times and the love we once shared, despite our disagreements and conflicts.

On the second day of Harriet's arrival, I suggested that she call my mother and confess to the awful lies she had made up against me and she did, without question. In addition to that, I had an interview with Dart Container in Plant City, which happened to be a well-paid job that consisted of hauling paper cups and other paper products to various cities. I was hired to start the following week, which gave me a reason to not have to worry about my present job, so I called in. On our 4th day of hanging out, Harriet requested to see the house that Sybil and I had. I told her tonight when Sybil was at work.

A little before midnight, Harriet and I pulled up into the driveway of Sybil's and my house. It was dark, in the house, with only a plug-in nightlight giving off a dull glow down the hallway. I slowly open Keevan's bedroom door. My stepson was sound asleep, so I quietly shut his door. Harriet was behind me, crouched over and following right in my footsteps. I hoped like hell Sybil wouldn't decide to come home early from work. I eased open our bedroom door and I cut on the light. Harriet slowly walked around, scanning the area. Harriet had a somewhat shitty smirk on her face as she looked at the bed. I met her gaze and immediately thought of taking Harriet to the bed, but that was not on my agenda. Suddenly, we heard movement coming from Keevan's room. I quickly shut off the lights. Harriet quietly rushed out the room, floated down the hallway and vanished. I just stood there in the room, prepared to act like I'd returned from work, but my son never came out. Again, the house was in total silence. I exited my room and tip-toed down the hall, searching for Harriet. I couldn't find her, but as I quietly crept through the house, she appeared behind me. I grabbed her hand and we left the house. On our way back to the hotel, Harriet complimented me on my desire to live a decent life. I couldn't help but wonder how decent I would have been had I laid Harriet down in Sybil's bed.

The following morning, after eating breakfast, Harriet asked me to remarry her. She promised that she would be a good wife this time. She seemed so sincere. I reminded her how wicked she had been before and how she had betrayed me during our first marriage. I thought about it for a while and I asked Harriet to swear on the Bible that she would be a good wife and never betray me ever again, and that we would endure until death did us part. She retrieved her Bible and placed her hand upon it. I grabbed my camcorder and recorded her swearing under oath that she had changed. She was, indeed, sincere.

After our agreement to remarry, I asked her if I should return to California or if she should move back to Florida. Harriet quickly agreed to reside in Florida because of my new job. I immediately called John, the man who renovated my home. Fortunately, I was on good standing with this guy, as well as Nations bank, so I asked him to set up a second contract for another house. I explained my situation and assured him that Sybil would keep up payments on the first house. John set up an appointment for me to look at another house and to see what repairs needed to be made. After I hung up, Harriet hugged and kissed me, assuring me that this time; we would be a happy family.

The plan was for Harriet to fly back to California and gradually pack her things, so that we could give John the weeks he needed to reconstruct the house to our standards. Harriet took a flight back to California, the same day that I started my new job at Dart Containers. That evening, I pulled up in my Ford Bronco and greeted Sybil as though I was exhausted from days of long traveling. Sybil greeted me with a tight, "I miss you" hug and kiss. Needless to say, she had no clue that my *job assignment* was fabricated. Furthermore, I informed Sybil that I'd be leaving my old job and joining Dart Containers Inc. She was happy to hear the news. Later that evening, the phone rang and Sybil answered.

"Honey," Sybil called out, "your friend, Clarence, is on the phone."

Everyone in my immediate family knew about me planning to leave Sybil except for Sybil. Not everyone agreed that it was a good idea. My father, for instance, felt that I was making a mistake. On the other hand, my mother said that she had heard of people remarrying and accomplishing a happy, lasting relationship. Personally, I felt that a man should follow his heart and not live in the past. The singer Johnny Taylor made it even more assuring that everything would be ok when I heard his latest hit entitled *Good Love*. The record seemed as though he was singing just for Harriet and I. Keitha, who was now almost seven months pregnant, drove to the mall with me to buy Johnny Taylor's cassette. As I drove back from the mall, I sang along with Johnny. Keitha just smiled at me, happy to see her brother happy. As I was taking Keitha back home to her mother, she asked if she could stay with me before she had her baby.

"Yeah, sis, you know that."

"Ma and them drink too much", she concluded.

To my surprise, when Keitha and I got to our moms, Tina and her mother Roxann were there. The two had walked from Roxann's mom's apartment which was around the corner. Needless to say, my decision to remarry Harriet came up. Tina, age 13, began recalling all the awful things Harriet had done to me. My daughter boldly told me I was stupid to go back to that witch, and she promptly turned her nose up at me. Like Father, like daughter, it seemed like she inherited my outspokenness.

"People change," I said, attempting to end our conversation.

"Harriet got his ass brainwashed!" Roxann intervened. "He thinks she got him last time! She's really going to get him, watch!"

Instead of becoming offended, I simply ignored Roxann's negative feedback and went about enjoying the day with my kids. Dell pulls up in front of the door honking her car horn and yelling for my kids to come. Roxann and I were left, feeling like unfit parents and I hated that more than anything.

My new job was what I hoped it would be and more. In addition, John the contractor was in full swing, repairing the odds and ends of my second house. Everything was going as planned.

On October 1, 1997, Harriet called and informed me that her U-haul and car trailer for her 1993 Kia Oldsmobile was loaded and ready for travel. I informed Harriet that in a couple of days, the utilities in our house should be on and that I'd be moving my things into it, so when she arrived, everything should be in place. Harriet whispered in that sexy voice of hers that she loved me and that she would be heading out in a couple of hours. I wished her safe travels and we both hung up. I gave a last look at the yard that I was about to abandon.

Boy, she must really love me to just pack up and drive 3000 miles to remarry me.

I then realized that it was Monday and Harriet would be rolling into Tampa around Friday sometime. Jeff said that he should be finished with the house by Tuesday or Wednesday. That meant that I needed to get busy. I felt a smile creep across my face; I had it all figured out.

Tuesday came and there was no call from Jeff. On Wednesday, I called him to see if the house was ready. The phone rang and rang before Jeff's wife finally answered. When I asked for Jeff, she asked me to hold on.

"Hey Toler, how are you doing?" Jeff asked in his slow drawl when he finally picked up.

"I'm okay, how are you doing?"

"I'm not doing so well, I was going to call you and tell you that our deal fell through.'

I suddenly felt a rush of disappointment and panic roll into the pit of my stomach.

"Toler, the bank won't approve Sybil to be in agreement with them because of her credit. She doesn't have good credit. Sorry, Toler that leaves you stuck with the house on State Street.

"Why didn't they say that the first time?" I asked.

"I don't know, I thought everything was okay," Jeff said.

"I'm in trouble; my wife is on the road. She's on her way here with her kids."

"Toler, I'm sorry, I tried! They just won't go no further."

"Man, what am I going to do?"

"When is she supposed to get here," Jeff asked.

"Friday," I snapped.

I was struggling to keep from yelling into the phone.

"I'll tell you what. Let me check with some other sources and if they can come up with something, I'll call you tonight. You'll be home, won't you?'

"Yes, yes," I answered, frantically.

"Ok, bud, I'll talk with you later."

The line went dead. My first intuition told me that Jeff wasn't going to call back. I pushed the thought from my head and placed the phone in its cradle. What was I going to do? After a lot of thought, I called around to only learn that decent sized efficiency hotels were costly. We're talking eight hundred to nine hundred a month. I only had nine hundred to my name. Of course, I could get a smaller efficiency room for seventy five dollars a week, but that was really nothing more than a hole in the wall. The thought of the children sleeping on the floor with the cat made me feel less than a man. I was overwhelmed with the prospect of having to find a place that wouldn't bruise my ego.

At 6:00 that evening, I got back home after a hectic day at work. I didn't have time to sleep because I was still calling and searching for a place for Harriet and I. Unfortunately, I had no luck and Sybil was now sensing that something was going on, but she said nothing. She watched me closely.

At 9:15, I finally dozed off with Sybil lying snug against me.

An hour and a half later, my eyes flew open and my brain came on like a television. My ex-wife and kids were cruising down the highway at this very moment to meet Daddy!

Shit! What in the hell am I going to do?

I thought and I thought. As I lay there, pondering, Sybil sighed a few times then turned her back toward me. Finally, she jumped up, apparently concluding that I just wasn't interested in her and stormed to the kitchen. We both had fallen asleep early. I got up and noticed that she and Keevan were eating. I notice Sybil didn't ask, nor attempt to fix me anything to eat.

"Where's my food?" I barked.

"You didn't say you were hungry!" Sybil shot back.

I started running my mouth at her and Sybil returned fire. The first thing came to my mind was to put her out, which would have relieved all my worries about finding a place for my ex-wife. But, I couldn't make myself do it. Deep in my soul, I knew I was dead wrong. That didn't matter, though. I had already made myself angry enough to call the police.

The officer arrived about 20 minutes later, got out of her patrol car and started walking toward the porch where Sybil and I were sitting exchanging words.

"What's the problem here?" the officer asked.

"I don't know what is wrong with my fiancée; he just got mad about some food!"

At that, I got up and headed to the bedroom to remove the .357 magnum Sybil had given me; I didn't want her to take it back because I had come to like the sense of security that the black hawk had given me. Moments after I had hidden the gun, I heard keys jingling as the officer approached me while I stood in front of the bathroom mirror, picking my teeth. The officer stopped at the doorway.

"Can you tell me what's going on?"

"Like I told ya'll over the phone, I want her out my house before someone gets hurt!"

"Whose house is this?

"This is my house," I said, arrogantly as the female officer's face turned a shade darker.

"How long has your girlfriend been living here?"

"That's not the point. The point is that I want her out of my house before someone gets hurt."

As I resumed picking at my teeth in the mirror, the officer glared at me like she wanted to sock me one. She about faced and took her jingling keys back down the hall. I actually giggled to myself, realizing how hot I had made the officer and she couldn't do a damn thing about it.

A couple of minutes passed and I heard the officer's keys jingle back up the hall towards me. Sybil was with her, but then she suddenly darted into our bedroom, leaving the officer to stand there, watching me. I gave her a cold, hard look to say that I didn't fear her one bit. Sybil came back and informed the officer that she couldn't find her gun. The officer turned and asked angrily if I had Sybil's gun.

I smirked and said, "Sure don't!"

Sybil interjected, "He got it, but that's okay."

The officer asked Sybil if she had all of her things, nodding toward the large bag Sybil was toting.

"I'll come back tomorrow and get the rest of my stuff," she said.

The officer looked around the room, presumably to find something for which I could be arrested, but she found nothing.

"I'll hang around until your mother can come and get you. You can wait by my car if you want," the officer said.

The officer looked at me and rolled her eyes before they left toward the patrol car. That was when I realized what I was doing to Keevan, the little boy who called me Daddy from day one. I truly didn't want him to let any of this affect his school performance by worrying about his mother and the crap I was doing.

"Keevan can stay!" I yelled from the screen door, but I got no response, just two sad faces looking downward at the sand they stood upon.

"Keevan can stay here," I repeated.

"No," Sybil muttered.

After they left, I started drinking like a fish.

I woke up early Friday morning, still feeling tipsy. I downed another beer and was drunk all over again. I didn't care and I hopped in the car to pick up a friend, Tony, and his wife, Dee Dee, who lived in Central Park near my mother. I picked them up with an agreement to pay them both to help me pack Sybil's things and also do some fall cleaning. On our way to my house, I ran into Roxann and was pleased to see that she was looking good. Roxann had gained her weight back, her skin tone was restored and she was well-dressed. I was in awe, actually. Rox informed me that Terry was sentenced to prison and she had been trying to change her act. I was so happy for her, but also a little sad. It was just the wrong timing.

Damn, why she didn't do this earlier when I practically begged for such a change, I wondered sadly to myself.

We made small talk. I asked her how our kids were doing and told her what I was doing and that I would pay her to help us clean if she wanted to join us.

"Yeah, but that whore better not come back here and try to mistreat my children again. I'll kick her ass!"

Tony and I chuckled.

"I ain't playing, big Toler!" she barked.

I assured her that Harriet had changed.

"She better" Roxann shot back.

Back at the house, the crew was in full swing, packing and cleaning for the funds I'd offered. A few hours in, I called a beer break and the four of us sat on the front porch, drinking Ice Houses while listening to some oldies. Suddenly, from out of nowhere, this big squeaky U-haul truck pulled up and slammed on the brakes, kicking up a cloud of dust. And out jumped Sybil's sister, Cint.

Cint, a big-boned, reddish woman who stood about 5'8 and was clearly the opposite of Sybil, slammed the truck door and stormed toward the fence entrance. As she fumbled with the latch on the fence, I immediately sensed that she was wired off of adrenaline and was clearly overreacting. Either that or she was drunk.

"I come to get my sister's shit!" she yelled.

Three men exited the van and another car pulled up. It was Sybil and her mother. Things were escalating and fast. Cint began walking toward the house and I moved in front of her like a dog protecting its territory. I was nose-to-nose with Cint and I ordered her to step off of my property before I put my foot up her rump. She knew I was ready for war at any moment and she made a complete about face and walked right out of my yard. I was angered by her hostile approach and I demanded that she stay the hell off my property while the move was in progress. Sybil and her helpers loaded up her things and not once did Sybil say a word to me. In all, I knew I was dead wrong. I felt it through my entire being. So when a feeling of guilt or compassion tried to climb to the surface of my mind, I immediately drowned it with alcohol.

During the move, my cell phone rang and it was Harriet. She informed me that she was in Louisiana and after she has rested, she would arrive in Tampa the following day around noon. I informed her that our house deal had went sour and that I was right in the middle of moving Sybil out. I told her that she and the kids should come straight to the house.

"I knew you would take care of business," Harriet said.

After Sybil and her crew left, my crew continued working and we finally got my house cleaned and back in order. I paid them for their labor and took Tony and his wife back home. Roxann rejoined me back at my place for a nightcap. We reminisced and had fun laughing together. Later, I broke out my favorite toy, my camcorder. After Rox and I made love, my body finally gave up. I woke up later realizing I hadn't slept much because Roxann was still wide awake, fascinated seeing herself being screwed on television. When I awoke again, Roxann's half nude body was curled up beside me sound asleep. I quickly glanced at the clock, 4:58 am. The thought of my ex arriving early made me jump up and get Roxann back to her mother's.

We got dressed and left. Rox gave me a peck on the lips and said goodbye, then mumbled something about some witch before walking onto her mother's porch. I waited until Rox's knock was answered before I headed back home to get some more rest.

I woke up a few hours later to realize my camcorder was still set up pointing toward the bed, and the tape of me and Roxann was still in the VCR. I hide it away, took a shower and dressed, thinking about my life at hand. I suddenly was startled by a loud ring from my house phone.

"Hello?"

"Hey Toler, this is Roxann. What's up?

"Nothing much, just waiting on Harriet and her kids to get here sometime this afternoon."

"Alright, I just thought I'd call," Roxann said gravely.

There was a moment of silence and then, the phone went dead.

For a moment, I felt I was making a bad mistake and I wondered briefly what it would be like to be with Roxann again. But in the end, I couldn't bare another disappointing round with her; the trust was gone. Besides, I was already in too deep with Harriet.

A few minutes passed and I was startled once again by the loud ring of the phone.

"Hello?"

"Hello, this is Sybil. I'm just calling to ask you if it is okay for me to stay in the house until I get on my feet."

"You should've wanted to talk about this when you had the chance but you didn't say anything. It's too late," I told her.

"Okay," she said softly and hung up.

"Damn!" I shouted as I stormed to the refrigerator for a beer.

I didn't want to drink until after my wife arrived, but hell, my emotions needed some help. The guilt, the inherent *wrongness* of what I was doing was really starting to get to me.

It wasn't long after Sybil called when I heard a car door slam. I looked out the window and saw it was Tony and his wife. It appeared that they had somehow managed to get their old clunker started. Tony had brought over more beer and the three of us sat on the porch and talked for a while. When they left, I found myself alone in the house once more. It was a strange, unfamiliar feeling and part of me wondered if it should stay that way.

CHAPTER 10

HOLIDAY BLUES

Finally, my ready-made family pulled up. The reality of it all hit me as they climbed out of the truck. There stood, a tired, dirty woman with a split personality, a flea-infested cat with an attitude, a U-haul full of junk, followed by a smelly car that wasn't paid for and two nappy-headed kids. I greeted them as expected and later that evening took them to a restaurant. Harriet's boy decides to drop an old cigarette in my glass of beer and laugh his ass off as I drunk it. This was my life.

The following morning, Harriet confessed that because of her fornication, she had gotten disfellowshipped. This meant that she was banned from congregating with members of the church. The church followed the Bible closely and according to *I Corinthians* **15:33**, "Be not deceived: evil communications corrupt good manners." The Kingdom Hall takes that to mean that we are the company that we keep. Therefore, members of the congregation shall not speak to those who are disfellowshipped.

I recall one day in 2004, nine years into writing this book, when I was at Wal-Mart. A Christian sister from the Kingdom Hall I attended was strolling down the aisle toward me. I knew her well and I went to speak to her. As I greeted her, she set her eyes straight ahead and kept walking.

She passed me with my mouth wide open. For whatever reason, the sister thought I was disfellowshipped. Being disfellowshipped under Jehovah's Organization is a humiliating experience. The punishment is designed to force a rebellious member to grieve and to lose all desire to continue down the path that caused such punishment. That day at the store, I experienced the humiliation of that shunning. This is not a permanent thing, however. The person is free to talk with the elders of his or her congregation and if they want to get their act together, they could have the ban lifted. One would only need to stop doing whatever it was that caused the social rejection. With enough faith and determination, Harriet could repair her reputation, whether or not she would was up to her.

Life with Harriet began immediately, which was probably sooner than I was really ready for. My conscience began to severely eat at me. Both on the job and off the job, I continuously thought about the unjust way I had treated Sybil. Every day, I drove this semi-tractor trailer down the high way in reverie about how I did my friend. At times, I found myself daydreaming that I had compensated Sybil with a new car and money for a home. The thought soothed my conscience a little, but deep down, I knew I didn't have the money to do that; it was only a dream. The fourth night after Harriet moved in, Harriet and I were at the dining table having dinner; Harriet sensed that something was troubling me.

"What's wrong, babe? Harriet asked. Our eyes met.

When I didn't answer, she asked me again. I looked down at my plate, then back at her.

"Talk to me," Harriet said, softly.

"I don't like the way I did Sybil. I never called the police on nobody before. I never treated anybody like that and Sybil didn't deserve that. Sybil never did anything to hurt me and I treated her like that!"

At that very moment, I wanted to blame Harriet because I knew that my actions were stemmed from the way she had treated me.

"Do you love her? Harriet asked.

I raised my head and looked into Harriet's eyes, searching for understanding. I could not describe what I saw in her eyes.

"No," I answered, gravely and proceeded to pick at my food.

Harriet was in full force preparing for our wedding day, which was set for December 24th. Every evening, I did a pit stop at Cozy Corner, a liquor store and bar that seemed to draw all the troubled in its district.

One evening after a long haul to Miami and back, I parked my assigned rig and headed to Cozy Corner. That night, as I sat slugging down cheap alcohol to medicate my conscience, I couldn't bear it any longer. I called Sybil at her mother's and told her my whereabouts and that I needed to talk. I went back inside and waited.

Shortly after, a man patted me on my shoulder to inform me that a lady was parked out front and asking for me. When I exited the building, I noticed Sybil sitting in a car that was not her mother's. I walked along side this burgundy colored cougar to greet its driver.

"Fine car you have here," I said with a beefy smile. Sybil smiled briefly and gave me a quick thank you.

"Whose car?"

"Mine," she snapped and looked away.

"This is nice."

I walked to the passenger side and proceeded to open the door. I suddenly heard two clicks from the electric latches.

"Oh, so you don't want me getting in your car?"

I walked back around to the driver side, hoping to say something that would change the way she felt about me. She was now letting up her window and she stopped about an inch from being all the way up. Our eyes met and there was only silence.

"Sybil, you can't say I didn't love you! I hope in your next relationship, you show your man that you love him, not just lie around and sleep and not communicate with him."

Sybil sucked her teeth and continued staring at me.

"You see, that's your problem," I said, feeling a slow burn within me. "You don't talk when you should."

I turned and walked off.

"You can't say I didn't try to love you," I said out loud.

I swung open the bar door. Sybil was now backing out of the drive way as I re-entered the bar.

"Bourbon and coke please! Make it a double."

As I sat there waiting on my drink, I knew I couldn't get angry at Sybil. Hell, I was grateful that she didn't give me a fight about the Ford Bronco truck she bought with her four thousand dollar settlement for the back injury she acquired. Sybil and I had only been talking for a month or so and she handed me her entire settlement so that I could purchase a car. She trusted me! And what did I do? I bought this Bronco and deliberately left her name off the title. It was times I let her drive when I really didn't want her to. And now, this house bit. She worked hard with me, day and night, painting and cleaning to create a nice home for ourselves. At the flip of a hat, I booted her out for another woman, and had to use a cop to do that. After all that I did to this woman, she hadn't said an unkind word to me, she just stared at me. If only she'd of cursed me out, or done something out of character, I'd of felt better!

The thought of what Harriet would have done to me if I'd tried her like that made me realize that I truly had a good woman. I remembered when I had prayed so sincerely to God, asking Him to send me a good wholesome woman.

"Bartender!"

I sat there for a couple more minutes, waiting for the bartender when I felt another tap on my shoulder and a voice saying that a lady was out front wanting to see me. The first person to come to mind was Harriet, but I trashed that thought because Harriet would have no problem coming inside and doing her own tapping on the shoulder.

I went outside and was surprised to find Sybil again. I walked to her car and looked down at her.

"Do you want to talk?" I asked.

"Yes," she answered.

I suggested a place to talk, so Sybil followed me to a wooded area that overlooked the Hillsborough River, which glittered vividly from the full moon that night. When Sybil got out her car, I noticed her shirt was wrinkled. This was very unlike Sybil, as she was always well dressed. I also noticed that she held a slight underarm odor, which was certainly out of her character. I embraced her, realizing that our break up had taken a toll on her. We sat as I affectionately held her in my arms. Sybil looked out onto the glittering river as I told her how sincerely sorry I was for treating her the way I did, that my actions stemmed from the way I was treated. I told her that I realized how awful I had become and to please understand and forgive me. I continued, saying that I had made a mistake breaking up with her and that I had gotten myself in a situation that would take some time to get out of, but I assured her that I would have her back at her house as soon as I worked on another house deal. Sybil listened quietly as I gave her insight on my strange relationship with Harriet, and that our relationship wasn't over.

Later, Sybil and I entered her car and we made love. Sybil and I started seeing each other about every other day. One evening, while talking with Sybil over the phone, she informed me that she was no longer living with her mother, that she had gotten her own place across town. Impressed, I started visiting Sybil at her home.

I recall a date Sybil and I had made, and that particular day I was running late. When I finally arrived, I noticed Sybil's house windows were busted out and trimmed with soot. An eerie feeling came upon me as I slowly got out of my truck and walked toward the door. I could smell the burnt rubbish from the house; and when I opened the door, my heart sunk when I saw the scorched room. The thought of Sybil being burnt to death caused my heart to pound. As I stood at the entrance of the doorway, I called out for Sybil. I heard the screeching of a door opening and Sybil appeared from the back bedroom. Her face was smudged with soot. This deeply touched me. Here was a woman whose house had caught fire, everything burnt and not the fire official, not even her mother, could make her break our date. As I wiped the soot from her face, I knew, without a shadow of a doubt, that I had agreed to marry the wrong woman. I suggested that Sybil move in with my father and stepmom, and so she did.

Meanwhile, Harriet was out spending money on her wedding dress, clothes and shoes for the kids and me, and arranging the wedding location and wedding invitations. She was acting like she was Princess Diana or somebody.

One night, Harriet and I stopped by my mother's for a quick visit. While there, I discovered that my mother was going through the same old crap with her boyfriend, Ivy.

The troubles that invaded my mother's heart began not long after Ivy seduced his way into her life. At first, he was okay, but he soon started disappearing on Fridays. He would return home on Sunday nights, dead broke. He got so bad that every now and then, he would stay gone two weeks at a time. To my mother, it wasn't about the money he wasn't bringing home; it was the honey because she adored him. Sadly, my mom went into a slump that led her to sit and cry practically every day.

"I wonder what Ivy is doing," I would hear her muttering to herself. All of this stress even created severe hair loss.

At that time, Ivy was 36-years-old, much younger than my mother. He stood 6'4 with dark skin and a slender build. He was intelligent and, admittedly, a fairly handsome man. He kept himself well groomed, but his drug of choice was crack. He was a sophisticated crack addict, if you will. I myself was around 32- years-old, but don't get it twisted. I wasn't about to let my mother keep getting hurt like that.

One day, after I returned home from work, Harriet informed me that Keitha called, saying that Ivy had returned after abandoning my mother for another two weeks. That very night, I drove across town to confront him and let him know that I wasn't going to sit back and watch him dog my mother out. When I arrived, I realized the two had gone to bed. I knocked louder than usual, Keitha must had left because my knocks were unanswered. So I went around to my mother's open bedroom window which was on the second floor.

"Hey Ma," I called. "Hey Ma!"

I heard my mother snoring. Getting a little angered and frustrated, I proceeded to climb the ledge and up into her window. Once I was halfway inside, I could see two body figures in the glare from the street light. Ma snoring as if she'd worked hard. Once inside, I walked to the bed and my eyes zoomed in on Ivy's feet that were poking out from the cover.

Who in the hell does he think he is.

I looked around for a stick or something but my eyes fell on a large pair of scissors. I grabbed them and turned back to Ivy. I grabbed his feet and pulled the startled man from under the covers. My mother felt the disturbance and she jumped up and ran for the light switch. By the time the lights came on, Ivy was on his feet, looking down at me. I had the scissors drawn up under his chin.

"Man, who in the hell you think you is!" I yelled at him. "You are not going to be treating my momma any kind of way, she ain't no play toy!"

"Bump you, little nigga! You don't run nothin' here, nigga!"

"You try me; I'll put these scissors in your ass!" I warned him.

'Toler, stop it!" my mother screamed.

Ivy and I continued yelling at each other until I suddenly withdrew the scissors, turned and knocked Ivy's cologne and cosmetics off the dresser before storming out of the room. My mother slammed the door behind me and warned me to not come back to her house. I think she even called me a bitch as I was pulling off.

I was disturbed by her response as I drove home. Did she not see that I was only trying to protect her, to show this man that the son wasn't going to allow him to dog her out?

After that, I stopped talking to my mother. The following day, I had Keitha come live with Harriet and me until she had her baby and got her own place.

A few weeks passed before my mom started calling me. Not long after my mom and I started talking again, Harriet and I visited her. I discovered that my mother was still going through the wringer with this guy. I looked into her puffy, dark, circled eyes. Her sad condition tore me up inside. Harriet walked over to me and patted my shoulders as I hugged my mother, telling her it will be alright. Evidently, Ivy had become more ruthless and desperate, to the point where he was stealing food from her freezer and selling it. He was also getting her drunk and taking her money. That night, as Harriet and I were leaving, I resigned myself to the fact that when Ivy showed back up, I was probably going to go to jail. I was going to split his wig.

Days passed and after work I would make pit stops at my father's place, Sybil would always be there. My father and step mother Vi, would look at me like I needed to be kicked in the ass for doing Sybil the way I did, little did they know I wanted to kick my own ass.

As for my mother, Ivy still had not been seen for the whole month of November. In the midst of this turmoil, she was gradually coming to grips with herself, at least that's what it sounded like.

On December 2nd, I planned a day to take my sons fishing while Keitha had her baby shower. That very morning, I ended up taking a belt to my boys' rear ends before the day even got started. Keitha's baby shower couldn't have been timed any better, because a couple of days later, she gave birth to a beautiful baby girl. Harriet and I broke out the video recorder, my favorite toy, and filmed my first niece exit the womb of her 18-year-old mother. Man, the things a woman has to go through! Hell, women should be called the stronger sex. Keitha named her daughter Leslie, after her baby's father.

It was December 24, 1997, at Sand Lake Apartments club house. There I stood, in my white tuxedo, waiting for our invited guests to witness our second wedding. As I stood sipping on cognac, I couldn't help but admire the large feast Harriet had prepared. The three-leveled cake and the champagne flowing into its sparkling fountain were fit for a king. I remember taking a moment to take it all in. Out of everything I saw, the sight of my mom and dad drinking and enjoying each other's company was the most satisfying thing I had seen all year. Meanwhile, the children ran about playing and dancing while the Justice Of The Peace waited patiently for the guests to arrive so she could start the ceremony, but no one showed up, not even a roach. After waiting a while longer, we proceeded with the ceremony.

My father, who was also the best man, made his entrance with Harriet. After our vows were sworn, the kids and my parents danced along in celebration with Harriet and me. When the music slowed down, Harriet and I danced alongside my father and mother. As we danced, there was a lit candle flickering beside Harriet's foot. The candle had been left on the floor from an earlier setting when I had sung a song to Harriet entitled, *You Are So Beautiful.* Trust me; American Idol would've had me arrested for attempting to sing because it was evident that God gave me a mouth to only eat with.

Harriet and I were slow-dancing beside this lit candle. I knew if she moved one more step, her gown would have gone up in flames. The thought of Harriet running and dashing into the front pool would've had my kids laughing there asses off. My family knew of the deceitful things Harriet had done to me in my first marriage, so seeing something like that would have made their day, especially Tina's. The tail of Harriet's dress was now only an inch from catching fire. Part of me wanted to let her catch fire and part of me didn't. After a moment, I diverted her step to safety.

Time seemed to fly! Even though nobody outside the family showed up, we were still having a good time. I think my 16-year-old son, Lil' Toler was sneaking drinks from the bar because he had taken off his tuxedo and was doing backward flips across the dance floor in his boxers. It was a good night and I let it pass. The kids were balling. Suddenly, it dawned on me. For our honeymoon, I'd made reservations at a hotel where Harriet was born, but the kids and all were having such a good time that I wasn't ready to pack up. The music was blasting and I wasn't feeling any pain. I noticed Junior, Harriet's son wasn't either. He was dancing hard. Man, I fell into laughter as he slung his hips dancing like some little twisted go-go girl. It was so good to see the kids really enjoying themselves. The next thing I knew, I saw a beer bottle sail across the room and land near us. I looked and saw that my mother had thrown the bottle and was now yelling across the room at Harriet.

"You see your bad ass son keep knocking down Lil' Johnnie (my youngest nephew) and you ain't saying nothing, bitch! You just stood there and watched him!"

Anyone could see that my mom was now pissy-drunk, but I personally didn't appreciate her wrecking my wedding. All of the bitter feelings that I held toward my mother throughout the years came roaring out. I screamed at her to the point that my father had to intervene. When my father got in my face, I redirected my rage to him. By this point, Keitha had gotten up, yelling and crying for my father and I to stop before it got physical. I happened to look over and spot Harriet across the room, bending down whispering in her son's ear. She looked back at us and there was that wicked look, a glare that I was personally familiar with and hated. I immediately started trying to defuse the situation with my parents.

We started loading up my truck and Harriet still showed no sign of being a supporting wife. It was as if I were her enemy. Sybil came to mind.

I got my family in my truck. As I was climbing into the driver's seat, Harriet suddenly grabbed onto my shirt.

"Where are you going?" Harriet asked, with a tight face.

"I'm taking my parents home!" I snapped and proceeded to get into the truck, but again, Harriet pulled me toward her. My mother yelled at her from the passenger seat,

"Let him go bitch! You ain't no mother fuckin' good!"

I attempted to shake Harriet loose.

"Let me go, bitch!" I yelled.

Harriet still clung to my shirt and she leaned toward my ear and whispered, "Tolerance, don't do me like this, let's go home."

In the end, I found myself sitting in the passenger seat of Harriet's car, allowing Keitha to drive my parent's home. I dozed off on the way home.

The following morning, Christmas, I was awakened by the ringing of the house phone and was immediately hit with a serious hangover. I looked to see Harriet lying beside me, staring up at the ceiling with "rocks in her jaws." That's an old term that my father would use when one's chin was lumpy because they were clenching their teeth together with anger and bitterness. I looked away, holding my head. My head was beating like a toothache. I rolled over to pick up the receiver and overheard Keitha and Ron's conversation about how I should have never remarried Harriet. Again, I looked at Harriet who was still lying there, staring at the ceiling. I got up and slowly walked to the family room, only to notice that the kids had rocks in their jaws, too. They were upset because I had reminded them earlier that I no longer celebrated Christmas. I felt bad because they didn't want to give Christmas up, but I refused to continue to live a lie due to tradition. I had explained to them that Jesus wasn't born on December 25th, that no one knows His true birth date. I tried to explain to my kids that there was no Santa Claus and that a person should give gifts throughout the year, not just on one particular day. I touched on a couple of more holidays that didn't have truth to it, like Easter, for instance. I reminded them that a rabbit does not lay eggs. It looked like the kids were not happy with my opinion. I sighed as I handed out watches, for the young ones to know what time it is. When I handed Tina her watch, she looked up at me as if, she wanted to shove it down my throat! Hell, I wasn't even supposed to be home to listen to all this bickering. I was supposed to be on my honeymoon in my birthday suit somewhere!

Needless to say, it wasn't a good morning.

Meanwhile, as that episode passed, I realized my neat, clean home had started to look like a dirty shack. Once again, Harriet and her kids didn't have any consideration, nor respect for what I had worked hard to establish. They practically damaged and smeared everything they put their hands on. And Harriet made it no better. She would sit up in the middle of the bed, eating candy and literally throwing its wrapper on the floor like she was at a park-somewhere.

One evening, my neighbor, Mr. Sunny, was walking past my house. He called me and I walked over to him.

'Your house was looking good, what happened?"

I looked at my trashed yard and back at him, shaking my head in disgust.

Again, I found myself complaining about cleaning.

"Oh well," Harriet said. "This comes with the package."

I must admit, I knew I was taking a chance remarrying Harriet, but I thought that we would have at least two good years together before we started having problems. Suddenly, I began to realize that her good no longer outweighed her bad. I knew that she needed to either get her act together like she had promised at the hotel or I would leave her for sure. Again, Sybil came to mind.

CHAPTER 11

HOW THE TIDE TURNS

On January 10, 1998 the winter felt like it was early fall. The cool breeze was refreshing to my soul as I drove my Bronco west on I-4. I sipped on a cold beer to unwind from a hectic work day delivering to the Dade County District. Miami customers were less snobby than most big cities, but the traffic there was hellacious. Later that day when I arrived home, I hadn't even parked the car when I could smell Harriet's fine cooking. Inside, despite our differences, we were able to sit around with the kids, laughing and chatting like one big happy family. Harriet had agreed to work and I thought that was a good idea; at least she would have somewhat of an excuse as to why the house remained neglected. That particular day, my mother came to mind, so I called to see how she was doing. Ivy ended up answering the phone and I felt a slow burn creep through me. I asked him who in the hell he thought he was to be running in and out of my mother's life like she was some kind of play toy.

"You worried about the wrong thing, bro!" he said.

Now, I was full blown angry! I quickly thought of my .357.

"Don't make me come over there," I warned.

"Come on!" he barked.

"I'm on my way!" I said, before slamming the phone down.

"Who was that?" Harriet asked.

"Ivy. He's back. I'm gonna go over there and see what's going on!"

I dismissed the thought of bringing the hand gun and instead, called Junior to ride along with me. I knew I would deeply regret it if I ended up shooting him. Within ten minutes, my stepson and I pulled up in front of my mother's apartment, got out and entered. I immediately spotted Ivy and our eyes locked. I looked away and spoke to my mother, who was entertaining Nicky, her gay male friend. But my eyes returned to Ivy, who was now getting up from the couch.

"What's up?" I snapped. Ivy looked at me with a smirk, as if I was a joke. "What's up with you?"

He stopped in front of me and looked down at me, trying to intimidate me.

"So, you think you just going to run over the Lamar family?"

Before he could answer, I hit him with a left, followed by a right and another left. Ivy's knees buckled and he grabbed for me. Our inevitable scuffle ensued. We slammed each other against the wall and couch. The lamp that I had given my mother crashed to the floor. Still clinging together, I got him in the middle of the floor and pushed away from his body before hitting him with another left. Ivy collapsed to his knees. His arms were covering his face as he rested face down on the arm of a chair that sat beside the huge project heater. I stood straddled over him looking down at him. I looked over at my mother who was still seated, her mouth wide open, stunned. Nicky was standing to the door, ready to exit at any given time. I looked back down at Ivy who still held his face down in his arms.

"Nigga, I told you I'm not going to let you do my mother any kind of way!" I barked at him.

I picked up a conch shell that was on the heater and cracked him in the back of his head and walked away. I called my stepson, who was standing in the kitchen entrance with my nephew Jonteral.

"Ivy got his butt beat, that's good for him," said my 10-year-old-nephew. I was now out of the house and unlocking the car door for Junior when, suddenly, my mother came rushing out the door,

"You're going to jail!" she screamed. "Ivy hadn't done anything to you!"

My mother was sneering at me as if she hated me.

"You going to jail," she repeated.

Ivy was now exiting the door. One of his eyes was closed and his forehead was covered in large knots. His face looked as though he had been attacked by bees. Ivy lurched toward me with a box cutter. I warned him that if he came any closer, I would shoot the shit out of him. Ivy stopped, he knew I will shoot if I had too; he turned back into the house without a word. My bluff worked, I left the scene.

The following morning, I was glad to wake up at home and not in jail. My swollen hands refused to let me forget about my fight with Ivy. But the thing that disturbed me was how my mother had yelled that I was going to jail. I felt my heart shift. I was hurt deeply. I then started thinking back to when my mom would yell and curse at my sister, just because she asked to eat, but wasn't allowed because Ivy hadn't eaten yet. Ivy always got the good food and her own kids got the cold-cuts. It was always about her man. That familiar slow burn came over me. I recalled a time when I was 16; she met this guy named LV. Actually that is how I got to know his son, Tony and his wife, DeDe. LV loved to drink his beer and liquor. He also seemed to enjoy keeping my mom in an uproar; he always had my mother crying and yelling at him. The guy seemed to get a kick out of upsetting her.

My mother would scream at him and LV would look at her and say, "Yes dear" and roll his eyes and resume drinking.

Mom would turn the bottle up to her head, sometimes spitting the cheap gin at him and telling him to go to hell. One day, I confronted LV and told him that if my mother ends up having a heart attack or a stroke behind his crap, I was going to do something to him. When my mother was sober, I expressed this to her.

"Boy, you ain't nothing but 16-years-old. LV is a grown man from the woods; he'll beat the shit out of you," my mother told me.

Being that LV's short stocky body was made up of rippling muscles, I started to believe her. But looks are deceiving because that very year, I got fed up with LV's crap and approached him, ready to go. LV suddenly grabbed me up in the air and tried to throw me down the flight of stairs that lead down from our bedrooms. I grabbed onto the rail and down the stairs we went, crashing out into the screen door and out onto the porch. I threw a couple of quick combinations, followed by a couple of hooks until we ended up in the front yard. Like Ivy did, L.V. collapsed to his knees and I caught him with a straight jab that jerked his head back and sent blood gushing from his mouth. My fist was up like a boxer, waiting for his opponent to get up. LV climbed to his feet, looked at me and paused before politely going back into the house to receive aid from my mother.

The point of the story is that my mom had a history of choosing her man over her kids. Not once after the fight did she ask if I was ok. All she said to me was that she didn't think I had it in me. Good thing I learned how to fight because if I didn't, she would've let LV beat the snot out of me and as the paramedics drove off with me, she probably would've yelled from her bedroom window, "I told you that you couldn't do nothing with LV, bitch!"

The following day after fighting Ivy, I went to my dad's house. I told him about the fight Ivy and I had and suddenly burst out in tears.

"That's your mother," my father said. "Don't hold resentment and hatred toward her – she's just in love."

I tried to understand, but I remembered that I was of no concern to her. As far as I was concerned, she didn't have to ever worry about me trying to protect her ever again! I deeply resented her, deeply.

Back at home, Harriet informed me that she landed a job at King High School. The job consisted of helping the school secretary. I was glad to know that we'd have extra income coming into the home, but the home itself would certainly suffer in the cleaning department. And that it did. The house gradually got filthier. The more I tried to do my chores and clean up behind Harriet and her two, the more I regretted that I'd remarried her.

Very quickly, I started holding resentment toward Harriet. I just didn't appreciate her coming back in my life and trashing out the living that I had tried to uphold. Harriet and her two began to look like the three little pigs and I was the wolf, ready to throw their asses out. I started huffing and puffing about the matter and again, Harriet made some lame excuse. I began to threaten to stop the kids' allowances. Later that day, Harriet must have realized how unhappy I was becoming. She agreed to enforce the chores and I concluded that things would get better.

March 7, 1998. If I'm not mistaken, I think that day fell on a Friday. I remember stopping by a liquor store and buying a pint of Paul Mason brandy to take home with me. It was early in the evening when I arrived. Keitha told me that Harriet and her kids had just left for the pet store to get Boneshaker a bag of dog food.

Good, I figured. It would be the perfect opportunity to unwind with a little peace and quiet over ice and brandy, followed by some slow jams to set the ambiance. I fetched my ice and headed for the family room, but I became instantly irate when I noticed the shape the family room was in. Clothes were thrown about. The tile was no longer white but a dingy, cloudy gray. There, near the entrance of the laundry room, sat a large garbage bag. I walked to the bag and discovered that it contained dirty clothes. I snatched the bag up to place it in the laundry room and I noticed sand, dried up mud and trash was piled around the bottom of the bag like leaves would have settled around an abandoned tire. Keitha then walked in and informed me that the bag had been sitting there for the past week.

"She's nasty!" Keitha said, shaking her head in disgust. "She won't even make Amy and Junior clean up behind themselves. That's why I'm going to hurry up and get my own place!"

"I know!" I replied. "This don't make no sense. I'm not going to say nothing to her. I'm through arguing. One day, she will come home and I will be gone for good. Just look at this living room! I worked hard to have nice things and this nasty heifer comes in and does my place like this!"

Keitha intervened. "It's a shame because she knows this is the reason ya'll broke up the last time. Now ya'll done remarried and she's still doing the same thing. She just doesn't care!"

I was getting angrier by the minute. So to get my mind off of Harriet's filthiness, I walked over to my little niece, who was sound asleep balled up in her blanket and slightly pinched her little, fat jaws. Keitha grinned.

"She's knocked out and I don't blame her. Junior is so bad, they be all in the living room playing, seeing that me and my baby is trying to sleep."

'That Junior, boy, he makes me so mad sometimes, I be wanton to knock him out."

"I have no problems out of him when you're here."

"Yeah, he acts up and tries to take advantage of women, but when he's around men he behaves."

Keitha agreed before disappearing into the other part of the house. I exhaled and took off my shirt to allow the cool air to refresh me. I then poured myself a glass of brandy and turned on the CD player.

Time passed as I relaxed deep into my recliner. The oldies was on point and sounded good to my ears. Soon too soon, I heard Harriet enter followed by the thumps of bags being set on the dining room table. I got up and walked toward the dining room.

"Hey babe," Harriet said with a smile.

"Hey honey," I said faintly.

I let a minute or so pass before I dove in.

"Harriet, why are clothes and trash piled up in the family room?"

Harriet sucked her teeth and rolled her eyes. She then slammed her purse onto the table and stormed past me grabbing the broom and dust pan and reentering the family room. I followed her and found Harriet sweeping like a mad woman.

"What's your problem?" I sneered before pushing her shoulder.

Harriet instantly went into rage repeatedly hitting me with the dust pan. I was now backing up and blocking her blows until I could go no further. With no other options, I turned and pushed her head onto the wall. She quickly dashed out of my reach and slung the dust pan at me. I blocked it from injuring my face with my forearm. She took her glasses off and smashed them on the floor. Then she covered her face with her hands while she cried angrily.

"Get out of my house! I've had it with you!" I yelled, as Harriet headed toward the back room. I trailed her closely, knowing she couldn't be trusted. Harriet tried to shut herself up in the master bathroom but I blocked the door with my body.

"I'm serious, Harriet. I want out of this marriage. So get your things and go. You got family, friends and old lovers, so just *go*!"

"Is this what I come way down here for?" she hissed. Her face was so contorted; that nobody would think to challenge her.

"Come on Momma, let's go," Junior muttered softly as his eyes shifted up at me.

Harriet growled and stormed out the door. I started grabbing her clothes and suitcases and followed her.

Outside, beyond the corner fence, she stood crying. It was a cry that I was familiar with. Harriet knew I hated to see her cry, so she wept loudly. I dropped her clothes beyond the fence and went to fetch another load.

After dropping the second load over the fence, Keitha stopped me with a question. Before I could tell Keitha that I was just only showing Harriet that I was not going to live like a pig, Harriet stormed in to confront me.

"Why did you put your hand on me?" she sneered.

Her nose was almost touching my forehead as she stood on her tiptoes to glare down on me. Her eyes were bright red, her teeth were gritting and her shoulders were raised and spread out like she was about to grab me at any moment. I looked at Keitha who looked back at me, as if she was saying that Harriet was about ready to kick my ass. I chuckled and looked back at Harriet.

If looks could kill, I would be dead.

Keitha suddenly started laughing and I chuckled even harder. Harriet glared at us both.

"You planned this to see how I was going to act, didn't you," she asked furiously as her eyes burned into mine.

A minute or so passed before Harriet removed her vicious glare. I was still looking at her, shaking my head to let her know that she should be ashamed of herself for displaying such a raging behavior after promising and swearing on the Bible that she had changed. What a joke! Nevertheless, Harriet's eyes locked onto mine again as though she wanted to put my ass in a sling. Suddenly, she stormed back out the door.

"Boy! Harriet is hot with you!" Keitha giggled.

"Hot ain't the word," I yapped, as I rubbed the knot on my elbow.

I went and poured the last bit of brandy I had left and sat down, pondering about what just had happened. Harriet's temper, followed by the wicked frowns she displayed was mind boggling. They were faces that would make any man wonder what kind of woman he was dealing with. The thought was scary and I found it ironic how part of me wanted to flee from her and go on with my life, while the other part wanted to apologetically hold her, kiss her and make wild love to her.

It's been said that a man can never figure out the ways of a woman. That may be true, but I will tell you a one thing that I have figured out; a woman that gives you oral sex all the time is not always trying to please you, nor is she so in love with you. There are some women out there who are looking to rob you of your mind, heart, and money. They try to make you fall in love with them and want you so sprung, you'll go for anything. The majority of men fall for it, especially if she is a good cook. You men, be strong and be smart!

The serenity prayer wasn't created for nothing!

I sat there in deep thought until my drink was gone. The anger subsided. I was about ready to apologize and hold Harriet like she expected. I got up to suck up to her once again, but when I got to the door, I saw that Harriet was gone. Before I allowed the painful feeling of Harriet and I breaking up to sink in, Sybil came to mind, but the thought of loosing Harriet was overwhelming.

Harriet will be back; she just went to vent, I said to myself.

Thirty minutes passed before reality struck. Harriet was known for vanishing after a heated argument. Her abandonment would often last for days, not to mention that she was also known to lay up with other men in the process. But no longer did my heart nor my booze allow me to accept the same scenario. Again Sybil's face came to mind. At that moment, I couldn't think straight. I knew that I made vows for the second time, *until death do us part*. I had no grounds for a divorce.

Forty minutes had passed and still no Harriet.

"Fuck that whore! Hell life is too short for this shit!" I thought.

I waited ten more minutes and that ten minutes seemed like an hour.

"Harriet ain't coming back," I mumbled as I reached for my phone to page Sybil.

Within five minutes, Sybil returned my call. I told her that Harriet and I had broken up, that Harriet was gone and I wanted her to come over so we could talk. Within a half-hour Sybil was at my door knocking.

"Come in!" I shouted.

Sybil walked in and our eyes met.

"What's going on?" Sybil asked.

We talked and I could feel myself calming down in her presence. During the midst of our conversation, Harriet walked in with the police. She nodded her head toward me.

"Mr. Lamar, your wife called with a complaint that you struck her and broke her eye glasses," the male officer said. Still a little stunned from the sudden entrance, I looked at Harriet who was standing near the door talking to a female officer. I glanced at Sybil, who seemed to be a little jittery.

"She's lying. I didn't break her glasses she broke her own glasses."

I heard Harriet suck her teeth as though I was lying.

"Oh, so I guess she bruised her own lip," the officer said sarcastically.

I looked again at Harriet and noticed a small bubble on the corner of her lip. I didn't know if I had done it when I pushed her into the wall or if she did it to herself. It could be proven by our kids and Keitha that it wouldn't be beyond Harriet to throw a fit and repeatedly hit herself in the face, pull her hair, kick and cry if things weren't going her way. Her tantrums were so regular that I got tired of stopping her from hitting herself. I started ignoring her and by doing so, the fits subsided.

The officer was now asking Sybil her name and if she witnessed anything. I intervened and explained exactly what happened.

"Have you been drinking," the cop asked.

"Yes, I had a couple of drinks."

The officer excused himself and walked back in the living room where Harriet and the other two officers were. The female officer approached and told me to put on my shoes. Once I did, I was quickly handcuffed and placed in the back seat of the police cruiser. The male officer stuck his head in the window and asked if I owned a .357 hand gun. I told him yes and he went on to say that Harriet had given it to him, so he decided to turn it in for safe keeping. I was told that when I got out, I had to go to the police station to retrieve it. I nodded and looked out the back window of the car. Harriet was approaching Sybil, who was now standing near her car staring at me.

"Tolerance been seeing you for a while hasn't he?" Harriet asked her.

Sybil got into her car without a reply and left.

I was booked in the Orient Road County Jail on a domestic violence charge. My bond was five thousand dollar and I needed to pay ten percent of that, which was five hundred dollars, in order to make bail. Consequently, knowing Harriet, she would soon drain me for every red cent that was available in my savings account. The feelings of hatred and resentment I once had toward Harriet once again resurfaced, but I was also scared of what the outcome of all this would be. Furthermore, I felt within my bones that she was going to try to destroy me. I rushed for my free call and called my cell phone. Harriet answered.

I could hear the engine of Harriet's vehicle in the background and I hoped she was on her way to pick me up. I took a deep breath and asked her to drop the charges, saying that I would lose my job if I was in jail.

"I don't want you to lose your job," said Harriet.

I went on to say that I loved her, but we just can't get along.

"I guess you can get along better with Sybil. You didn't waste any time getting her to the house. I wasn't gone an hour."

"Sybil came to pick up her mail that came to the house last week."

A moment of silence fell upon us.

"Where you going"?

"Why?" Harriet hissed.

"I'll lose my job if I don't get out."

"Well, I didn't call the police until I came back and seen Sybil's car."

"I figured that," I said blandly. "We're both just repeating the same old thing here. Look, there is a ninety nine dollar special on plane tickets to California. You can just draw the money out the bank."

To my surprise, Harriet's mother suddenly intervened.

"He's right; they do have those ninety nine dollar specials."

I realized that I was talking on a three-way connection and that for the first time, my mother-in-law, the Wicked Witch from the West, was in an agreement with me. Harriet didn't want to hear that, so she immediately started getting mouthy with me. Before I could say anything, her mother jumped in and snapped.

"Won't you shut up and listen? That's your damn problem. You won't listen!" she yelled.

Harriet yapped a few more words and said she had to go and hung up. I redialed, but she wouldn't pick up. I called home, but couldn't get through there, either.

After a long weekend without hearing from anyone, I was awakened, along with four dozen other inmates for PP court (Preliminary Presentation Court). We all marched down a wide corridor with the hope of getting our bond lowered or released on our own recognizance, which would allow me to salvage my job and see what Harriet was up to.

The PP court was a fair-sized room with rows of benches and microphones that hung from the ceiling. A 36 inch TV, that showed the judge, hung on the far right wall. On the far left there was a smaller screen, and there sat a zealous state attorney, fingering through his files.

"Good morning men. I'm Judge Heinrich"

"What in the hell is this?" I muttered.

"This is TV court," the inmate next to me said. "This saves them from transporting us to and from the courthouse."

"So I got to talk to a fuckin' TV?" another one snarled.

"Sit down and shut up before I get you with contempt of court!" the judge on the larger TV yelled.

The judge's dogmatic voice proceeded to spit out his rules and regulations. An officer who stood in the corner of the room began calling everyone's name in alphabetical order. When he was finished, the judge called individuals to stand before him. This judge didn't play. His voice roared through the set and he commanded everyone's undivided attention. The judge lowered bonds depending on the charge; the more serious the charge he would grimace and slam his files, making it loud and clear that the inmate wouldn't be going anywhere for a long time. I could feel the blood drain from my face as the inmate next to me was called to stand. I intensely searched the screens in the hope of seeing my father, stepmother and Sybil, but the monitors were limited.

"Tolerance Lamar."

I stood up.

"Yes, your Honor."

"You're charged with domestic violence, your bond is set at five thousand dollars."

I then noticed Harriet appear on the smaller screen. Harriet had come to drop the charges.

"Who are you, ma'am?"

"Tolerance Lamar's wife. I came here to let you know that I'm scared of him."

"So you don't want him to get out of jail? The judge asked.

"No!" Harriet answered.

"Your bond, Mr. Lamar, has been raised to ten thousand dollars! That will hold him for a while," the judge said.

"Thank you," Harriet said, before walking off the screen.

"Damn bro," one of the prisoners murmured. My chest tightened.

"Next!" the Judge yelled.

I was speechless and overwhelmed with a feeling that Harriet was trying to buy time to clean me out like she had before. I knew that I had to get out of there. I only had one hope and that was to get to my cell and call Ms. Bennett, my kids' grandmother, and have her call my father to go pick up my payroll check. I knew I had a full week in but wasn't sure that it would be enough to cover ten percent of a ten thousand dollar bond.

When I finally got to a phone, I couldn't get through. Turns out that Ms. Bennett had a block on her phone. The thought of my house being gutted made my stomach churn. Hours began to drag and I had no luck at reaching anyone on the outside.

At 4:00 pm, to my surprise, my name was announced to roll my things up; somehow I had made bail. With in an hour, I exited the door to my freedom. On the outside, Sybil was waiting on me, and she ran up and embraced me. Behind her, my father and Vi were smiling. I hugged and kissed them gratefully.

"You bonded me out?" I asked my father.

"No, Sybil bonded you out."

I looked at Sybil, who was still gazing at me and smiling.

"Thank you, honey."

"You're welcome. That was almost my entire income tax refund, but I love you too much to not stick by you."

I placed a warm kiss onto her lips.

"We were going to get you out Friday, but we were told that your bond would probably be lowered. Thanks to that witch you married, the judge upped your bond.

"Bond is now ten thousand dollars, that should hold him," Sybil mocked. My father and Vi chuckled.

"So the bondsman wanted a thousand?" I asked.

"Yep, ten percent," Sybil confirmed.

The four of us got into my father's vehicle. When we pulled up in front of my house, I noticed my bronco was parked in the same spot. My house looked so lonely and neglected, my heart shifted at the thought of my past. I fumbled for my house keys. I exited the vehicle and took the lead through the metal fence. Filled with curiosity, I inserted the key and unlocked the door. We entered to find that Harriet had pre-planned to return because her and her kid's things were gone; whereas some of my things, furniture and other valuable items were near the door ready to go. Boneshaker was now scratching on the door in the laundry room.

"We beat her to the punch!" I said and rushed to the laundry room.

"Yep, she was fin to get you again!" my father said.

The four of us talked a little more on my dilemma before my father and Vi headed out, leaving Sybil and I alone. I then called the police and reported my cell phone stolen and paged Harriet a message to end our marriage peacefully. I then changed my locks. I also called my kids and informed them that I was still planning to get a loan from the bank to add rooms to the house like I had previously planned and that I loved them.

The following morning, Sybil and I got up, ate breakfast, and then drove out to my employer to get my paycheck. I also informed them of my plight and my supervisor understood enough to grant me a couple of days off. Again, I used the telephone booth to call my cell phone. Finally, Harriet answered. Sybil noticed me talking and she got out the car and walked toward me. Harriet told me that an officer had called her and that she would drop my phone off at the sheriff's station and I could pick it up there. I thanked her and told her that she could have the house; I would get my things and leave.

"I have other plans," said Harriet.

"Well, we need to talk, so we can get an understanding."

"I'm doing something right now and I got to go."

"Where are Amy and Junior?"

"They're in school. I got to go!" Harriet repeated.

"Alright, I guess I'll talk to you later."

"Bye," Harriet said. I wanted to tell her I love her, but Sybil was looking me right in my mouth. The line went dead.

Sybil and I got in the car and headed to Nation's Bank. I came to learn that Harriet had taken money out of my account, but thankfully, she didn't take it all; that itself was confusing. I then went by the Sheriff's office and picked up my cell phone, then picked up Sybil's son from his grandmother's. We headed to my father's house to pack Sybil's things. In the middle of all these errands, I realized that I was confused because part of me still loved Harriet and part of me disliked her. As for Sybil, I knew she was not my type, yet she was a good pain killer.

The following afternoon while Sybil was at work, I went to Harriet's job and called her from the phone booth that stood in the lot where she worked.

"Hello, Harriet, I'm just calling to let you know that I don't really want to end our marriage like this."

I then took a deep breath and let my feelings flow. I recalled the promise that I had made to my children. I refreshed her memory about how I was trying to regain custody of my kids so they could come live with us. But, most of all, I explained how my daughter, Tina, was at a vulnerable age of 14 and that she really needed her father. I begged her to please drop the charges and pick up where we left off.

Silence fell between both ends.

"I don't know what I'm going to do," Harriet said dryly. "I got to go... my boss keeps looking at me. I got to go. Page me later."

The phone went dead.

Later that evening, I arrived home and was about to exit my car when Keitha greeted me and asked if I would like to go on a dinner date together to get my mind off of things.

Regina, my neighbor from across the street, yelled between giggles that Harriet had come over talking about how she loved her husband.

"She's full of it," Keitha sneered.

"If she loves you bra bra she would do the things you ask of her. She hasn't changed a bit," Keitha concluded.

I will admit that I felt a little better to hear that Harriet had come by and left word that she loved me.

"She ain't no good for you bra bra."

My head hung at my little sister's voice. I exhaled.

"I know," I replied.

Keitha then turned and headed back into the house; I grabbed my cell phone and paged Harriet. I stood by my vehicle waiting for Harriet to return my call, when I spotted my neighbor walking across the street toward me.

"Did your sister tell you that I seen Sybil too?"

I shook my head no as she continued.

"She is glad to be back home because she was smiling from ear to ear!"

We both chuckled as she walked back to her yard.

Moments later, I realized Harriet hadn't returned my call. I finally gave up. I was just tired of feeling the way I was feeling and I knew it was best that she hadn't called back. Seven years of heartache and pain was enough. I went inside the house.

As the days passed, I began making plans for my future with Sybil. We resumed fixing up the house by painting and so on. One evening after work, Sybil angrily informed me that she caught Harriet parked in front of the house while Amy and Junior peeped through our windows. Both had sleeves of unopened paper cups that I had sitting on the corner of the porch in their hands. When she pulled up to park, both of them dash to their mom's car.

"Put it back," Sybil said she yelled.

Harriet then poked her head out of the car window and loudly reminded Sybil that she was the wife. The women apparently passed words back and forth before Harriet drove off.

I had Sybil note the incident so I could later inform the judge that while Harriet had requested a restraining order, she was continually driving by my house, stalking me. For the first time, I did not call Harriet to beg her back. Instead, I tried to weed her out of my life.

On March 15, 1998, Keitha frantically woke Sybil and me from out of our sleep to inform us that Harriet had called H.R.S. and given them the videotape of me whipping my son and her son with a belt. After shaking the cobwebs clear from my head, I recalled the incident that happened three months ago; a morning when I decided that my son Lil' Toler was due for a good ass whipping.

"That dirty heifer," Keitha fumed.

She was mad because I had finally stopped running behind her.

Oh well, I thought. *She'll get over it.* Sybil and I rolled back over and went back to sleep.

CHAPTER 12

SAD EYES

During the month April, a few days after I had received a court date for the incident with Harriet, I arrived home from work and was greeted by three dismayed faces.

"Bra bra!" Keitha yelled as she rushed toward me. "The detectives been by here about that tape Harriet gave them."

"Dad, they came around Dell's house asking me and Toler questions, and they checked Toler for welts," Tina intervened.

"Honey, they say they want to talk to you, they left their number for you to call them when you got home." said Sybil.

Sybil then momentarily disappeared down the hall and returned with a card. I called the number immediately.

"Mr. Lamar, do you recall whipping your son?"

"Yeah, I whipped him and will whip him again. What's the problem?" I asked, feeling a slow burn inside me.

"We are on our way to ask some questions Mr. Lamar. Please don't leave."

"Alright," I said before the line went dead.

"Who in the hell are they supposed to be?" I fumed as I slammed the receiver back into its cradle.

Suddenly, I realized how quiet the family room had gotten. I mumbled a few more words and proceeded to take off my boots. I glanced at Tina, who quickly looked away and started biting her finger nails. At the same time, Keitha looked away and exhaled. Sybil was the only one who never broke her stare. Honestly, I felt like I hadn't done anything wrong, I tried to speak with confidence that everything would be okay so they can stop looking as if I was going to jail or something. I walked toward the back room. It wasn't a good fifteen minutes when one of the girls yelled that the detectives were outside.

Outside, behind my fence, stood two Caucasian males, staring down at the face of my 80 pound Rottweiler name Boneshaker. The younger officer, who looked to be in his mid-twenties, was now fiddling to open the fence while his partner stood beside him.

"Tolerance Lamar?"

"Yes sir," I said as I approached them and proceeded to unlatch the gate for them.

Boneshaker was still wagging his nub, ready to lick 'em to death. *I should have left the fence open for that dog to go and get lost, sorry mutt.* I closed the gate behind us and started to walk toward the porch. When I asked what was going on, the older detective started reading me my rights. The younger detective took a hold of my arm and I just stood there in dismay as I listened. The shock was interrupted by the clanging sound of handcuffs.

"Wait, can I get my shoes?"

Both men's eyes glanced toward my bare feet.

"Sure, we'll let you get your shoes" said the arresting officer.

The men closely followed me onto the porch where Keitha's sad eyes met mine. The men and I entered the house and walked with me into the family room where I had taken off my boots. As I put back on my boots, I glanced up to see Tina still sitting in the same spot looking downward and chewing on her nail. I suddenly begin to feel weak. It was a feeling that I never want to experience again. Out of nowhere a female voice got all of our attention as she stormed in the house and actually sneered at Keitha and Sybil who were standing near me. And when she fixed her eyes on me, she said, "Is this the guy?"

This Caucasian woman identified herself as a high ranking detective for the Hillsborough County Police Department. She was medium-built in stature and crowned with puffy sandy red hair. She went about as if she was The Big Bad Pussy Cat.

"Take him to my office for questioning," she demanded.

I was then escorted out the door.

"Because your neighbors are watching, I won't handcuff you," said the older detective.

"Thank you I appreciate that," I said faintly.

Later during questioning, I tried my best not to show how scared I had become.

A detective placed a form in front of me that clearly read, in big letters, that I would be released after questioning. After reading this, I recalled what my grandma used to tell my sister Rena and I.

The truth will set you free.

I started talking fast, spilling my guts. I even demonstrated on the floor the positions my boys were in and what actually took place.

"Take him to booking and his wife will be joining him because she just sat there and watched," said the red head.

That homey the clown looking heifer just tricked me.

I was booked on two counts of aggravated child abuse. My bond was fifty thousand dollars. The next day, while I was still in a daze, I called Sybil. She informed me that I was in the papers and on the news and that Harriet had to turn herself in within 24 hours. I got off the phone and fetched the day's paper and learned that Harriet had fabricated that I was performing sex acts on her children. Harriet's despicable mission had backfired on her. As I read the article, the look of Harriet's distraught face plastered next to mine made me look and feel like a real dummy because I had many premonitions about this evil woman that I ignored. My mind drifted back to when I was 16 and a man told me, "If a woman does it to you one time, she will do it to you again."

I recalled the mess she made of my name in California. Harriet had once again cast lies on me. Suddenly, my wife's venomous attack made me light headed and I couldn't read anymore. I trashed the article. I had to lie down and I wished that this was only a dream.

Sure enough, the next day Harriet was on the news and in the papers, arrested with a fifty thousand dollar bond like me. Ambivalently, I wondered what would become of Amy and Junior. What would become of me and my kids? I was angry with how the media had assassinated my character as if I was a danger to kids.

"You are both charged with two counts of aggravated child abuse," Judge Heinrich announced over the speaker as Harriet and I stood in two separate courtrooms. I stood passively staring at the big screen as the Judge fingered through Harriet's file.

"Oh, I see the picture here: you get angry with your husband and try to get even and consequently, you get arrested as well," mocked Heinrich. "Does she have any priors?"

"No, your Honor, only one arrest, a misdemeanor."

Keitha, who was actually sitting in the audience witnessing our hearing, later said that when the judge called Harriet's name, she stood with two big plats sticking straight out from each side of her head and her thick eye glasses were fogged.

"She looked shot out!" Keitha expressed.

"Mrs. Smith, (Harriet's maiden name)," the judge continued, "I am going to release you on your own recognizance until your court hearing. As far as you, Mr. Lamar," the Judge's voice deepened, "You are in big trouble. Look to be here for a long time because your bond will remain at fifty thousand dollars. Next."

I was completely demoralized. My legs started moving toward the metal door. Apparently, the media was addicted to my case. Seemed that the nightmare I was experiencing literally moved to Elm Street. Things started happening really fast. I couldn't keep up with the unfolding drama. For instance, I read a clipping from a news article stating that it looked like I was performing some ritual on my boys. In addition, Sybil was getting attacked by the media. Her statement was printed, saying that I was a good father and that I wouldn't hurt my children. On the other hand, I was extremely hurt by other fictitious statement and viewpoints. I was stunned to see the lengths that the media went to make their papers and broadcasts interesting by slandering people. I never realized this until I was the victim. I felt so lost and alone. The next thing I knew, an officer came and escorted me to a one man cell, the reason being to keep the other inmates from learning my charge. If they found out, I might become the victim of a hate crime that may lead to getting brutally beaten or even murdered. I can remember crying uncontrollably because the media had portrayed me to be this monster. The way some officers looked at me made me truly feel like hanging myself. But, I knew I couldn't do that.

I can still remember the times when I thought about how stupid I felt for allowing myself to trust and let Harriet back into my life, knowing she could care less about my kids' welfare. My children needed me, and I had little or no hope. I knew my family couldn't afford a fifty thousand dollars bond, and if they could have, I would have feared getting shot due to a drive by. If it wasn't for Sybil and my father, I don't know what I would have done. And poor Sybil, I really took her through it. I went as far as asking her to page Harriet on her three-way line and once we were connected, I left a message to Harriet asking her to help me, saying that the inmates may try to kill me. I ended the message with *I love you.* On the other line, I heard Sybil make a deep sigh, and yet, not once did she scold me nor leave me.

A week or so passed and I was back on the camera before Judge Heinrich for a bond reduction. The four hundred dollar street lawyer, my dad and Sybil had scraped up, was standing tall on the big screen to represent me, but when I was called to stand and my lawyer heard the denial by the Judge, followed by *next,* that sorry bastard turned an about face, saying nothing in my defense. Later that evening when I called Sybil, she told me that my lawyer walked away leaving an icy remark that I would *be lucky* if I didn't get twenty years!

I slowly placed the phone back into its cradle. I couldn't sleep, but I had to go lay down. It was becoming clear that my life was pretty much over and the reason behind it was eating me alive. I felt flashes of hate toward Harriet, knowing she was out trying to get herself unhooked by acting like a battered, confused wife who felt that my discipline was egregious and she was only trying to seek my comeuppance. I knew that wasn't the case, hell, she encouraged the discipline. It was about winning and losing. Either she won or everybody would lose. Sadly, my children were the ones losing. I couldn't get mad with anyone but myself because I knew how sadistic Harriet could be.

What can I say? *You reap what you sow.*

Days followed and I finally was able to talk to another lawyer that my father and Sybil managed to provide for me. The mere opening of my cell door was a relief to my soul. I was escorted to a small room where I sat face-to-face with a lawyer named Hershock. This clean cut short-in-stature white male appeared to be in his early forties and it was clear that he was no Public Pretender. He exuded professionalism. I immediately thanked him for being willing to help me, and between my father and me he would get paid; being, that I bonded out to go to work. Hershock explained to me that my case was highly publicized and that the media was having a field day ripping me apart. He also told me that the tape that was given to HRS was my biggest problem, being that I couldn't deny whipping my boys.

"They're calling it torture," said Hershock

"Torture," I repeated. "I didn't even put a welt on them, I didn't hurt them!"

I could feel tears begin to trail down my face onto the wooden surface of the table, creating small puddles.

"I can't believe this," I cried. Hershock waited patiently until I got my composure before he asked me to explain what happened.

The truth will set you free; I heard a voice whisper inside of me.

"My son and daughter were over for the weekend."

"Your son and daughter don't live with you?"

"No, not at that time. I was making arrangements with Nations Bank for a loan to have two rooms added to my house. I was arrested two days before I was to have a hearing with the bank."

"So, your son and daughter live with their biological mother?"

"No, their mother has been on drugs ever since I left her. She's been using crack for over five years now and there doesn't seem to be an end in sight, so my kids are living with their aunt who is on the mother's side of the family."

"So, you were going to try and get custody of your kids?"

"Yes! I had legal custody once before."

"What happened?" Hershock asked, as he wrote something down on his pad.

"I lost custody when I dropped my kids off by their grandmother's and didn't return. I thought that the mother would see that I wasn't going to take all the responsibility. I thought she would take a stand and get our kids. I thought wrong!"

"I see," Hershock muttered. "What's the mother's name?"

"Roxann Stone"

"And you have two kids by her?"

"No, four."

"Four?" he repeated, looking up from his pad. "What's the other two names?"

"Terran Lamar and Terrance Stone. My oldest son and daughter were over for the weekend. Sometimes, Terrance and Terran would come over and the other two would stay with their aunt. My wife couldn't handle my four and her two at one time, so that particular weekend, my two oldest were over. Actually, they were over for the weekend and the following week. Tina was out of school because of school procedures, but Lil' Toler was already out because he had gotten suspended for bad conduct. Anyway, both wanted to stay the week with me and..."

"Tolerance and Tina?"

"Yes," I replied.

"Sorry to cut you off. Go ahead tell me what happened."

"Well, I noticed my son's cocky behavior, always talking noise to his mother, calling her stupid in her face and he..."

"Who, his biological mother?"

"Yes."

"I see, go on," Hershock muttered.

My son started getting too disrespectful toward his mother and me. He even started wearing his pants below his butt, showing gang signs with his hands and whatnot. I really felt that I may have serious problems with him, but I ignored the thought because I was grateful that they were in my company. Wasn't long Lil' Toler started challenging me by mocking that he would be able to knock me out in about a year or so because of his big hands. I'd grin with a remark like, 'you'll never be able to handle me boy.' Periodically throughout the day, Lil' Toler would make sarcastic remarks, insisting that his punch would soon be powerful enough to knock me out. I'd wave him off as if he was just talking and continue to entertain my family. That whole weekend Lil' Toler was acting like a 16-year-old thug, cupping his crotch, giving gang signs, trying to get fresh with his stepsister Amy.

I took a moment to catch my breath. Hershock patiently waited for me to continue. So, the weekend was over. Every day when I came home from work, my wife, Keitha and Tina would come complaining to me about Lil' Toler's disruptive behavior. It was either how nasty he had been talking or how hardheaded he was being. But, I'd be so tired that I wouldn't say a word to him, I kept putting it off until I wasn't so tired. One night, I think it was that Thursday, I was on my way home from work when I decided to stop by my Mom's and I just so happened to run into Roxann. She told me that a couple of weeks past, Lil' Toler had hit her in the head with a broom stick and threatened to throw hot grease on her. My first thoughts were Toler was probably mad with her because she never would leave the drugs alone, knowing that she had to stay clean in order to regain custody.

Nonetheless, I realize through a repentant experience that there is no good explanation for one to strike their mother. I mentally noted that I would definitely have a long talk with Lil' Toler that coming Saturday when I was off. The next day, when I arrived home, again, everybody was complaining about Lil' Toler. Junior, my wife son started being disruptive in school as well. Tired and hungry from the rigors of the day, I told Harriet to write down all the things Lil' Toler had done and I'd deal with him later.

The following morning, I took my wife's car to work and returned to find myself again bombarded by everyone complaining about Lil' Toler's behavior, only this time the complaint was about him taking my money out of the ash tray of my truck.

"I told Lil' Toler that was your money, but he took it anyway!" said Keitha.

This time I approached my son and asked if he had taken my money from my truck. He claimed it was only a dollar in change and he thought Harriet said he could have it.

"He's lying," yelled Keitha.

Again, I was too tired to fuss with him, so I went to my room to bathe and relax. While I was in my room, Harriet and the girls accompanied me. Later, Junior entered and started agitating his sisters. I was enjoying their company because it was a good feeling to see them all together, but he was pushing all of our buttons. Lil' Toler soon entered the room with his slow, thuggish walk. This is when I noticed his swollen nipples; they were sticking out the holes in his shirt. He stopped in the center of the room displaying gang signs.

"What's wrong with your nipples" I asked.

"Why you want to suck 'em?"

Harriet and the girls looked at me like, are you going to let him talk to you like that?

I was stunned by my son's verbal blow. Lil' Toler, with that mischievous grin, turned and left the room. Exhausted, I ate dinner and went to bed. The following morning, I woke up thinking about what my son had said to me. All that day, Lil' Toler's sarcastic remark taunted me. Later that evening, I got off work early. Happy to be off, I decided to go home and spend time with my family. I thought it would be fun do some karaoke with them and record it. I set up the camcorder in the far corner of the family room and called my father to come over to join us for the event. It turned out to be a lot of fun and was very memorable.

The following morning, I was awakened by a blatant confrontation. When I gathered myself to where I could make sense of what was going on, I realized that Lil' Toler and Junior were arguing. I heard Toler's dominating voice threatening to knock Junior out. He was fussing and carrying on like he was the man of the house. At that moment, I had had it with Lil' Toler's behavior. I suddenly hurled out of my bed and put on my shorts. I knew if I tried to whip him, he would try to block every lick and then later boast about it. The boy had a slick mouth. No doubt, he'd brag, saying he blocked my licks or that it didn't hurt and he flashed that mischievous grin. So I decided to retrain him so I could give him an effective discipline. This would also prevent me from having to chase after him and perhaps cause serious injury by falling on one of the glass tables that sat throughout the house. I got up, went outside to my boat and cut two 20 inch straps from the rope that was in the storage box. I then went to my wife and asked her to give me the list that she had been compiling on Lil' Toler's ugly behavior. Harriet quickly saw that I was finally going to get on Lil' Toler's butt. Enthusiastically, Harriet went to get the list and returned with the list, saying not to forget about Junior. Harriet elaborated about how terrible Junior had been acting in school and recalled the several times she had to leave work and go to the school to get him for biting, spitting and throwing temper tantrums. So, I asked her if she had written up a list for him, too.

"No," Harriet said, "but I will."

Harriet went on to say that Junior had deliberately blamed her for his behavior because she didn't give him his medication, trying to use the medication for an excuse.

"I'm sick of him," Harriet concluded.

Therefore, I went back out to my boat and cut two more straps for Junior because I didn't want the discipline between the two boys to look unjust. I went back inside and Harriet was sitting at the kitchen table writing up a list for Junior. When she finished I took the list and added questions for their sisters to read off to them. I entered the family room and set aside the glass coffee table to make space for the discipline and placed two chairs for the girls to sit before their brothers and read off the questions to them. Toler had eleven questions and Junior had about eight. I then called for Tina and Amy and told them to take turn and read off the questions I had written up for each brother. I handed them their list and showed them their seat. I then called for Toler and Junior.

When the boys entered the room, I told them that we were going to play a game and that they had to lie down on the floor.

"What kind of game?" Lil' Toler asked.

"A spelling bee. When Amy or Tina spells a word correctly, I'll take a knot out of this rope. Whoever gets untied first will win five dollars."

"You gonna tie us up?" Lil' Toler asked.

"Yep," I replied.

Junior's eyes lit up and he made an *Ooohhh* sound, indicating he wanted to play. I then told the boys to lie down on the floor so they could get ready to play. They both hit the floor. I restrained Lil' Toler's feet and hands. I then turned to Junior and gave him a little knot, again, just to keep Tina from making opposing remarks that I tied up Lil' Toler and not Junior. Although Junior was no threat, it was Lil' Toler who needed restraining. I proceeded to pull down Lil' Toler's pants below his buttocks to embarrass him.

"What are you doing?" Lil' Toler asked, panicked.

"You'll see," I said in a voice he knew wasn't a game.

Both boys fell silent and their eyes followed me. Harriet had now seated herself on the couch beside the boys, whereas I sat at the foot of them. I instructed the girls to read off from the list all the things their brother's had done. Tina had to read off to Toler, and Amy, to Junior.

Tina's first question was asking Toler, "Why were you playing sex games in school and to your step sister Amy?"

He gave this lame excuse that he was just playing. I then verbally disciplined him on the issue. Next it was Amy's turn to read Junior's first question, which was regarding him not taking his pill, and he felt that it gave him the reason to cut the fool.

I simply told him, "I am your pill!"

I began to think that this verbal discipline would be beneficial to teach the kids the dos and don'ts, so when they have their own kids they would have some idea of what not to allow. So I decided to turn on my camcorder that I had set up in the corner from the night before. Harriet also intervened by raising her hand to speak and giving her input about their behavior. After all the questions were discussed, I told Harriet to fetch a belt with a pot of water. This was to bring the element of fear to the discipline, so that the wayward child wouldn't want to receive another discipline like that again. Harriet brought me the belt and water. I asked her to dip it, and to hand it to me. As the water dripped their faces instantly tightened with fear. Mission accomplished.

I truly believe that a parent needs to make sure that their discipline exudes some level of fear. This is only when you're dealing with extremely sarcastic and disrespectful youngsters. If you don't exude fear, you're just wasting your time. The child will take you for a joke.

After I gave the boys a verbal discipline and a thorough ass whipping, I proceeded with the routine that I had previously planned for that day. We went fishing.

While we were on the water fishing, Lil' Toler and I had a father and son talk. He actually listened and in return, I listened to him. Lil' Toler started smirking and said that the belt was mostly hitting the couch and not his butt. Still, I sincerely tried to get him talking so I could better understand his behavior and disrespect towards his mother and I. Junior was now about to jump out of his seat to say that he had gotten loose. They both giggled. I smiled and turned to hear Junior's input. After the discussion, I felt that I had reached them and that their bad behavior would stop.

Life at home took on a drastic change for the better. Lil' Toler had started respecting adults, he stopped stealing from people, he stopped with the sexual gestures; he stopped calling his mother names to her face and didn't dare strike her. His past school behavior no longer existed. And Junior became so disciplined in school that one of his teachers wrote us to say thank you for setting things straight with him. Another teacher happily called to say that Junior had changed his behavior. I was not only proud of the boys' corrections, but proud of myself for being the source for such change.

Weeks passed and suddenly, my second marriage to the same woman derailed. Once again, I found myself constantly complaining to my wife for allowing the house to get so filthy, the same reason that destroyed our first marriage. This time, I wasn't going to go through the same crap. Either she was going to get with the program or she was going to get the hell out. Like before, Harriet stood toe to toe exchanging words with me. I eventually asked her to leave.

Harriet saw that I was going to stand my ground and not stoop to her level. She flew into one of her fits and started hitting herself in the face. Her glasses crashed to the floor and broke. She then yelled for her kids and stormed out of the door and drove off into the darkness. I waited about 45 minutes for her to return. I began to feel guilty because of the marriage vows I had made and how only infidelity or death would justify breaking them. Because of Harriet's disloyal, promiscuous past, I knew that it would be days before Harriet would show her face. I called Sybil to come over and help me get over Harriet. Within 30 minutes, Sybil was there. We sat in the family room and started talking about my dilemma. The next thing I knew, Harriet and the police were in the house and confronting me about striking Harriet. Harriet coaxed the officers to believe I was a no-good, brutal husband and lo and behold, I was arrested on a domestic violence charge. The following morning, at my wife's request, my bond was increased to ten thousand dollars when it was initially five thousand dollars. Thanks to Sybil though, I was still able to bond out.

Angered, Harriet came to my house to harass Sybil. She wanted revenge and her quest to get it led her to give HRS the tape of me disciplining our boys. I was eventually arrested again and charged with two accounts of aggravated child abuse, that's why I'm here.

"That's quite a story," said Hershock.

He agreed to help me, but he informed me that my family would have to come up with more money for his retainer fee and that he would get back with me as soon as he heard from my father to discuss the matter.

After about four weeks in the county jail, I finally got in court. My attorney knew his stuff. He had what I considered to be a no-nonsense approach in representing his clients. Furthermore, a male judge was sitting in for Judge Hawkins; that in itself was a relief. The judge reviewed the tape of me disciplining my boys. After the review he reentered the room, seated himself, and said that all he saw was discipline. My bond was lowered from fifty thousand to fifteen hundred dollars.

Fortunately, Sybil and my father were now able to post bail for me. While I was at the counter to sign for my personal property, the officer informed me that they had recently placed another charge on me: felony for the possession of a firearm and that carried a bond of twenty five hundred dollars and I couldn't be released until it was paid.

Another tremendous shocker was the realization of how dirty the Judicial System can be. Meanwhile, my father and Sybil were again beating their heads against the wall trying to meet this additional bond. A day or so later, my father was able to get a title loan on my truck.

On April 30, 1998 I finally made bail, and after the hugs Sybil informed me that Boneshaker was missing. Immediately, I figured that Sybil didn't lock the gate, although I didn't have room to complain. It was like I had just left the pit of Hell. I was exhausted and relieved that the humiliation I had endured in the county jail had ended. I had been segregated from the regular population for my own safety and placed on lockdown in a section in the jail that was normally reserved for murderers and rapists. I can still remember the men staring out of their cells at me as if I was a member of the demented elite. It took all the strength I had inside to keep the system from making me feel as though I was inhuman. I found myself still fighting back tears, even though I was en route to my home.

I later received a letter from the courts informing that a hearing was set regarding an extension on the restraining order Harriet had filed against me. Considering her previous lies and her evil disposition, I assumed her reasoning behind this was to cover her tracks so as to solidify her role as a submissive and physically abused housewife.

Finally, Harriet and I were summoned for an arraignment hearing on child abuse charges, where we were both called before the Honorable Judy Hawkins. Two hearings were set and I just straight out told Sybil that I would attend the hearings alone because I didn't want to piss Harriet off any more than I already had. Besides, it wouldn't look good in the judge's eyes to see me accompanied by another woman.

During the hearing, I'd hoped to speak with Harriet, but the bitch wouldn't even give me eye contact. She had no problem rushing past me, swishing her ass which was not her normal walk.

On June 2nd 1998, I had my hearing concerning Harriet's restraining order. We sat before another male judge and Harriet was engaged in showing a cause for an extension. I can remember the look Harriet gave me before we were seated; it was a look as if she wanted to kill me, a look that made me no longer hope for eye contact. Yet, despite what Harriet was telling the judge and how she felt about me, I gloomily told the judge that I would like to end our marriage as friends and not enemies because deep down in my heart, I was saddened by the way our marriage was ending. In return, the judge replied that the manner in which we conclude our marriage was up to the two of us, but until she dropped the restraining order, I could not have any contact with her, not even by phone. He then concluded with the consequences I would experience if I violated this. I shook my head in agreement and continued to look downward.

"Mr. Lamar, do you understand?"

"Yes, your Honor," I said as I raised my head.

When I left the courtroom, I was about to unlock my truck when I sensed someone staring at me. I looked up across the street and there stood Harriet. Short in stature, Harriet's reddish complexion glowed vividly against her lengthy black hair. I exhaled passively and proceeded to enter my truck.

"Do you want to talk?" Harriet yelled from across the street.

"Where," I replied.

"I don't know it's up to you" said Harriet.

"We can meet at Shell's Seafood," I offered.

She gave a quizzical look and suggested that we go park in front of the sheriff's station and talk. I agreed, so Harriet walked to her car and followed me to the sheriff's station. We both parked in the lot and she got into my truck. Harriet immediately suggested making sure that no one knew of our visit. I concurred. Harriet began saying how sorry she was for getting me in trouble like she did, but it was the way I had made her feel. She then asked me to tell the judge that I was drunk when I disciplined our boys.

"I wasn't drunk," I objected, "and I'm not going to tell the judge that I was."

Harriet then flipped the script and grew suddenly sad. She began to speak about HRS and how Amy and Junior were being separated from each other. She then lifted her head up with confidence and said that she would soon get them back. I felt her pain. Sympathetically, I asked her not to go against me in court, that my kids needed me as well. And if she loved me, she would not end our marriage this way because that is what Satan wanted.

"I know Satan is busy," she mumbled.

Harriet's eyes caught hold on the yellow envelope that was sitting in the console.

"Give me some money. I see you got your income tax."

"I only have a few dollars," I muttered as I dug out my last five dollars and handed it to her, letting her know the envelope was not from a tax return.

"I see you got new rims and tires on this truck and a new stereo system."

"I had these things on layaway."

I then found myself gazing into Harriet's wide, bedroom eyes as her wet tongue slowly slithered across the rim of her red curvy lips. Like a pig waiting for slop, my lips plunged onto hers.

My hand roamed into her pants meeting her wet vagina.

"I love you, Tolerance Lamar," she murmured as we kissed. Tarzan was now pressing hard in my pants and he wanted out.

"You want to kiss it?" I asked looking down gripping my stiff bulge.

"I want to and I don't want to," said Harriet as I started to unzip.

"No," she grimaced looking back toward the sheriff's station. Then she whispered, "You want to see it?"

"Yeah!"

Harriet then pulled her pants down a little more, which allowed me to get a clear view of her healthy, hairy trap. I must be honest: Harriet's seduction was working because I was about ready to do whatever she commanded.

"Let's go somewhere else," I suggested. Harriet said that she had to be somewhere, that she had another man and that it was love at first sight. Although she went on to say that we could see each other, she made me promise that I wouldn't interfere in her new relationship.

"Promise me, Tolerance Lamar!" she demanded.

Harriet eye's beamed sharply into mine. I exhaled, as though it was the hardest oath to make. I gave her my promise. Harriet then pulled away from my lips and said she had a song that she wanted me to hear.

"You want to hear it?" she asked childishly.

"Yeah," I said.

"The tape is in my car, I'll go get it."

She left the truck and returned and popped her tape in the cassette deck, then turned facing me, pretending she was holding a microphone. She proceeded to sing along with this song, "I'm Still Wearing Your Name" and she put emphasis on the part that things were not the same.

I went along with the twisted sister like I was enjoying her singing, but really, if she was on American Idol, Simon would had thrown his Coca Cola cup at her. But still, I was relieved that we were talking and kissing. I thought that this could be the beginning of the end to all the betrayal and lies. It might even possibly bring our marriage to a peaceful end. When the song was over she said she had to go, so we exited the truck. Harriet and I resumed kissing as her back rested against my truck. Harriet again concurred that she wouldn't go against me in court. No doubt, she knew my discipline was needed and that it was out of love, not malice. Harriet went on to say that she would call me that evening. I'll never forget during our final kiss and hug, I said to myself, *who in the hell does she think she is!*

We departed, and when I got back into my truck, I noticed Harriet had placed the five dollar bill in my console among my tapes. Forty minutes later, Harriet called my cell phone, talking and laughing as if there were no more bad feelings lingering. I must admit, I hadn't felt better in months.

The following morning, I received a call from Harriet giving compliments on the looks of my new boat, a 17-foot off shore that was taking up space in my yard. I offered her a day out on the water, but she declined, stating that I'd never get her out there so I could drown her.

Propitiously, it seemed that we were now on good terms and I happily told my mother of Harriet's remorseful words. My mother warned me to be careful fooling around with Harriet. I knew my mother's words should not be ignored, yet I wanted to stay on the good terms that had been established. And not only that, understand that when a person loves another, that person may have the tendency to want to forgive and work it out.

However, that particular morning when I checked my mail, I discovered a subpoena for an arraignment hearing regarding my domestic violence charge. To make things worse, the same week, I received another court order for the fight I had with Ivy, my mother's old boyfriend. This was scheduled on the same day of the first hearing, just different courtrooms and times.

The day of the hearing regarding the fight with Ivy, my mother showed up. Not once had my mother ever came to court to support me, but during this particular incident, she did. I was somewhat curious. I wondered if my mom was there because she felt bad that she was the one who had called the police, and now that Ivy had abandoned her weeks ago, perhaps she had a change of heart and wanted to support me. Or maybe she figured this was her chance to catch up with Ivy?

Heartbroken and bitter, my mother admitted that Ivy was stealing from her to buy drugs and that she would tell the judge that I was only trying to protect her. As we waited for my name to be called, I hoped Ivy would be a no show. As for my mother, I think she felt the opposite. Luckily for me, Ivy didn't show, so the case was dismissed. My mother managed a smile.

I wasn't out of the woods yet, as I had to make another court appearance that afternoon and to my surprise, the domestic violence charge was dropped.

Now, this really threw me for a loop! Was it that Harriet dropped the charge because of our last encounter or the officials learned that she was fabricating her story? Again, I scanned the room for Harriet. No Harriet. I was brimming with relief. Today was a good day; weight was lifted off my shoulders. I almost looked forward to the next court hearing.

Weeks passed and I hadn't heard from Harriet and what she had up her sleeves remained a mystery. Finally, the setting for the next court hearing arrived.

Division B was crowded like always. I seated myself directly across from Harriet. People all around me looked deep in thought as they sat waiting to be called before the Honorable Judy Hawkins.

After 15 minutes of sitting, Harriet suddenly got up and went to the restroom. A minute or so later I got up, headed to the restrooms and waited outside the door for her. When she came out I tried talking to her.

"I can't talk right now," she muttered without eye contact and re-entered courtroom.

I retreated back into my seat.

When Harriet and I were finally called to approach the bench, I had this familiar unpleasant feeling that my psychopathic wife was going to switch out on me again.

The fact that I was not able to come up with the balance of my lawyer retainer's fee, Hershock announced to the judge that he was resigning from the case. Harriet's lawyer said that he and his client were prepared for trial. I glanced at Harriet. She sat there stone-faced as if I wasn't there.

The judge informed me that I would be appointed a street lawyer on the courts expense. I was then handed a business card to my assigned attorney. Hershock wished me luck and again gave his word that he would come back to represent me if I could come up with the money for my fifteen thousand dollar case.

Hell, selling my boat and truck wouldn't come close to that, so I set an appointment with this appointed attorney, whose name was John Boduski.

John looked as if he was in his mid to late 30's, stood about 6 foot tall and was stocky with blond hair. He and I reviewed the tape of my discipline. John concluded that he'd call up some professional who would show the cause of my actions because it was pretty clear that my intentions were good. We would therefore stick with the not guilty plea on the two counts of Aggravated Child Abuse that is characterized under malicious punishment. John continued that he would show that my discipline was out of good intentions not malice; however my charge could still be considered child abuse, which is a lesser charge.

"But my intentions were good!"

"We have to get the judge to see that," said John.

"To discipline, a parent can strike a child on the buttocks and buttocks only with an open hand until the hand stings; this indicates to draw back, to stop striking."

Well, isn't that some shit, I thought.

"As for the felony possession of a firearm, I probably can get that to run concurrent."

John's professionalism wasn't as superb as Hershock, but he talked with confidence and this set me a little at ease.

Again, I called my wife and left a message for her to please return my call and that we needed to talk. I waited another hour and called again, but this time I left the following message: "What is wrong with you Harriet? I will appreciate if you return my call!"

Hours and hours passed and there was still no response.

CHAPTER 13

TEARS OF A CLOWN

C uriosity was getting the best of me. What was Harriet up to? She once mentioned the name of the restaurant she worked at, which was in the Tampa Bay Mall. I just couldn't remember the name of it. For a while, I was beating my head against the wall, trying to recall the info Harriet had told me. Finally, it dawned on me. I grabbed the phone, called information and got the number.

"Can I speak to Harriet, please?"

"Jussa minute."

The first thing that came to mind was that she went from working for the school board to a measly restaurant. She was also about to lose her late model Oldsmobile. Not only was the Kia finance company in California looking for it, but the car was also about to fall apart, due to previous accidents. The woman and her two kids seemed like they demolished everything they get their hands on.

Within a minute or so, Harriet picked up the phone and said, "Hello?"

"Hello," I replied.

When she realized who I was, she stuttered, as if I had startled her and immediately slammed the phone back into its cradle.

Now, I was sorely confused and at the same time, more convinced that something was mentally wrong with that sister! She was like some sort of witch in disguise. I was sick and tired of the whole ordeal. I was tired of trying to get Harriet to see that we could end our marriage like two reasonable adults. The whole scenario was shameful and embarrassing. I knew God didn't approve of such betrayal toward one's spouse. Satan was probably sitting back laughing his ass off. I truly didn't want to end my marriage this way. To be totally honest, I was willing to go as far as sucking up to Harriet to save our marriage, despite what people thought about how stupid I was. But, Harriet had other plans.

I left a message on her phone.

"Harriet, you promised on the Bible that you would stick by me, I'm your husband and if you go against me, telling lies so you can get off the hook, God will curse you, God don't like ugly."

During the blistering month of August, I had an appointment to meet with John. At John's office, he informed me that Harriet's charge of aggravated child abuse had been dropped. He went on to say that it was good that they had dropped the charges knowing that the evidence showed that she was involved, yet they decided to let her walk, leaving me holding the stick. Therefore, I should get some sort of relief, hopefully probation or something.

During the days that followed, thinking about my painful situation was almost unbearable. I guess God was with me because during this terrible time in my life, I drove an 80-ton semi to and from cities and never got into a crash. A week or so after my last visit with my lawyer, I received mail from an unknown agent. I opened the envelope to learn that my wicked wife was still out to finish me off because now, she had filed a lawsuit demanding money and the dissolution of our marriage, or else. I didn't have a problem with the divorce, nor the money that I didn't have, but my assets? The things that I acquired before I remarried her, I don't think so! And all the lies within the suit, it's like I was married to the devil's daughter!

On September 23, 1998, the day of my pretrial, I made it my business to leave for court early because Judy Hawkins snarled at me earlier, warning me not to be late. So I made sure that I was there early. It was only a pretrial, so there was no need to drag my family along. There I sat, waiting for my lovely wife, Harriet, to appear. Finally, god's angel appeared and seated herself across on the far end of the room. John entered the room a short while later. He spotted me and walked toward me. He wanted to know if I was still in accordance with our agreement. I told him I was and he gave me some insight on what would basically be said to the judge. That's when John and I noticed the Tampa Tribune news reporter sitting in the corner with his camera. John suddenly informed that he was going to ask the judge to keep the cameras out of my case because the cameras could hurt me.

"How," I asked.

"It can give the judge a reason to use you as an example by giving you more time than you deserve."

"All Rise! The Court of the Honorable Judge Judy Hawkins is in session," yelled the bailiff.

John suddenly retreated among a body of court officials, and then we all took our seats. Meanwhile, as I waited for my case to be heard, I sat and observed Harriet's attorney. He was very good, and he clearly had favor with Judge Hawkins. I sat there and wished that he was representing me instead of John. Oh well, all I could do was hope for the best.

Harriet's attorney concluded one of his cases. He then placed his papers in his briefcase and walked over to Harriet. Harriet whispered something in his ear, and then removed a cassette tape out of a Walkman she had been holding and handed it to him. Her attorney then walked to John and whispered something in his ear. John looked over at me and shook his head in disbelief. Harriet's attorney departed into one of the court's adjoining rooms. I didn't know what the tape was about, but obviously it had something to do with me. And then, suddenly it dawned on me.

No, she didn't, I know she didn't have the nerve to record me calling her when she had initiated calls to me first, I thought.

My attorney approached me.

"Your wife has a tape of you calling her," he whispered.

I was devastated.

"What do the tapes say?" I asked.

"I don't know. I'm about to go and listen to it now. I'll be right back."

John headed toward the door that the defense attorney entered. I looked over at Harriet. She stared straight ahead. At that moment, I again realized that the woman I'd married didn't give a damn about me. That nasty bitch! As I glared at the side of my wife's cold, betraying face, I saw something I had never seen before, her mother's evil face. At some point, Harriet had become a younger version of her sadistic mother.

Ten minutes later, the defense attorney and John returned to the courtroom. My wife's attorney walked to the bailiff and whispered something into his ear. The bailiff then whispered something to the judge. The judge nodded in agreement. About that time, John approached me and informed that the message Harriet had recorded was threatening in nature.

"Threatening?" I murmured. "I didn't threaten her."

The first thing came to mind is that I was being set up, that someone had forged my voice.

"You heard me threatening her?" I asked.

"I heard you say that God will curse her."

I quickly explained that Harriet and I were practicing God's Law from the Holy Bible and that *Malachi 2:16* said that God forbids married couples treating one another treacherously.

Again, John gave me that look that said, *you married her.*

"The court is taking this tape to be a threat, which can put you in violation of your restraining order."

I was scared, angry and disappointed.

"What about how she had called me and how she had harassed Sybil? We met and talked. She even kissed me and wanted to have sex!"

"When did this happen?"

"June 2nd. She asked me if I wanted to talk. She set me up!"

"Okay, I'll see what Judge Hawkins has to say, I'll let the judge know that your wife agreed to all of…"

"She violated her own restraining order," I interrupted.

"Yeah, I'll be right back," said John as he headed toward the court officials.

Judy Hawkins slid her glasses on the bridge of her nose and looked at me from above its rim. Anybody who knew about this judge knew that wasn't a good sign. My name was called to stand before her. Harriet's attorney informed the Judge that he had a tape recording of me calling his client, who was now a state witness. He continued saying, "Recently, Mr. Lamar was court ordered to refrain from having any sort of contact with Ms Smith."

Judge Judy frowned.

"Bailiff, take him and put him on the bench."

The bailiff standing next to me grabbed my upper arm and started walking me toward the jury box. The bailer cuffed me and told me to have a seat. I mentioned for John and he came.

"I'm going to jail?" I asked frantically.

"I don't know. The judge will call you after she clears her docket," John said.

I was scared and confused. I looked over at my wife who sat in clear view, chewing gum as if she was enjoying a show. Ten minutes later, John returned and told me he didn't think the Judge was going to let me go because she doesn't like when people violate the conditions and orders handed down by her. He then stated that the State is willing to make a deal.

"What kind of deal?"

"Six years."

"Six years!" I exclaimed.

"Six years, or go to trial, which was now an unpredictable 50/50 chance, being that your wife is now a state witness against you. And this tape of you calling her is not good."

"So, if I lose I'll get more than six years?"

"From experience working with Judy Hawkins, if you lose she'll probably give you the max of 14 years."

I was speechless.

"You need to decide what you want to do. I'll be back" John said and headed back toward the occupied table.

I exhaled. Despite the handcuffs, I was able to take my cell phone from my waist. I called Sybil. I told Sybil that they were trying to lock me up and give me 14 years and that she needed to get down here. I also called my father. I attempted to call my mother to let her know what was going on, but a court official noticed me talking and quickly reported it to the bailiff, who came and confiscated my phone. Thirty minutes later, Sybil popped up and seated herself across from Harriet. Not long after that my father, Roxann, Toler and Tina appeared and seated themselves behind Sybil. And there, they all waited, watching to see what the judge's next move would be. I immediately motioned for my lawyer and asked him to let me speak with my father. John agreed and waited for the appropriate time to ask the judge to allow my father to speak with me. I just couldn't believe the court was serious about sending me to prison for an act that was born out of love and concern for my son and a genuine desire to disrupt the destructive path in which his life was headed. On top of that, I didn't hurt either of my boys. Why were they out to get me? Why couldn't the court see that my wife was doing all of this out of revenge? I looked at Harriet and shook my head. I inhaled and lifted my head up. My lawyer must have gotten the go-ahead because he knelt down and whispered to my father who slowly got up and approached me. The expression on his face was as though his car had been totaled and he had no insurance. My father sat next to me as John stood and explained my dilemma. My father turned to me. His eyes were sad.

"Son, you better take the six years or you might end up with fourteen."

My father looked downward, shaking his head in disbelief. I tried to convince my father that I wasn't guilty of the charges, that I only gave the boys a good whipping that they needed.

"Son, I understand, but they got a tape of you tying the boys up."

"Yeah, but I had to restrain Lil' Toler because he would block and kick and then brag about it later. He had become a threat. I mean, the police will restrain a person if they have to."

"I know and if he didn't cooperate, they'd take him and beat the shit out of him without a second thought," Pop murmured.

I went on to say that the tape only showed little of me spanking the boys, that 90 percent of my discipline was verbal. I didn't even put a welt on them.

Pop was now glaring at Harriet.

"Look at that slimy bitch," he said. "Sitting there like she is so innocent. Somebody needs to take her and..."

We were interrupted by John letting me know that I needed to make my mind up for the panel. I noticed my sister Keitha entering the courtroom.

"Panel, what is that," I asked.

"A group of people to be selected for jury," said John.

I looked at Sybil and my family, then over at Harriet. I noticed in the far corner behind Harriet was the channel 28 news reporter, fiddling with his camera. I looked back at Harriet and felt a slow burn flowing within me. At that very moment, I hated her.

John told me that he would be right back and that I needed to tell him my decision upon his return. I tell you, I was so confused, I didn't even know if I should live or die.

"This is a damn shame that you can't even discipline your own children," Pop grumbled. "If you were white, they'd give you probation or some kind of parenting classes."

"I know," I faintly replied. "John says I have a 50/50 chance. I got family to speak on my behalf, and if I can prove that my intentions were good, I should be able to win, right?"

"Son, I would take the six years, you can't see what they're trying to do! If you lose, the judge will give you the max! You know they don't want us on the streets."

Silence fell between us as I lowered my head. Finally, I took a deep breath and motioned for John, and told him I would take the six years. I again looked at my children and they looked as if *they* were going to prison. Sybil just stared at me from a distance. I told John to get my cell phone and give it to Sybil and my truck keys to Keitha, and he did. Sybil's face became tight. She got up, walked over to Keitha and politely took my keys out of her hands before retreating back to her seat. Keitha looked at me and managed a smile. John immediately returned and asked my father to return to his seat. My thoughts were running like wild race horses to the point where I wanted to just lay down. I asked John to ask the judge to give me time to go home before sentencing so I could get my affairs in order, like my mortgage and storage. John agreed to ask the judge for a two-week furlough.

Finally, my name was called. I stood face-to-face before the judge who frowned at my very presence. John stood beside me and told her about me agreeing to take the six years, and that I was asking for a furlough to take care of my personal matters before sentencing.

"I don't see that happening. I have a tape here of Mr. Lamar calling threatening his wife."

"Threatening her?" I repeated.

"Yes," the judge barked. My head dropped as I knew I did not threaten to hurt anybody.

The judge continued, "You were court ordered to have no contact with your wife."

"She'd called me and came by my house. She violated her own restraining order!" I said.

"Your Honor," John cut in "my client has informed me that Mrs. Lamar has been seeing my client and she even had sex with my client." She ignored him.

"Put Mr. Lamar in custody and I will call him back out after I clear the rest of my docket."

The bailiff immediately grabbed my arm and jerked me toward the far left door that led to holding cells. I stopped midway and looked at the judge.

"My heart was in this,"! I said to her. A stronger tug by the bailiff got me walking toward the door and down the hall. As I was being escorted by this asshole, a female officer was escorting her prisoner to Hawkins's courtroom a few feet ahead of me. The black female prisoner was taking very short steps because of the shackles on her feet that were connected to a chain running to her handcuffs. As they were about to make their pass, I noticed that the prisoner was somewhat cute and we made eye contact.

"Ain't you Tolerance Lamar?" the prisoner asked while we were still in motion.

"Yes," I replied.

She smiled. "Your sister and I is locked up together. She was talking about you the other day. You let the good woman go for the bad one."

"Yep," I admitted as I was pushed around the corner to a holding cell.

The bailiff shoved his clanging keys into the metal door and it opened. I was pushed inside. The bailiff took off my handcuffs and opened a holding cell that had bars an inch and a half thick. A cage fit for a powerful animal, but sadly, the cages were only filled with Blacks and Hispanics. Again, a familiar feeling of being inhuman ate at me. I found a spot to sit and I felt the pain of betrayal rush through me. A pain I should have been used to, yet it still hurt as badly as the first time. And on top of it all was the agony of knowing that I was going to prison for six years.

One inmate noticed that I had on fresh street clothes and he asked what they got me for. I told him I was in there for disciplining my son and I got charged with aggravated child abuse. Six years in prison or go to trial and take a chance of losing and get 14 years.

This ended up sparking a lively conversation. The majority of the men, especially the older ones, complained that kids today were extremely rebellious, and strict, stern discipline was sometimes needed because, if not they'd run over you. They offered their opinion by saying that I should have taken it to trail, tape or no tape. One guy even believed that the tape was going to help me, providing what I said was true. One black dude stood up and said that if it was his son and he had hit his mother, his son never would have had the opportunity to tell him to suck his shit because he would have split his head to the white meat.

"Who was your judge?" a Hispanic man asked.

"Judy Hawkins," I replied.

"Oh shit! She's a bitch!"

"She's a bull dagger. She don't like men," one said.

"She show don't," said another.

"If you take it to trial and lose, she's gonna give you the max," one said with conviction.

The Hispanic man reiterated, "That bitch ain't nothing nice, especially with drugs dealers."

"She hate drug dealers because her daughter got strung out on drugs. If I didn't have any drug charges, she might have cut me some slack."

"Shit," someone else sneered. "Not that bitch. That bitch is nasty. I know because she was my judge once."

"She's always been fair to me," another person said.

"I heard she don't like men and I got to go in front of her," said a middle-aged man whom sat crouched over, looking down at his feet.

Another black dude chimed in with a loud angry voice, "Man, she's my judge and she tried to give me ten years on a domestic charge. My lawyer got it down to five. They patted my wife on the back and she's the one that hit and tried to cut me with a knife!"

Everybody looked at him as if he might snap at any time.

"Hey man, take it to trial," someone else said. "If you lose, file an appeal. Give the fourteen years back!"

He sounded convincing, but the thought of losing the case and catching fourteen years, I couldn't even bear the thought.

"Just the thought is making me sick," I admitted.

"Who is your lawyer?" someone asked.

"John Boduski."

"Private or appointed?"

"Appointed."

"Man, you're in trouble. They all work together."

This seemed to be the only thing everyone agreed on.

"I can't chance getting fourteen years. I'll have to take the six. Man, I can't believe this shit happening to me!"

The voices in the cell seemed to roar. One man that was pacing the room made a comment that he couldn't believe that you can't even discipline your own child anymore. He wondered aloud what the world was coming to.

"When they go out and rob and steal, they want to shoot them in the back or lock them up like an adult, like they did me when I was sixteen," I said angrily.

Suddenly, we heard the keys jiggling. The outside door opened and my lawyer walked up to the cell and looked in. I went up to the bars to talk with him and I immediately noticed that his face was dark pink. I looked into his eyes, in the hope that something good would come out his of mouth.

"Toler, they backed out of the six years. Now they want eight years, and they made it clear that they won't go below that."

I felt weaker than before as my heartbeat increased.

"Eight years?"

John went on to say that we were going to take it to trial, that I still had a 50/50 chance. He felt that there was a chance to convince the jury that what I did had been an act of discipline, not aggravated child abuse.

I stared straight into his eyes looking for a sign of hope. At that point, I felt the jury was my best decision. Besides, I couldn't just stand there and let a judge take away eight years of my life without fighting. My situation was becoming scarier by the minute.

"A 50/50 chance," I repeated.

"Maybe a little more," John said.

I pondered for a few moments and said, "Let's do it."

Ironically, though that was the hardest decision of my life, it was made in just a few minutes. John left to tell the judge that we were taking it to trial and that we are ready to pick the jury.

Twenty five minutes later, the bailiff reappeared and opened the cell door.

"Tolerance Lamar, let's go," he said as he hand cuffed my hands in front of me and slammed the cell door behind us.

The unjolly green giant practically shoved me through the metal door leading out to the corridor. In the corridor, the bailiff told me in a harsh voice to take off my dress shirt and suspenders and that they had a shirt and tie to wear before the jurors, as if my clothes weren't fit. I remember gazing at the tie and shirt dangling in the bailiff's hand.

"Hurry up and get that shirt off," he shouted.

Apparently I was moving too slow because he snatched at my suspenders, popping them from my slacks. His huge hands repeatedly pushed me against the wall as he roughly unbuttoned my shirt. I felt helpless and violated. Tears began to drip from my eyes. The bailiff yanked off my shirt.

"Here, get this on," he ordered.

He thrust a white, long sleeved dress shirt, that wasn't any better than my own blue, into my hands. The bailiff sneered at me as if I had committed murder. Again, I felt that my life was over.

"Hurry up, we don't have all day," the bailiff growled.

I stuffed my shirt tail into my pants and started buttoning it up. The bailiff pushed my hand out of the way and started buttoning the shirt. My head was bobbing back and forth from his rough assistance.

"Put on this tie," he said, coldly.

I took the tie and slung it around my neck; wiped my wet face and made an attempt to tie the tie. I looked up at the hard, lumpy, red face of the bailiff, trying to digest it all. I remember the tears streaming down my face as I fumbled trying to tie that ugly tie. I never was any good at it, so I just tied it in a knot. The bailiff started hastily guiding me toward the door to the courtroom. I began to feel weak, as if my very life was rapidly exiting my body. The bailiff shoved me out into the court room. John saw the bailiff and me walking his way and he immediately asked the judge to at least let me tuck my shirt in properly. I was pushed back near the hall door. John walked up to me and turned me around and tucked the front of my shirt neatly into my pants. I wasn't even aware my shirt was hanging out. As he re-tied my tie, he muttered something about how he hated his job. I mustered all I had within me to pull it together. I didn't want my kids to see the despair I was in. And I especially didn't want to give Harriet the satisfaction. I wiped my eyes, took a deep breath and held my head up. John pointed me to the table where I was supposed to sit. I heard my kids crying over the official's voices. I glanced over at my kids. Tina's tears were streaming down her face and Lil' Toler's eyes were bloodshot red as he sniffed sadly. I tried not to cry, but I eventually failed as I wiped my unwelcome tears. After I was seated, the judge looked my way and asked me if I was ready. I shook my head yes.

"Are you sure?" she asked again,

I nodded yes.

She then told the two bailiffs, the one who had been shoving me around earlier and a black female to clear the courtroom and bring in the jurors. She then ordered my kids to leave her courtroom because of their constant sobbing. Within a couple of minutes, the courtroom was empty, leaving only the judge, the state prosecutor, court officials, and John and I. The angle I was sitting in made it clear for me to see Harriet staring at me through the small window of the door everyone had exited. I looked at her in somewhat of a daze. The light glared off Harriet's eye glasses as she continued to look in, I broke her stare by looking off. I dried my eyes; I really didn't want her to run back and tell her family and friends that I was crying.

A few minutes later, the jurors started entering the courtroom. One behind another, I watched the thirty individuals who had my freedom in their hands be seated. For a moment I was seeing double.

Something was wrong with this picture.

I was struck with doubt and uneasiness because there was only one black person and she looked too young to be able to relate to my situation; the rest was all white! These white people don't understand the black generation, and I doubted that they believe in corporal punishment. The white friends I knew ran over their parents. The thought of catching fourteen years in prison made my stomach churn.

Moreover, my attorney's request to have the cameras removed during my trial had been ignored; I saw the cameras of two major news casters set up in the north and south corners of the courtroom. It was evident that the judge was looking to show her tough stern demeanor and use me for an example. I looked toward the exit doors and there it was again, the reflection of light glaring at me through the small window. I looked away. At that moment, there were no words to describe how I felt. Yet, there was one thing I knew for sure and that was that Harriet, without a shadow of doubt, was the most deceitful, sadistic woman I had ever loved.

The State Prosecutor proceeded to elaborate about the discipline I had given my sons. He painted a picture of me being malicious toward my boys, that what I had done was egregious and I was nothing but a violent man. The things he was trying to make me out to be really hurt my feelings and the rules forbidden me from saying anything in my defense. I had to sit and listen to the garbage that the state was telling the jury panel. But finally, it was my attorney's turn to present a rebuttal for what was said.

John began to tell the jurors why the discipline I had given my boys was needed. As he was explaining, without warning, this white woman in her mid-40s burst out into tears, exclaiming that she couldn't handle it, just the thought of spanking a child brought her to tears. John quickly got her removed from the list.

Consequently, the white lady was a fine example of the way mainstream white Americans feels about physical discipline. I believe that's why you hear a lot of door slamming and yelling in their homes; mom is up stairs begging the kid to open the door. The child will yell "I hate you go away!"

The state prosecutor and John selected fourteen jurors, thirteen white and one black out of the thirty candidates.

Here it is, 2014 and it still disturbs me today for what I had to endure.

I was put back in the holding cell for recess. Fifteen minutes later, John came to me saying that he didn't think we would win. The 50 percent chance of victory had dropped to 10 percent when considering that the black female juror said that she was childless and was a victim of child abuse. He said that I could enter a plea to open court and that the judge would make a decision based on that. I shook my head with confusion. I didn't know what to do. One thing I did know is that tall white men with dull red necks and cowboy boots accompanied by old white ladies whom still wore pearls and hair in a bun on top of their heads, are usually not fond of blacks. Hell, I almost fainted when they entered the courtroom.

"Can we pick another jury? Get some black people who can relate to my situation, like someone who has children and know how it is living in the ghetto."

"I'll ask the judge, but I don't think she'll agree being that the panel was properly selected."

John said that I could have a chance if he called my family and friends to speak on my behalf. That might help convince the jury that my intentions were good.

"You think I could win?"

"It's a possibility, but I can't promise you anything."

"What about the psychologist you were talking about?"

"One would be scheduled to see you but that's down the road. I need to tell the judge what we're going to do. Go on or back out!"

John saw my frustration and he gave me time to think about what I want to do. I was placed back on the docket for the following day. That meant I had to stay overnight in that jail. Later that evening, I got a return visit from John. He discussed my dilemma and the chances for a new jury; he concluded that he would let me know back in court.

Back in court, I sat in a crowded holding cell waiting impatiently for my lawyer. Finally, John appeared with a sad face…

"If you can't get me a new jury, I'll get my father to get me a lawyer that will argue the fact that I need a better jury selection because this is not fair! No offense to you. You being court-appointed can only do so much." The holding cell got quiet.

"I'll see what the judge has to say," said John.

"Thank you" I replied dryly, talking as if I got money; knowing damn well my family was broke. John left letting the bailiff know that he would soon come for me. Ten minutes later, the bailiff came, handcuffed me and escorted me to the courtroom.

My name was called and John immediately joined me as I stood before the Honorable Judy Hawkins.

"Your Honor, I've discussed with Mr. Lamar that the offer of eight years was still open and that the state was at the bottom of the guidelines. I told him that he could walk up here and accept eight years in Florida State Prison, he could come in here and enter an open plea to the court, or he could prepare to go forward with the trial tomorrow," John said.

"I, I don't wanna get anybody upset with me," I said. "It's just a hard decision. I don't understand when your kids go out there and rob somebody, or when they go out and steal something, the police wanna shoot them down or try them as an adult. But, when you try to keep them in order and let them know that *hey, you're not gonna be acting like this*, I whip him and I have to go to prison for eight years."

"Uh-hum," the judge grumbled. "Well I understand, but all I care about is that you understand that after this meeting ends, the state will no longer be in a position to offer you eight years and you correct me if I'm wrong Mr. Grey, but if you are found guilty, Mr. Grey is the state prosecutor, he's going to come up here and say, *I want you to sentence this man to 14 years*. Am I wrong or right?"

"No Judge, that's right," said Mr. Grey.

"Then, it'll be up to me," "I will have sat through the trial, so I'll have some sense of what everybody's talking about. I haven't seen the video and I haven't seen any of the other evidence." said the Judge.

"Right," I said.

"Just let me finish please, Mr. Lamar. If you don't accept the state's offer or if you don't enter a plea at this point, there isn't going to be any other option. If you decide in the middle of the trial, for instance, you want to enter a plea, your only option is then to enter an open plea to the court, and then I'll sentence you the way I think, anywhere from, I guess probation, community control or house arrest to 14 years. Do you understand what I'm saying to you?"

I nodded my head, yes.

"I think I'll be better, even though I know you're a tough judge, um, I don't like the way this, this jury, we got different types of children, they got the; the first class and second class, I got the third so, I'm, I don't think they can relate to my type of kids. You see they could tell their kids to go to their room, you tell mine to go to their room you better not have a window. They'll leave. Umm, I think I'd be better off with, with you. Even though I know you're tough something is telling me not to go with this jury."

"Well, you need to make that decision."

"Yes, your Honor."

"All I'm telling you is that... Why don't we do this, do you have a docket?" the judge asked looking toward the prosecutor. "You are not going to be here this afternoon is that right?"

"Right Judge," said Mr. Grey.

"When are you leaving because if he's going to enter a plea, he needs to enter it? If he isn't going to enter it, he doesn't have to enter it, but I need let these jurors know."

My lawyer jumped in suddenly.

"There's - there's one issue," he said. "I just want to put on the record right now that Mr. Lamar raised a question about the jury. He's brought up options that if he brought family in and they were to hire somebody else, that he could get another shot at jury selection. I've advised him that there was nothing improper with the panel in the way that it was brought down here. It's unfortunate for him that there weren't some people from his neighborhood or people of his specific race. There were some black jurors, but we discussed why we did not select those black jurors. One did not believe in punishment. The other one, feeling that she had been a victim of child abuse herself; this is the jury we have, and I cannot do anything else about that, and this court and the state's not going to allow us to pick another panel."

"If you don't want this jury to decide whether or not you're guilty, I don't have any problem with that. All I'm telling you Mr. Lamar, is that it was very clear that you would have until this morning to make up your mind."

"It's your call," John said to me.

"Give him the opportunity!" the prosecutor said.

"Yeah, give me the opportunity to have a fair shot. Mr. Grey, if your son tells you to suck his body parts, you wouldn't appreciate it either. I just want, I just want y'all to look at what I was trying to do, don't look at me as a criminal. I am a good citizen. I'm a truck driver. I deliver to these stores and these restaurants around here, I am not a criminal! I was losing my son's respect. He was playing sex games, he was stealing and he was wearing his pants all down like gang members giving peace signs. I knew I had to do something."

"Sir," the prosecutor said. "Believe me, I understand you probably did this with the best of intentions; but unfortunately, unfortunately you went about it the wrong way, that's all I can say to you."

"Well, this is the deal, you are going to have to make a decision" said the judge.

"Eight years?" I said.

"Or open to the court and at this point I'm prepared to honor the cap for eight years that's it."

"What is a cap?" I asked.

"It's the most time you could get. I could sentence you anywhere from supervision to eight years, at most. Otherwise, you can take the eight years that the state offered."

"Okay. That's if I go to trial, right?"

"No. If you go to trial, you're opening yourself up to anywhere from probation to 14 years because I haven't seen any evidence. And if I think the evidence is really terrible, frankly at the end of a trial, I'm going to sentence you to 14 years because I think it's that bad. But, if I don't think it's as bad as the State thinks, then I'm going to use my judgment and I have to listen to what everybody says, in addition."

"And with a plea open to the court, the courts are willing to honor what the bottom of the guidelines offer by the state at this point," John said. "With a plea open to the court after reviewing all the materials and evidence, you could get anywhere from your supervision possibilities to eight years."

"Right, but that's it, and it's closed after 1:30."

"That's about as clear cut as it can be," John said.

"You can open or you can enter a plea at any time in the middle of trial, but there would be no cap, absolutely no cap."

"I understand, Your Honor" said John

"I'm not going to hear half of the evidence. They may persuade me in a different way to do something else. So, I'll see you back here at 1:30. If you can make it closer to 1:15, it might be helpful."

"Okay," said the prosecutor.

"I want him separate from everybody who's coming in this afternoon, absolutely separate, okay? Thanks a lot."

"See you at 1:15."

The Judge agreed and court was over until after lunch.

The bailiff touched me on my shoulders and nodded his head toward the door leading into the holding cells. John said that he would be with me in a minute as the bailiff shoved me to start walking.

I found myself in an empty cell. Fifteen minutes later, I heard the dangling of the bailiff's keys, followed by John's voice. I rushed to the steel bars to meet him. John and I talked between the bars; only this time he had forms for me to sign. He said that he was confident that I had myself a hanging jury and that I should go with the open plea offer asking mercy to the court.

At 1:15, I re-entered the courtroom.

"Are you all set?" the Judge asked, as she peered over the rim of her glasses at John and I.

"Yes, Your Honor, at this time, Mr. Lamar is going to enter a plea of no contest open to the court on the two counts of Aggravated Child Abuse, one count of Felony in possession of a Firearm and the Misdemeanor Battery, which is attached in the information."

"Let me stop you," the judge said. "I'll take a guilty best interest plea, but I'm not going to take a no contest plea."

"Okay," John replied.

"Not on these facts."

"What's the difference between a guilty plea and a no contest plea?" I asked.

"No difference unless there were civil proceedings and there's not going to be a civil proceeding, so it's not going to have any effect on your sentence or what your record will look like," John whispered.

"What…what… what battery, misdemeanor battery," I asked.

"The domestic violence against Harriet," John said.

"That was dropped!"

"I've gone over this, Your Honor," John said.

I looked up at John, thinking, *what in the hell are you talking about you went over this with me?*

John continued, "I've done… I've done four plea forms in front of him."

"Okay. Is there a Domestic Battery here?"

"Yes, ma'am," the prosecutor said.

"Fine, he can plead no contest to that."

"Okay," John said.

"Alright," the judge said. "I understand what his position is, but not on the other."

"It was dropped, but then it was amended," John answered. "It was combined into the new information with the Felony in possession of a firearm and brought into the courtroom, so at one time, it was dropped."

"Okay he can plead no contest to that. I don't have a problem with that."

"Well Your Honor," I said. "That was dropped because I did not hit her. She hit herself and knocked off her own glasses."

"Okay, you don't have to enter this plea. It's is your call again."

"Mr. Lamar," John said, as his neck and face began to turn red, "I've put four forms in front of you. In fact, the last three that I put in front of you, I went over each one; each one with you within the last two days. They were Aggravated Child Abuse, Felony in possession and Battery."

"Well, I went to court for that in courtroom ten and they said it was dropped."

"It was reinstated. Is that right or not?" the judge asked.

"I'm not... I'm not certain," the prosecutor said, as he flipped through his files. "As far as I know, he's got a domestic that goes with the Felony in possession that stems from the same incident. They may have, in fact, not processed it in Misdemeanor Court because he had this other charge and so they brought it over here. So, technically, it was dropped, but not forgotten, if you will."

"That... that domestic violence also was a lie. She said I had a gun which was not true. That gun was in my closet," I said. "I'm not going to plea, I'm... I'm already taking a plea of child abuse, which is hard for me to do because I was trying to give my son the discipline that was needed, and now you're asking me to plea to..."

"Mr. Lamar..." John whispered.

"Domestic violence?"

"Mr. Lamar, maybe I've been wrong here, but are you capable of reading?"

"Yes sir."

"Okay, have you been able to read any of these plea forms that I submitted to you?"

"I've read all of this here," pointing to the upper section of the plea forms.

"I did not read down there, I'm sorry, sir. I thought it was Aggravated Child Abuse and the Firearm charge. I didn't know Domestic Battery was down below."

"Perhaps we could explain to him that the practical effect of the misdemeanor is two points," the prosecutor said. "I don't know if that will make a difference to him. It basically has little to no effect."

"Well then, maybe the state wants to let it go?" the judge said.

151

"I'll do that. If he'll sign it, I'll do it."

"Okay," John agreed.

"I appreciate it," I said, "Her daughter even admitted that she hit herself."

"Okay, just enter the plea of guilty to the aggravated child abuse and the felon in possession because you feel it is in your best interest to do so," John said. "I need your initials, then my initials."

When I was done signing the forms, John collected them from me.

"Let the record reflect that Mr. Lamar has initialed next to 'I am pleading guilty because I feel it's in my interest to do so,'" he announced to the court. "I've initialed that as well and we're acknowledging that that is the plea he is making before the court."

I raised my hand to speak.

"Put your hand down, please. You are pleading guilty in your best interest to two charges of Aggravated Child Abuse. Each of those is punishable by up to 15 years in Florida State Prison. Do you understand that?"

"Yes, your Honor."

"You're also pleading guilty in your best interest to one charge of being a felon in possession of a firearm, which is also punishable by up to 15 years in Florida State Prison. Do you understand?"

"Yes, your Honor."

"How far did you go in school? Did you graduate from high school?"

"My son was born when I was 15 and I dropped out of school then."

"Your son was born when you were 15?"

"Yes, a week after my 15th birthday."

"Okay. Do you have any questions at all about the rights that you gave up?"

"I have the right not to..."

"You have a question?"

"Yes."

"Go ahead," the judge said.

"I have the right to not... um; to not, um, I can't think of the name of it."

"Incriminate yourself?"

"No appeal."

"I discussed the issue of an appeal," John interrupted. "For most purposes, since there's not going to be a trial, there's not going to be very many issues for us to review on an appeal; however, from the date when the judgment is imposed, we could appeal the judgment and have thirty days. And, at that time, if he feels that there was something improperly handled for his sentencing, I would discuss that with him and discuss with him whether or not he had the right to that appeal. If he felt that he still wanted to file a notice of appeal, I could file the notice of appeal."

"Do you understand what your attorney has just said?" the judge asked.

"Yes," I answered out of false pride, though I was still confused by most of the legal terms. On top of that, I couldn't really think straight because I was feeling overwhelmed with it all.

"Do you have any other questions?" the judge asked.

"No ma'am," I said.

"You understand that you are giving up your rights to have a trial? We're already picked a jury and you're saying now 'I want to enter this plea, I do not want to go forward with a trial.' Is that correct?"

"That's correct!" I strongly replied, as if I knew what I was doing. In actuality, I was feeling as dumb as a box of rocks. The only thing I knew about the law, at that time, was that law meant that the police were coming!

"You know that at trial, the state has the burden of proving your guilt beyond a reasonable doubt?"

"That's correct," I repeated.

"You know that at trial, you don't have to say a word. If you want to testify, you can; if you don't want to testify, nobody can force you to. You understand that?"

"Yes, your honor."

Apparently, no matter how intelligent I tried to make myself sound, my facial expression must've sent off the wrong signal because the judge slowly asked me again, "Do you understand what your attorney has said?"

"Yes," I repeated.

"Has anybody threatened you, pressured you in any way or promised you anything to get you to enter this plea today?"

"No, your Honor."

"Okay. Are you taking any drugs?"

"No, your Honor."

"Alright, establish a factual basis for the record, please."

"Yes Ma'am, as to case number 98-6717, the charge of felon in possession of a firearm, the defendant was found to have in his home a Ruger .357 revolver on a television stand in one of the bedrooms of the home. The testimony at trial would be that this was his gun and he also told the police that when he got out, he was going to shoot her, referring to his wife, Harriet Smith. As to case number 98-9254; the defendant did, at some time, most likely during the month of December, did repeatedly strike two children, Tolerance Lamar and Junior Combs with a belt, causing some welts on their buttocks and legs. He did videotape that entire process. There is no question as to who did it, and he is clearly on the tape doing it. That also occurred in his home here within Hillsborough County. They are both under the age 18 and one is his son, and the other is a stepson for whom he had accepted custodial familial responsibility during that period of time."

"You're prepared to stipulate that the State could establish a prima facie?"

"Yes, your Honor," John said.

"Now, Mr. Lamar, one further matter. You are pleading open to the court. By that, you understand that I've agreed that I would not sentence you to any more than eight years that the state offered you. You could get anywhere from supervision to eight years in Florida State Prison on these charges. Do you understand that?"

"Yes Ma'am."

"Okay, is there anything else anybody wants to put on record at this time?"

"Your Honor, Mr. Lamar had requested that when we get to the sentencing hearing, he would like to have two of his children that were present, um…Lil' Toler, who is the oldest boy, and Tina, who is his daughter, to testify and speak to the court. And because of their age and the fact that we're going to probably have the news cameras in here, he would like to see if we could do that off camera, so the children would not be exposed to that media or be placed on the news for any statements that they had to make in court."

"You're going to subpoena these children?"

"I actually had subpoenaed them for trial, and I'll probably subpoena them again for sentencing" said John.

"Well. I guess that's going to be a subject of discussion. I'm not certain that I want to hear compelled testimony of the victims in this case."

"Well, I think they would come down. I think they would come down on their own accord, too."

"Well, if you can satisfy the court that they would come down on their own accord, then I certainly would listen to what they have to say; but I don't intend to put anyone, let alone a child victim, under compelled testimony on behalf of the defendant in a case."

"There may be positions that were from the act itself; we do have video tape depositions of the children which I think point out the relevant issues of the impact upon them of what occurred during this time that would be relevant for sentencing. I may just allow the court to review those tapes."

"That's fine," the judge said. "And I haven't closed the door to these folks testifying live; I certainly would see them off camera. I don't intend to make a spectacle, especially out of the children's testimony."

"Thank you."

I raised my hand.

"Yes sir, Mr. Lamar."

"Your Honor, it's... it was already hard for me to have made this plea, for which I know my intentions was right and... and my discipline had worked very much because the kids started acting better; Lil' Toler stopped talking nasty and Junior's teacher called and wrote a letter stating that his behavior has been much better. I don't... I mean, it's hard... I mean, I been a bible student for years, your Honor, and it's hard for me to accept the lies that I been continually hearing. Now if everybody wants me to cooperate like I'm supposed to... and I want to... I would appreciate if the lies just stop. I mean the lies of welts and the threatening with gun. I didn't put no welts on my sons."

"The welts," John murmured.

"The welts, okay."

"One of the children having testified as to having welts; the other child testified as to not having welts" said the prosecutor.

"Right, see the children's mother is against me, as you can see. Whatever she tells her child, he's gonna do it because he has done it before."

"It is Harriet's child?" said the prosecutor.

"Right," the judge said.

"The one that's making the statement to the injury," John said.

"Okay, okay. Well, I'm going to review any and all material that you want me to. If you want me to see or review anything, I'd much prefer to get these things in advance, so I'd appreciate it if you put whatever you can together. Furthermore, I'm going to give you a sentencing date. He has a prior record, obviously: A felon in possession charge."

"Right," the prosecutor said.

"Mr. Lamar has discussed with me, and I've advised him that since there is a history of violence that's in his past …"

"That's when I was a teenager," I intervened.

"Late teens, a teenager… it would have some impact on the court that for the majority of his adult life, he's been living as a law abiding citizen." said John.

"Well, I was going to order it anyway, so it's good that we agree. October, um… 19th, it's a Wednesday at 2:00."

"Your Honor, one of the issues that happened yesterday was the allegation of the phone calls to the ex-spouse," John said.

"Right"

"And the orders previously imposed by this court would still review those transcripts and see if that was the order Mr. Lamar was under that said he could not contact a witness in that indirect manner."

"I will do that now, but I wasn't going to jump to the conclusion that a juror would not have acquitted him. So I'm going to do that" said the judge. "Because if there is a sentence that would cause incarceration, Mr.

Lamar is going to be requesting that I request this court for a furlough, or I'm sure he's probably going to have me back here next week, even perhaps with request for bond pending the disposition of this case for sentencing.

Well, I'm going to ask the court reporter once I find out exactly who the court reporter or reporters were, because there are several dates in question to transcribe. I am not going to let you out at this point, Mr. Lamar. I want to review what I said to you and what you said to me. It's actually to your benefit because my recollection now isn't going to help you get out."

"Well, Your Honor, I understand that," I said. "But, before I am sentenced, I'm going to need time to get my personal matters in order. I have a home and a boat. Nobody in my family knows how to drive a truck and boat, so I need to get those in storage. I need to get with my bank about my payments, so Sybil, my fiancée, is able to keep the house note up."

"Okay," the judge said.

"It's something that I need to really to take care of. I just wish you grant me that one day."

"Okay, well, I'm not going to mislead you. I'm not certain what I'm going to do, but what I urge you to do is start thinking about alternative ways that you can make these arrangements."

"Alternative ways?"

"Alternative, that means that if you are held in the county jail until you're sentencing date, you're going to need to figure out some way to work with this woman you're talking about and any family members to get your affairs in order. That's what I'm saying, clear?"

"So, I won't be granted…?"

"Your Honor, I'm sorry, but what time was the sentencing on the nineteenth?" the prosecutor asked.

"Two o'clock," the Judge repeated.

"I'll provide you a packet of the tape and reports," the prosecutor said.

"That's fine," Judge Judy Hawkins said. "Next!"

And, with that, the hearing was over.

CHAPTER 14

AMBIVALENCE

The camera man kept the camera trained on me until the bailiff escorted me away. There was so much pain and disappointment to the point where I didn't know if I was coming or going. When the bar doors slammed behind me, I leaned against the wall, then collapsed head first onto the bench. A sharp ache began forming in my skull as I laid there looking up at the ceiling light. I looked toward the metal toilet. I took the roll of toilet tissue and placed it under my head. And there I lay, waiting for the day of my fate.

What happened to my life, I thought. *What did I do so wrong to deserve this?*

At that point I wondered if John was working with the judge. I got so depressed; I just stared blankly at the wall. Finally, I was transported back to Orient Road County Jail. Unlike the ten foot by eight inch one-man cells for dangerous and crazed men, I was placed in general population which was a huge dorm that had stairs leading to the one-man cells. Being that the jail had been recently built these particular cells were larger and cleaner. Each cell had a real-looking toilet and sink, not cold metal toilets like the older cells. Above the sink, there was a metal mirror that you could clearly see yourself in; below that there was a small metal shelf to hold your toothpaste and brush, along with two studs for hanging your towel and wash rag. Next to the slab of concrete sat a plastic burgundy chair, a wastebasket and a light brown wooden desk. I marveled at the three foot light mounted above it.

"If you don't belong upstairs, I advise you to not be up there," the dorm officer yelled.

I immediately left the vacant cell and returned back downstairs to a two-man cell. My roomy was a crack head, waiting to be sentenced. Living with a filthy, grown stranger in a compact room wasn't easy, especially when he started farting during lockdown. I couldn't wait for the opportunity to get a one-man cell upstairs. Condos, they called those cells, and to get one you had to have good conduct and had to have been in a two-man cell for awhile. The officials called the different sections of the jail *pods*. The pods consisted of holding forty cells; twenty man cells downstairs and twenty condos upstairs.

I was in pod 3-Delta. Each pod was designed to hold about 60 men, but due to the jail being overcrowded, some inmates would be assigned to a plastic mattress on the floor.

As soon as I got in the pod, I got a message from Gayle King, who hosted a talk show out of New York. The officer handed me her 1-800 number and I made the call. I told her the reason I was in jail. Gayle response was that she wanted to help me that I needed to be heard. I agreed to speak on her show; she concluded that she'll be getting back with me. This gave me hope that the judge might get some insight on what I was trying to achieve when I disciplined my sons.

The day after, Montel Williams left me a message, but I never could reach him with the number I was given. Nonetheless, part of me had hope and part of me still felt very bitter and angry knowing that I could actually get prison time for trying to get my son's attention and stop their foolishness. I was angry because the individuals that were seeking to send me to prison knew how destructive the youth of today can be. Teenage crimes are rising at an alarming rate. There are kids killing each other for control on corners. The four letter word we call 'Love' has been bastardized into another four letter word: Cash.

Everyday, our kids are being introduced to drugs and lives are being ruined before their very eyes. Our juveniles are committing crimes, such as murder, assault with deadly weapons, burglary, auto theft, shoplifting and robbery. Many of our teens drop out of school like flies. Their grades start falling and if their parents don't take a stand, the pride in doing well in school completely evaporates. The futures of our young people are being destroyed before they can even start building it and when a parent shows enough love and courage to do something about it, it seems like the parent gets negative backlash.

I sat in my cell and thought about these things every day. I thought about how, back in my days, a tough rebellious child got the tough ass whipping and tough love that was needed. Of course there are lines, causing bruises or breaking of the skin is child abuse and unacceptable. No, I'm talking about a good rearing that the child wouldn't want to get again, and would also provide a good learning opportunity where the child would clean his or her act up to avoid another confrontation.

I couldn't help but think about how I had tried to explain to the prosecutor, that I had to discipline my son in order to get his attention and stop his bad behavior. The Attorney's reply had been that he understood, but that I had gone too far. I just didn't understand it; I didn't even leave a welt on my son, but I had gone so far over the line that it was recommended that I spend eight years in prison. I was crushed. My kids had already lost their mother to crack and the state knew this. Apparently, they don't give a damn. My children were at the age where they really needed guidance.

I thought about the parents out there like myself who love their children and have enough courage to take a stand against their child's bad behavior. From the quiet of my cell, I commended them. I laid there and wished there was a way I could help parents understand the importance maintaining their composure. I was a living example of how if you slip, the law would grip and the grip of the law is cold and unpleasant.

When a prison guard passes my way, I couldn't help but wonder how a police officer had the right to restrain a teen when they felt threatened. They could even hogtie them and it would be justified. But, when the parent restrain their child, its a crime. The local newspaper had proven time and time again that the police had no problem beating or tasering the hell out of our teens. The playing field is so uneven that it's hard not to let it get the best of us.

Despite the anger I felt from my situation, I felt a stirring desire to help others. If I had the chance, I wanted to talk to other parents and remind them that we all have jobs to do with our children. The law, HRS, Department of Children and Families and others organizations have no doubt put a huge dent in the modern family dynamic. However, loving parents shouldn't let the fear of getting arrested force them to stop disciplining their child. I would hope that parents would be smart and give their child an appropriate discipline. I would like for them to continue to train their children, despite our unbalanced judicial system.

Parents with extremely bright children should also understand that when they act out, it may be from boredom. Discipline should not always be the first option. In this case, it would be wiser to encourage the youngster to read and give them games that will stimulate their mind. In other cases, a child who consistently misbehaves should be evaluated by a physician to see if Attention Deficit Disorder (ADD) or Attention Deficit Hyperactive Disorder (ADHD) may be the cause. Parents shouldn't shrug off their child's misbehavior as simply a matter of kids being kids.

Consequently, if I would have been aware of my child's association, and applied all of what I've mentioned, I probably wouldn't have gone through this painful ordeal. I also came to realize that the old saying, *Think before you speak* had a lot more truth in it than I ever realized.

When I asked my son, "What's wrong with your nipples boy?" in front of his giggling sisters, perhaps I embarrassed him. My son was in his late teens and was probably going through adolescence stages. So, should I have been surprised by his disrespectful reply? I'm certain now, that I should have called my son to the side and asked him about his swollen nipples like a concerned father should. If I had done that, I probably wouldn't be in the predicament that I found myself in.

My thoughts were interrupted by the small speaker mounted in the light fixture of my two-man cell. I climbed down from my top bunk and headed for the officer station like the speaker commanded. I was told that I would be moving upstairs in a one-man cell and I did so happily.

A day or so later, one of the officers, Officer Ponds, had a message informing me that the Channel 13 newscaster would like to interview me.

"When," I asked.

"Today at 5:00 pm."

I asked him what time was it. Looking at his watch, 2:15 he said. I agreed to do the interview. The officer then said that he'd let them know and left.

At 4:50, Officer Ponds returned and walked me down to the Captain's room where the interview was to be held. I entered the small room and was greeted by Jennifer Jones, a black female reporter, along with a cameraman. I must admit, it was good to see a reporter of color. This gave me hope that she'd be able to relate to my dilemma that led me to perform this harsh, but much-needed discipline on my son. I took my seat and she handed me a microphone and asked me to clip it onto my shirt. She informed that the interview would be replayed on the 6:00 o'clock evening news.

Jennifer Jones proceeded with the interview.

"Mr. Lamar, your wife turned in a videotape of you chastising your two boys and you were charge with two counts of aggravated child abuse on your biological son and stepson, and you are now waiting for sentencing. Is that correct?"

"Yes."

"We understand that your boys were getting out of hand, and you felt you needed to step in, but why did you record it?"

"Well, ma'am, it wasn't like I had the camcorder for that specific reason. The camcorder was already set up to make a family tape of karaoke with my kids. And when I got on my son and stepson, I felt that the verbal discipline would be beneficial for my son to look at when he got older and had kids. I felt that a lesson could be taught."

"I'm afraid..."

"So the media just showed me spanking them?"

Jennifer nodded yes.

I suddenly felt the slow burn of anger building in my chest.

The video had only been partially shown for the sole purpose of making me look bad. I inhaled and tried to digest it.

162

"Why did you tie them up, Mr. Lamar?"

"You can clearly see on the tape that the discipline was mainly for my 16-year-old. My stepson was no threat, but my 16-year-old was. His cockiness and how he kicked and blocked the licks and then the way he would taunt was the reason I had restrained him. I felt that it was necessary."

"I see. The video also shows that your wife wet the belt to cause more pain."

"No. The reason she wet the belt was to scare him. I wanted to scare him; I wanted his eyes get as big as Kennedy fifty cents. I wanted fear in this discipline. Dealing with my hard-headed son, fear was needed. I knew what I was doing; I didn't even put a welt on them."

"Mr. Lamar, how would you feel and what would you have to say to society if you get prison time?"

"Well, I would be very hurt and angry because of the judge's decision, knowing that the majority of our black kids, who are living in the ghetto, are rebellious due to a lack of discipline by their parents. What I would say to society is 'parents don't let your teenage children intimidate you to the point that you end up going through what I'm going through.'"

Jennifer smiled, as if she understood why I performed the discipline. She looked at me in a way that I thought said that she would help me if she could. She asked if I had anything else to say. I told her that I had something to say to my wife. I looked into the camera and said: "Harriet, you're wrong, but that's okay because God don't like ugly."

The interview was over. Jennifer wished me good luck and I was escorted back to my housing dorm. I felt optimistic and hoped that the judge would finally understand my motives and not send me to prison. In the meantime, I went about minding my own business, keeping out of trouble and pondering what would become of my life. Sometimes, I told myself that it wasn't as bad as it seemed. A few times, I went downstairs and sat among other restless souls, but I quickly grew tired of listening to the inmates always yapping about drugs, women and violence, so I eventually just stayed in my condo. There, I would draw colorful pictures of the way I felt on envelopes, then write a letter and mail them to Sybil.

One evening, my conscience led me to write Sybil's mom, asking for forgiveness for the way I had treated her daughter and that I would never treat her that way again.

Sybil's love proved to be unconditional. During my wait, she visited me almost every day. Her love and loyalty was unbelievable. I must have been out of my mind to trade her for a promiscuous, wicked woman like Harriet. The more I realized the pain I had caused Sybil, the worse I felt.

Again, I was approached by another news broadcaster whom wanted to interview me. This time, it was Channel 28. Officer Ponds let me know that if it had been him, his boy would've been picking his teeth up off the floor. A female officer who had learned that my son had struck his mother told me that if it had it been her child, he would have got the shit shot out of him. And yet another officer said that if his son would have invited him to suck his body parts, that he would have made him wish he was dead.

Such response from these officers made me feel like my discipline had been mild. This made me feel better. I agreed to do the interview and I requested a haircut. Although haircuts were only given on Thursdays, I was an exception. I was given an inmate barber of my choice, which made me feel a little important. The inmates in my dorm wanted to know why I was getting special treatment. When I told them, they start calling me *The Celebrity*. I was again escorted to the Captain's room and I was greeted by the reporter of Channel 28 News, this time a white male.

The set up was similar to my prior interview. I was seated and given a microphone. The reporter did his introduction and then the questioning began.

"Mr. Lamar, you are facing time in prison for beating your two sons with a leather strap soaked in water. Do you have anything to say?"

"Yes, I want to clarify that I did not hurt my boys. It was only a scare tactic to get my older son's attention. And the belt was not soaked."

"Isn't it true that the boys were tied up, forced to get on the floor and were beaten on their naked bodies?"

"No, that is not true. I only hit their buttocks. You have a copy of the tape, don't you?"

"No, not at this present time."

"For one thing, I didn't hurt my boys in any fashion or form, and yes; I restrained the boys only because of my oldest son. I gave my 8-year-old stepson a little knot to make the discipline look fair and to not show sides, but he was not a threat. I exposed their bare butts to embarrass Lil' Toler."

"Your son?"

"Yes… because he wanted to be so cool. I wanted the girls to laugh at him."

"The girls?"

"Yes, his sister and stepsister. I also exposed the butt so that he would feel the licks. I wanted my discipline to count for something and earn respect!"

"Mr. Lamar, you stated, on the day of your arrest that you were only trying to turn your son's behavior pattern around. Isn't love more effective than tying a child up and beating him with a wet belt? If, Mr. Lamar, you had another chance at correcting your child, would it be different this time?"

"Love is very much needed and I have shown that. I love my children, the type of son I have, you have to display more than just love; you'd have to show him that you mean business or he'll run all over you. But, now, knowing how the laws have changed and what to expect, yes, I would do it another way, and that's by calling HRS and telling them to come get him and raise him."

I don't remember if I asked the reporter if he thought I deserved to go to prison or if he volunteered his opinion because he concluded the interview by saying that he didn't think I deserved prison, just probation and some sort of parenting classes. We shook hands and I was escorted back to my dorm.

The inmates stared at me as I entered the dorm. Some smiled and teased me by saying, "There goes the Celebrity!" I managed a smile.

Someone asked how it went. I told him that it went okay, but deep down inside, I was disturbed by that interview. Something about that reporter wasn't right.

The following day when talking over the phone with my mother, she informed me how Channel 28 was talking bad about me and how they played the video of me disciplining my boys in slow motion, making it look way worse than it really was.

"They are not on your side," my mother said.

She went on to say the opposite about Channel 13 and that they had managed to stay neutral through it all. Nevertheless, I wasn't surprised about what Channel 28 had done, I just felt down, knowing that some people were looking at me like I was a horrible father. The more I thought about it, the more depressed I got. I felt that if I got out, I wouldn't be able to sit in my front yard and not get shot at by someone who felt that I needed to be killed because I was labeled a child beater.

If heartache was an instant killer, I would have already been dead. I had to keep telling myself that I was a good person. The following day, John came to inform me the status on my case, and he made it clear that I was not to accept any more interviews until after sentencing. He concluded that I could hurt my case by doing so. Later that evening I spoke with Sybil over the phone, she said that listening to the Channel 28 News had spoiled her day, not mention how all the bills were piling up. Unfortunately, her job at the nursing home wasn't cutting it. Furthermore, Sybil told me that my 14-year-old daughter Tina, was out of control. She had threatened her former foster parent's husband by saying, "If you hit me, you know where you going!"

My insides flamed with resentment and anger, knowing that the judge had sent the wrong message to our children. I fear that the law would create another epidemic in our society, a conundrum, in fact. The current laws and societal views have taken the necessary discipline out of the homes, leaving a responsible family structure stuck in a twisted battle for control over their offspring. Many of our growing children would slip through the cracks because of the laws that are restricting parents from giving a good whack.

I turned to the Bible during my stay in jail and the Holy Scriptures helped me realize that I wasn't a bad person because even God approved of the rod. But still, the thought of me going to prison and Tina headed down the wrong path depressed me even more.

I was overwhelmed with mixed conflicting thoughts and I had to do something. So the following morning I called Sybil and ask her to call two-way to New York and ask for Gayle King. So she did and I was able to speak with Gayle. Coincidentally, Gayle had me on schedule that week to do her show by satellite. Despite what John had said, I was run to do the show in hope that the judge would understand my purpose and not send me to prison. Furthermore, I needed money! I needed money to help Sybil with my bills, so I asked Gayle if I would be able to receive money to do her show. After the long distance call, I felt a little better. Although the money I was to receive wasn't very much at all, but it was better than nothing. The real help would be me being on her show explaining my case.

On October 10, 1998, around noon, Officer Ponds informed that Gayle King wanted to interview me.

"When," I asked.

"In one hour," he said.

I was then given a fresh haircut and escorted to the captain's room. Gayle King had suggested that I prepare to be seen nationwide by millions of viewers. I asked God to help me speak the right words and not freeze up with nervousness. I took a deep breath before I entered the small room. The room was clustered with equipment that was far more sophisticated than the local media's had been. Cameras, monitors and phones sat in its position as I was greeted by three people who pointed to where I needed to sit. When I was seated, they got back to checking on their equipment. A big camera was then turned in my direction and my face appeared on a large monitor. I was given a clip-on microphone and a pair of ear plugs so I could hear Gayle.

One cameraman told the other to phone Gayle.

"We're ready," one of them said into his hand receiver. Minutes later, I heard my earplugs make a cracking sound.

"Tolerance Lamar?"

"Yes," I replied.

"This is Gayle King. Do you hear me loud and clear?"

"Yes," I repeated.

"Good, how do you feel?"

"I'm ok!"

"That's good. The show is about to start in 60 seconds. Are you ready?"

"Yes," I muttered.

One of the cameramen pointed to a timer on the screen. A number ten appeared, and then started counting down to zero.

As I sat before the cameras, I felt a sense of importance. I almost felt like a celebrity. But the distinguished feeling quickly disappeared when Gayle King informed her audience:

"Our story today is about a man out of Tampa, Florida who is now incarcerated for two counts of Aggravated Child Abuse. The authorities received a videotape of Mr. Lamar beating his son and stepson with a wet leather strap while both boys' hands and feet were tied with rope. We have Mr. Tolerance Lamar on air by satellite to see what he has to say."

"Mr. Lamar?"

"Yes."

"I have seen the tape of the whipping you gave the two boys. What did they do to get such a whipping?"

"Well, it was mainly for my 16-year-old son. He had started getting very disrespectful towards his parents. He started stealing from me and acting like a real thug around my wife and daughters. He hit his mother in the head with a broom stick and threatened to pour hot grease on her. And when he invited me to suck his body parts, I knew I had to put my foot down and stop his behavior."

"Yes, your son's behavior was no doubt bad. But, tying his hands and feet was awful! Why didn't you just take their privileges from them, and send them to their room?"

"My kids didn't come from the Little House on the Prairie. If you sent my kid to his room, he would have gotten out of the window."

"Doctor, you have seen the tape as well. Now, Mr. Lamar explains his discipline as if he did what any other father would do. Is this rational or what?"

"What looks like a duck quacks like a duck!"

My ear plugs exploded with laughter by the audience.

The Doctor went on to say, that, to punish a child, take the electricity. Gayle looked dumfounded. Take the electricity Gayle repeated.

"Yes, such as video games and television…

He will get what he deserves," she concluded.

I felt an enormous wave of heat and I was about to tell the doctor that if she had those two boys over for the weekend, she would be singing a different song, but I remained silent.

"Okay, Mr. Lamar, we thank you."

I could tell that I had been switched to another airwave and she informed that she would mail a copy of the show like we agreed and good luck. The ear plugs went dead.

I felt numb at that moment. I realized that she didn't give me a good minute to explain myself. If I recalled correctly, she said she wanted to help me. The cameraman told me thanks for my cooperation and he held his hand out for me to hand over the mic and earplug. I was in a daze as I sat staring at the fuzzy screen. I didn't respond until I felt a hand tugging at my shirt to unclip the mic. I handed him his earplug and headed toward the officer who was waiting to escort me back to my dorm. As I was being escorted, I tried to ignore the pain and emotional turmoil that was churning inside of me. The fact that some people didn't believe in physical discipline might result in me losing my freedom. I would be looked down upon. The world seemed so unfair. I entered my dorm and forced a smile telling the inmates that the show went fine. As I headed for my cell, Officer Ponds suggested that I write a book.

"Yeah," I murmured, as I climbed the stairs and shut my cell door.

I lay there, staring at the ceiling, wishing that this was all a bad dream. I felt so exhausted like someone was pumping the life out of me. I was drowning in a pool of negative feelings. I felt like dying.

My days were beginning to drag and I found myself at my lowest point in life. Less than a week before my sentencing, a psychologist was set up to see me. I was told to be seated and the psychologist proceeded to ask me about my past, like how my life was growing up and what type of discipline my parents administered to me and my sisters. As I talked about my past, a different set of feelings emerged and I thought about how my mother treated my sisters and I. Tears began to fall and I started sobbing. After I got myself together, I went on to talk about the abuse my mother endured at the hands of my father and how my sister and I were taught to fail. The doctor continued to question me and with some of the things he asked, I wanted to make up a lie. But my Grandma Alma's voice kept coming to mind, saying *God hates liars* and *the truth will set you free.* The doctor listened intently as I poured out my life. I even demonstrated how my discipline was administered and I tried my best to explain that my discipline had good intentions. When the evaluation was over, he told me that his recommendation would go to the court for sentencing and that he was recommending probation and family counseling. He then told me that this was not always granted, but there was a good chance that the judge would honor his recommendation. That was the first time in a while that I got a good night's sleep.

CHAPTER 15

THE LORD IS MY SHEPHERD, I SHALL NOT WANT

October 29, 1998 was the day of my sentence. It was not looking good, as I was going before a female Judge who by all intents and purposes, didn't like men. She had even been dubbed as Judge *Hang 'em High* Hawkins by many of the inmates. I was scared for my life. John, my lawyer, didn't help, stating that from his experiences working in Judge Hawkins's courtroom, she'd probably give me what the state suggested, which was eight years, because I was taking an open plea and not going to trial. If I went before the court and apologized and showed remorse, she might let me off with house arrest, which is what John said he was going to request. However, the look on John's face was not convincing.

Words of my ex-mother-in-law, Ms. Bennett, came to mind.

"The Lord is my shepherd, I shall not want," she quoted, encouraging me to say this just before I enter the courtroom.

The Lord is my shepherd, I shall not want.

The bailiff, John and I entered the courtroom. With my feet and hands shackled, I short stepped my way to the bench where all the jailers were to be seated. I scanned the audience. My family members were sitting across from Harriet, who was chewing gum nonchalantly, as if she hadn't notice my presence. Junior was snuggled up under Harriet's arm like he was a little, bitty baby.

I also noticed my own kids weren't present.

The court room was now full of the good, the bad, the ugly, and the damn phony. Man! The Young and the Restless didn't have anything on this crap!

Finally, my name was called to approach the bench. My family came up and stood behind me.

"I have two letters written on behalf of Mr. Lamar," Judge Hawkins said. "Have you had an opportunity to review this PSI with Mr. Lamar?"

"Yes, your Honor, I have a few corrections that we'd like to make on the record," John said.

"Sure."

"Page number one shows three charges. That battery was not passed by the State Attorney's office in the introduction of Mr. Lamar's plea. And page three, in the defendant's statement, the final line says, 'This all came about because the defense's son took a stick and hit his mom in the head.' I think when you're refuting that statement, you're almost going to get the impression that this was the precipitating event, that this happened and therefore, the punishment happened. That happened some time before and we want to make that clear to the court that this was an additional misbehavior of the child that lead to it, but was not something that happened instantaneously within the events. And I'd also like to get down to page nine, the recommended disposition."

"Yes," Judge Hawkins said.

I glanced over my shoulders at my kids' mother, who looked like she was under malnutrition. Sybil stood in front of her with a rueful stare.

"I think that this is something I'll cover as we go through this sentencing hearing," John said. "There is a classification by this evaluator that my client has shown no remorse. Discussing this case throughout, as he perceived the events at the time it happened, he thought he was doing the proper acts. In hindsight, there's a remorseful position right now, and he's always taken the position that when it happened, he did not feel like he was doing something from a malicious intent. I just want to focus on those issues that have been listed in that PSI at this point, but otherwise, we're ready to go forward with sentencing. There's something the defense would like to bring forward. Mr. Lamar would like to address the court, and family members would like to address the court, and when I may proceed, I will."

"Proceed right now."

"Your Honor," John said, "first of all, we did have a Psychological Evaluation by Dr. Gamache in this case and he talks about a realm of possible sentences. He does not direct the court into one possible sentence or the other, such as incarceration or rehabilitation, but he makes the issue of rehabilitation as a viable resource. Mr. Lamar wanted this court to see all the materials, everything that a jury would have seen to make the determination of the severity of the offense and the appropriate punishment or rehabilitation. The defense's position is that the Court should use rehabilitation, or a form of supervision, as compared to incarceration. Incarceration does one thing; it takes Mr. Lamar out of the environment, away from the family and away from his kids, which causes no intervention with the family and with those children for Mr. Lamar. Supervision, on the other hand, as followed with Dr. Gamache evaluation, would provide Mr. Lamar with access to a Family Violence Intervention program, Domestic Violence Psychological Counseling and Family Parenting counseling. With these facts and circumstances, it is clear that Mr. Lamar is not only rehabilitated, but his family and his children are rehabilitated. We're talking about a type of offense that is cyclical, from generation to generation, and by simply removing one individual, we have cured nothing. But, if this court uses the power of supervision, we can, hopefully, provide treatment and remedy not only to Mr. Lamar, but to the entire family under a structured setting. Mr. Lamar clearly would like that reunification with his children. I think also that when we look at Dr. Gamache's evaluation, he, even on page six for the impressions or recommendations, phrases that certainly one can empathize with Mr. Lamar's parental dilemma to the extent that his statements are truthful. Well, this court has received and will hear from individuals in the courtroom that this is not fiction by Mr. Lamar of the oldest son's misbehavior. We have, and it's been provided to the court, and the state has received the copies too under their own subpoena, the history of Lil' Toler's incident reports and student referrals of his misbehavior over the last two years in school, and this is on a monthly basis. I've also got twenty two incident reports. It's not fiction of Mr. Lamar's perception of the misbehavior of his child. The hitting in the head with a stick to the biological mother is not fiction. The biological mother is here and she'll inform the court the behavior that this boy demonstrates. I don't want to put him on trial because that's not the focus, but it does give reason and it does give support and it does tie in with Dr. Gamache's impression and evaluation that if these statements are true, then one can certainly see why Mr. Lamar was behaving in this manner, not that it was appropriate. Dr. Gamache doesn't say it's appropriate, and nobody in this courtroom is saying it's appropriate, but with appropriate supervision, this person could be trained to deal with this in a more appropriate basis. Those children can also be trained to deal with it in a more appropriate basis. We've got this tape labeled *Family Sessions*. At the time it was made, I think it's an egregious thing, first of all, and why that the tape was even made."

I looked up at my lawyer, jolted by how he had just flipped the script by stating that what I had done was outstandingly bad and that he didn't know why I made the tape!

"In the psychological evaluation," John continued, "we see his mother's own version of why the tape was made for the history of the case. This was a novelty to Mr. Lamar. The camera was new to him. I mean, I think he would have filmed anything. I think he would have filmed paint drying. The camera was for almost every event, and it had been previously on for the video taping of a karaoke session. It had been set up, not for the purpose that this is going to be part of the psychological tool with the children. It's unfortunate that it was videotaped because it has caused such disturbance for these children. Mr. Lamar will inform the court that he does have remorse for what happened. He thought he was acting appropriately at that time. But, if he could have seen where this would have gone and the exposure it caused his children, he wouldn't be standing here today. He's not proud of this at all. That tape is an isolated incident of a moment in that day. We also know through the depositions, the videotaped depositions of the children interviews in the case, that that wasn't the entire day. When that ended, Mr. Lamar went fishing on his boat with the children the rest of the day, there was no more punishment. It was two controlled sessions of the punishment; it wasn't a continuation throughout the day.

Going back to the term, *Family Sessions*, I think that does have some appropriate titling because it is an educational demonstrative tool for this individual to have and hold for the rest of his life for what he actually did as he goes through any type of court-ordered supervision. I think the demonstrative purpose of that tape has a reverse benefit of instead of being for the children, it's for Mr. Lamar.

I know the courts are going to be concerned by some, or at least I was concerned yesterday, when I received some fax coverage of the current supervision in California. I think in order to interpret what that probation is we have to know the history of what lead to probation. The history is this: It's a relationship where Mr. Lamar has been married to Harriet Smith two times. The first time here in Tampa, the relationship went awry and he'll explain what happen in the relationship. She left him. She took his belongings and his vehicle and left for Georgia. The children were left stranded at a day care. She was gone. She eventually came back remorseful and apologetic. She came back to the relationship and then again, a few short months later, disengaged and went off to California.

Again, when she decided that the relationship should be back on, again, like a light switch, she contacted Mr. Lamar. In love and joyousness about this call, he traveled almost immediately to California to reunify with the family. And again, Ms Smith, like a light switch, determined when the light should be on or should not be on. She was not pleased with Mr. Lamar and she got a temporary restraining order. He does the heinous act of taking flowers and sticking them in her mailbox. He was leaving and she actually came out, I believe, and said that you *were under arrest* and the police came."

"It was a citizen's arrest!" I said aloud.

"Mr. Lamar, be quiet, please," the judge said.

175

"He was given some community service work and three years of unsupervised probation. He was to make no contact for three years. That was the extent of it. He wasn't given a probation officer or a location to report to like we normally do here, under terms of probation; it was unsupervised court probation. He was out of the house with no means of family support; he was living out of his work truck and living on the streets in the climate of San Francisco. He was cold and eventually he left California to come back to his home in Tampa and, again began working and reunifying with his immediate family. The next thing that happened was Harriet Smith flipped her switch again and decided that it was time to have the relationship again. Clearly, by the next act, we can see that he did not violate any court order because she was the one who travelled three thousand miles across country to reunify with him. I don't know what powers he could have had if he was consciously, willfully violating any type of supervision to draw somebody three thousand miles across country. So, I think it's important to understand what happened there in that case. Immediately, when it came across, it was very shocking, yet after having a conversation last night in the jail with my client, the factors in it aren't as shocking. So your Honor, at this time, I'd like Mr. Lamar to address the court."

I stood and cleared my throat; feeling like this was my last shot at proving that I wasn't some horrible monster.

"Your Honor, I guess by me being on the road a lot… I'm a truck driver… I was just ignorant when it came down to the law about discipline. I had custody of my kids. We were doing fine and I married *her*. Things were going good until she started tipping out with her first husband, which is what started our problems. Well, anyway, I was in love, but we ended up getting a divorce. She called me again to get back together, and I saw the same scenario in my second marriage. That's when I told her I want out of the marriage. At that point, that's when I pushed her away from me."

I remember having to take a deep breath as a slow burn was welling up inside me. I got control of my emotions before continuing.

"People don't want to listen," I said. "They only listened to the lies that this woman had been saying. I told Harriet that I wanted out of the marriage and that's when this child abuse came about. I never, ever hurt my child, none of my children. I only did my best. I never even put a welt on my son. I saw my son acting like a thug. I wasn't used to him acting like that. He had already hit his mother upside the head. He had given her hard times. He has a nasty little mouth. His teacher called yesterday stating that somebody better come get him before she ended up on TV with child abuse charges. I saw my son getting very nasty with his mouth, very disrespectful. He started challenging me, he started wearing his clothes below his buttocks like thugs do, doing the gang signs, and he started smoking and stealing. I knew that I needed to do something. I kept putting it off. This woman here, every time I got home from work, she would complain, Toler this Toler that.

I didn't want to get off from work and have to chastise him, so I kept putting it off. The night he invited me to suck his body parts, I was already on the edge with him. He started saying that he'd be able to knock me out within a year. I heard that cocky voice, and saw that his hands were bigger than mine and his feet were bigger than mine, so finally I disciplined him. I restrained my son because I knew he would be kicking and blocking, I pulled the pants down to show the buttocks because I wanted to embarrass him okay, and before all that happened, this woman stepped in, my so-called wife and said to me... and I quote..., *Don't forget about Junior.*

That discipline wasn't for Junior, that discipline was for my son. My son was a threat, not Junior. But, she wanted him in there, so I added him. I gave his rope a little knot. I didn't have to restrain Junior, but I just did it because of his mom's request and to be fair. My daughter, Tina, was there, she was very outspoken and I didn't want her to say I was taking sides. My wife asked me to not forget about Junior because he was acting up badly in school, so I proceeded with the restraining and I pulled their pants to their buttocks for show. I wanted the girls to laugh at Toler since he wanted to be so cool and cocky. The water bit with the belt, was just a scare tactic. I felt at that time fear was needed in this discipline. My son took everything as a joke. I apologize for doing it the wrong way, but I felt at that time that I needed to give my son some good discipline. Before I started, before I even raised my hand with the belt, I verbally disciplined him. I said, 'Why are you doing this? If I didn't love you I wouldn't care. I can't tolerate you acting like this in my household,' all this is on the tape.

I just couldn't allow him to keep on. He had also struck his cousin in the jaw. He even started talking about having sex with his stepsister, Amy. I knew I had to quickly handle that matter before it got touchy. I felt like I had to step in. I apologize to my boys if I did it wrong. I'm a father, not a criminal. I just want the courts to realize that my kids didn't come from the Little House on the Prairie. I mean, my kids came from the ghetto. With my type of children, you have to give them a good discipline because they won't take it seriously, especially my boy. I know him. I know what was needed for him. I apologize if I did it the wrong way. It will never happen again, even though it did change his behavior pattern. During the same month, Harriet and I start getting calls from his teachers thanking us for getting involved because his behavior was better. Junior's teacher also called and wrote letters thanking us for stopping Junior's spitting, kicking and talking back. I just tried to do what I felt as a father, Your Honor. A lot of people said that if that would've been them that he invited to suck his private part, they would've knocked him out. The camcorder... the camcorder was already in the family room from the night before when we were doing karaoke. The firearm... the best of my knowledge was, once you turn an adult, your teenage record is gone. I didn't know that I couldn't ever have a gun around me. That gun was given to me. A certain person wanted me to keep the gun because her son was seventeen and was into smoking reefer, and she didn't want him to get a hold of that gun. I kept the gun in my closet and it was in a holster. I never ever threatened nobody with it. I don't know how that popped up. I'm hearing something about how I made a threat with the gun and that's a bunch of lies. I'm not a threat to society, your Honor. My kids need me, they already lost their mother. I took her to Acts, I took her to Dacco to try to get her off the drugs and she keeps going back. At the time I got arrested, the following Thursday, I was getting a loan from the bank for twenty thousand dollars to have rooms added for my children. I'm asking you please let me gain my fatherly image back, and it won't happen again. My kids, I mean, this has been blown out of proportion, your Honor. I'm not a bad person. I just felt that I was losing my son because like this ad here says."

I raised my chain-cuffed hands to holdup a newspaper article.

"This article clearly states that crimes are being committed mostly by teenagers. It states right here and you know as soon as he goes out there and robs and steals from somebody, he is going to jail and bound over as an adult. Then, whose fault will it be? It won't be mine... I tried, I just done it the wrong way and again, I apologize; I'm a father and I have always been one. I tried."

"Thank you, Mr. Lamar, is there anything else?" John asked.

"No."

"There's also Mr. Lamar's fiancée, Sybil Gordon is it?"

"Yes," Sybil said as she approached the bench.

"Okay, will you please state your name for the record?"

"Sybil Gordon."

"Miss Gordon, could you please convey to the court anything you wish to share on Mr. Lamar's behalf at sentencing."

"Yes. Good afternoon, your Honor, I'm Mr. Lamar's fiancée. I'd like to make a statement in court to say that Mr. Lamar's is a good person. He's a good man and he loves his kids. Everyone makes mistakes and it was a mistake that he made. He was worried and he gave discipline to his kids. And I would like the court and you, Your Honor, to just give Mr. Lamar a chance to try to get his fatherhood back and get him into some type of program. I believe he just needs some type of class to make a change in his life, and try to better it. For my sake, can you let the court know also to release him because right now I'm working, but I need the help from him. Also if there's any possibility, can the court do that on my behalf."

"Your Honor, also in the court is the biological mother of the oldest boy, Lil' Toler. Will you please state your full name?"

"My name is Roxann Stone."

I noticed that the judge sneered at the sight of her and I immediately realized that the judge was against me and everything I stood for. Roxann's frail body made me feel shameful for her, and I could only shake my head as she looked into the judge's cold eyes.

"One of the issues I brought up is Mr. Lamar's discussion of the poor behavior of Lil Toler," John then looked down toward Roxann. "Did you perceive or witness any of this?"

"Yes," she said. "My son he hit me in the head with a stick and he was fixing to throw some hot grease on me. And Lil' Toler is a very disrespectful boy and he will make you mad enough to knock him out – that's how bad he is. And Tolerance, he's a good father. I have four kids and I was with him for 13 years and he never abused any of my kids."

"You don't have custody of these children, do you?" the judge asked.

"No ma'am, I used to have custody."

"But you don't have them because you were an addict?"

"Not then, I wasn't. It was just that someone went around lying, saying that I left them in the house by themselves, even though at that time, I wasn't doing drugs."

"Okay," said the judge.

"Your Honor, also present before the court is Mr. Lamar's sister."

"Ma'am, would you please state your full name."

"Keitha Lamar."

"You told me that you'd like to address the court. Is there anything you'd like to share?"

"Yeah, my brother never did nothing to hurt his kids and he has never made no threat to her."

The Judge grimaced and I began to feel despair.

"I stayed with them when she came and when she left and there were no problems. My brother is a very good man. I would like to see him get released."

"You were in California with your brother and his..."

"No. When she came down here, I stayed with him."

"She was there that night," I added.

"When she came in town, I was there with my brother until she left," said Keitha.

"I see, Thank you," the judge said.

"There was no problems and no threats, it was just a happy family," Keitha concluded.

"Also present in court is Mr. Lamar's parents, Mr. Lamar Sr.," John said.

"Sir, is there anything you'd like to share?"

"Good morning, your Honor."

"Sir, if you could just state your full name."

"Tolerance Lamar Sr."

"Thank you."

"All I would like to say for my son is that he just about said everything, but your Honor, what I would like to say is I know my son pretty good and he really had no intention of just hurting his children, nor doing them harm. He actually didn't know any other way to get this boy to respect him and respect his mother. So Your Honor, what I would like to say is that I'm very confident, if he could just get some kind of parenting class or maybe just have some way to guide him in the right way of discipline, I'm confident that he'll never do this again. I know it was just a mistake. He thought he was doing something the child needed."

"Actually your Honor," I said. "I mean, once I got a report from his teacher, I actually felt that I had done a good job. I really did. I mean, his behavior pattern changed to where I really felt I had done a good job, but I apologize again and I see that I have done wrong because I have suffered."

I could feel tears welling in my eyes.

"I've suffered," I repeated.

"I'd like to give everybody an opportunity to address the court, is there something you'd like to share, ma'am?" John asked.

"My name is Viola Fumes, Tolerance's stepmother. Tolerance has always been a very nice person, but he has had problems in his marriage. When he first married Harriet, she left him alone, took everything out of the house. He tried to go back to her, the last time when she left him, she left him nothing. She took all his personal belongings, his new car; she even took his fishing rods. She left his kids all alone in school and he didn't know what had happened. He didn't know HRS had got them. She did him that way!"

"I had her arrested in Georgia and she had taken everything to her first husband!" I added, angrily.

"Ma'am, is there anything you'd like to share?" John asked, moving on.

"Yes. My name is Barbara Lamar and I'm Tolerance's mother. I feel like he was just chastising his son. If he doesn't stop him now, his son is headed for a lot of trouble because you cannot talk to him. He talks so much trash to you and he doesn't pay attention to anything you say. So what he did was a little drastic, but I bet he'll pay attention to him now."

The Judge grimaced as if my mother was a fool.

"Thank you, your Honor. Before the State speaks, I would like to focus on some of the things that clearly have been lies by Harriet Smith. First of all, when she was in the spring facility, she made allegations that she wanted out of this because this man was doing sexual acts with those children and that he was videotaping the sexual acts. That was the initial report. The investigation began on that belief. When they got the tape and saw what happened and conducted the interviews and found out that wasn't true, they questioned Ms Smith. She recanted and actually denied that she ever made such a statement, that the law enforcement had conjured that up or made this heinous accusation by mistake. Clearly, the relationship seems to be in power of Harriet Smith, when it's on and when it's off. She's the one that can come back from Georgia, she's the one that can come from California, she's the one that can get on the phone and tell him to drive to California. This has been a relationship where she's engaged every encounter in this relationship. Harriet Smith, as she claims from the PSI, when she's been asked or when these matters have been discussed with her, she feels that she has no responsibility. She's got her own son down there on the floor, too. Now, she'll sit in court today with her arm around the boy and looking like a proper parent, and it is just inconsistent. The fact that you'll also allow your son to be restrained on the floor with a belt and have the whipping going on and participating with the dipping the belt in the water… those two acts are inconsistent, and I think it speaks to the credibility of what Mr. Lamar is stating of the history he's gone through with her. I don't hold Mr. Lamar on two pedestals for his act, but I also don't hold Ms Smith on a pedestal for her acts either, Your Honor. I think both of these people have responsibility here and unfortunately, because the state has dropped all charges against Ms Smith, the only person who can be court authorized for this supervision is Mr. Lamar.

There's one statement in the PSI by the person that now has custody of these children, Dell Tolbert, who stated that Lil' Toler is always a nice boy at home, that she doesn't have any problems with him. It's completely inconsistent. She told an attorney that Lil' Toler is a problem child and that when you discipline him and you put him in a room, he's likely to crawl out the window and take off. I think the child's behavior is a factor. I think it's a factor that is consistent with the recommendation by Dr. Gamache. Mr. Lamar recognized it, and unlike many fathers who might have simply avoided or escaped parenting responsibilities, he did not disown his children. He simply applied a very poor form of discipline which he felt had been instrumental in his own upbringing. There's no other history of this abuse occurring any further on this date, Your Honor. There's no other history from that date to the date of the arrest, and this wasn't something that happened immediately upon the taping. This tape lay in the house for over three months before Harriet Smith decided to use it against Mr. Lamar. We're asking to break the cycle, not by incarceration, but through education for this man and his family, and that can be done through supervision. Incarceration won't be a tool that can help the family. And the family that we're focusing on is clearly his biological children. Your Honor, at this time; the defense doesn't have anything further. Thank you."

"Mr. Grey," the judge said.

The prosecutor then stood up and buttoned his jacket.

"Good afternoon, Judge. I'd like to start out by saying that I am sure, based on the voluminous requests that you have made of me in this case, I know that you have reviewed HRS reports, old State Attorneys files, school records, health records. I mean, I could go on for ten minutes listing all the things that I know you, Your Honor has reviewed, so I'm confident that whatever decision you make is going to be a well-informed one. Having said that, I think that, what we have here is a person whose only remorse is that he has to answer for this incident. He stands before you today saying that you know that it worked. It's justified because it worked, because the kids behavior turned around. I find that appalling and disgusting. The children, both of them, as you, Your Honor knows misbehave. One has attention deficit hyperactivity disorder. They misbehave. They're not the best of kids. Their misbehavior did not warrant the malicious punishment by Mr. Lamar. In all the things that I reviewed, there is one thing that jumped out at me, Judge, and that's the word 'temper.' This man has a temper and when he gets mad, he goes off. He's got a history of doing that and he's got a criminal history that goes back to the early eighties. Any challenge to his authority, he is going to take action, whatever it takes, and in this case, it happens to be the abuse of his children.

There's been a lot said about Ms Smith who's sitting in the courtroom there. She's been cast as the source of all these problems, and she's been described as a switch. Well, I suggest that the finger on that switch, Your Honor, is Mr. Lamar's temper. You know she is a dependent person. She tried to love the man, but the guy just keeps going off. He has beaten her, he has abused her, he has gotten in trouble in California for violating an injunction and he clearly does whatever he wants to do without regard to the law or anyone else. He is standing before the court trying to portray himself as a martyr. Well, the court knows that he doesn't even have custody of these children. He abandoned these children. That's how he ended up without them in the first place."

Even now, as I'm revising this manuscript, it burns me to hear the lies that were said to make my situation worse. Back then and even today, I remember how that prosecutor made me regret the time when Harriet and I had split up. Immediately, I was the mother and the father to all four of my kids. Heartbroken and stressed, I made the worst decision in my life. I left my kids with their grandmother in the hopes that their mother would come to her senses and help me with our kids. Sadly, Roxann never showed up.

I say that to say this: that prosecutor talked as if he was a perfect man; when in reality, I bet he had fallen weak for a woman at some point in his life. But we will never get to know of it. The difference between him and I is that he was fortunate enough to go to college and learn the skills to talk against a person, no matter what the circumstances and the facts of the case were. True, I lost my kids by dropping them off, but my attention was simple. Selfishly, Dell, Roxann's sister was in need of funds, she quickly got HRS involved and I lost custody to her. I was a weak son of a bitch! I should had taken a stand and held on strong for my kids, not fold and run behind a woman. This happened decades ago, and it still hurts my heart.

I can still picture my daughter, Tina, who is now an adult with three kids. On her good day, I will get a smile and a hug; on her bad day, a sneer, followed by an icy remark.

"You left us to take care of somebody else's family!"

I remember my beautiful daughter, Theresa, riding in the back of a pickup truck as her mother and her lover drove away into the sunset. I remembered my sons struggling with school, struggling to educate their minds.

This is a cruel unforgiving world and to be honest, suicide was on the horizon for me. But, ultimately, I knew that when you fall, you have to get back up, forgive yourself, and continue to strive to be the best person you can be for you. Damn what people think, they will never be satisfied regardless! Goodness will be your witness.

But still, it was hard to sit there and quietly listen to that prosecutor defame me.

"He's nothing more than an absentee father who now wants to make everything right in one full swoop by exerting his authority," the prosecutor continued. "He is not a martyr, he is not a symbol and he should not be held up to parents who struggle with the issues of corporal punishment and whether or not to use it. This is just a complete affront to those people, and I am personally offended that he stands here before you saying, 'I was trying to do the right thing; I was only trying to do the right thing. My kids were going to be in a gang and this is the only way I can keep them out of the gang.' I find that offensive. He is nothing more than an abuser who is disguising himself in the cloak of parental best intentions and I ask that you sentence him accordingly."

"Your Honor, just a brief response if I may?" John interjected.

"Sure."

"We want to make it clear that the children are not on trial. The children's behavior is not the issue that we think justifies. We think it's not an excuse, but it is part of the reason we brought up those issues with the children. Also, my client has shown remorse, he has apologized even in his own statement. He can see that at this point and he has apologized for what has happened. I think the court could follow the plan by Dr. Gamache. Clearly, supervision would allow the domestic violence intervention program, psychological counseling, intervention family counseling between the children and the father."

"Number two on the final page of this recommendation, where it says that there could be severe restrictions imposed on this contact with the custody of the children, that clearly is already going to occur and will continue to occur, regardless of what sentence this court imposes because children and family services are already involved in the child's wellbeing and the child's supervision. And finally, we would concur with the final issue that my client would be discouraged and forbidden from consuming any intoxicants throughout the supervision. Mr. Lamar, apparently you want to address the court with something else?"

"Yes Your Honor, I never beat my wife before."

"I beg your pardon?" she asked.

"I never beat my wife."

"You never hit her?"

"I pushed her Your Honor."

"How about anybody else? Did you ever hit anybody else, Mr. Lamar?"

"I pushed her, Your Honor."

"Yes, think long and hard because I'm listening to everything you say and Mr. Lamar, I think I know an awful lot about you, having spent many, many hours reading all of these files okay. So before you answer me –"

"Yes, your Honor."

"Make sure whatever you say is accurate."

"Yes ma'am."

"Okay?"

"Yes I… I was trying to protect my mother Your Honor, and I got in a fight with my mother's boyfriend."

"Yes, anybody else Mr. Lamar?"

"Not since I've been an adult"

"Since when?"

"An adult your Honor."

"Really? Tangy Biggum ring a bell?

"That's a lie Your Honor."

"That's a lie?"

"Yes your Honor."

"There was a charge."

"She's a pros…," I stopped myself from speaking, as I sensed the judge was subtly trying to inform my wife and Sybil of my cheating, which had nothing to do with my case.

"That's a lie? You never grabbed her, never ripped her shirt, she's wasn't four months pregnant at the time?"

"That's a lie Your Honor."

"Okay, we've got that down. In 1993, there was a trespass charge. You were yelling and screaming in an intoxicated state. Is that correct or is that a lie too?"

"No. I was trying to talk with my wife, Your Honor."

"I beg your pardon?"

"I was trying to talk with my wife," I repeated.

"Trying to talk to your wife, there was a restraining order."

"Okay, See, the problem with you Mr. Lamar, from my perspective is that you have a skewed view of life. You don't see what the rest of us see, okay? But I see, and I'm not trying to embarrass you, but I see a man who hasn't had custody of his children since 1992, for very good reason from what I can see, having read all of those dependency files. The only custody or any contact you were supposed to have was supposed to be supervised. I see a man who's had a history of violence."

"I haven't hurt anyone, Your Honor."

"Excuse me? Well, I guess we'd have to decide what the definition of hurt is, and I'm not getting into an argument on this? From my perspective, when you hit somebody without their permission, you hurt somebody. Now I'm not going to get into it with you, I'm just telling you that this is part of your problem. Just for clarification, I asked Miss Hossman to check your status in California. Mr. Lamar, did a judge tell you to show up for jail in California?"

"There is an active warrant for Mr. Lamar in California," said the prosecutor.

"I was not aware of that Your Honor," John said.

"You had to show up for weekend jail. Does that ring a bell, Mr. Lamar?"

"No your Honor."

"No."

"That's not true. They gave me community service and that was it. They said I can't get in anymore trouble within three years."

"Well, are you in trouble within three years? Yes, because for one, you didn't comply with the last judge."

"I had to come home, Your Honor. I didn't have no family. I didn't have anybody there. I slept in my truck."

"You have a justification for everything that you do."

"Well, that's the truth Your Honor, I'm sorry, but it's the truth. I didn't have anywhere to stay."

"Ah huh. The other problem you have Mr. Lamar, is you don't listen to what a judge tells you. You don't remember anything about any jail in California?"

I was flabbergasted to see how the judge was accusing me of running off on a jail sentence in California, when the term 'weekend jail' is only another name for community service. I had no probation, and no jail time, only thirty hours to do on weekends.

And the wife beating I was accused of! It was unbelievable to see how the court was giving wrong critical information during a decision of taking someone's freedom!

"You do remember that the judge in California told you don't get into any more trouble. Well, you're in a lot of trouble in the state of Florida. I doubt that judge knows you are not in California, that your back here in Florida."

I could only shake my head. I was too shocked for words.

"No? This judge or at least another judge earlier told you not to have any contact with your wife!"

"He told both of us, your Honor!"

"Well, I just listen to some tapes."

"Your Honor, if I just may briefly," John said. "I'd like to advise Mr. Lamar that the court is speaking. Mr. Lamar, at this time, you should refrain from interjecting comments."

"That's alright," the Judge said with a smirk before looking coldly my way.

"No, I was only trying to explain, I'm sorry," I apologize.

"Maybe we'll get the time that you can explain, but right now, you're interrupting and that is what I'm trying to prevent." said John.

"That's fine," the Judge said. "As I was saying, I listened to the tape again. I listened to it yesterday and I listened to it again today. My problem with you, Mr. Lamar, my real concern about putting you on immediate supervision is that I don't have any confidence that you will listen to me or anybody else. You will do what you think you need to do! You have shown that's your track record. You do not listen. You were told not to contact Ms Smith, I listened to the tape. Forget the language, forget the implicit threats!"

What threats? I thought. There were no implicit threats or bad language. Yet, I remained silent, realizing I would only make matters worse.

"You were simply told in March, or before March, not to have any contact with your wife and it is clear that you did. You've been told time and time again not to do these things!"

"Your Honor, I can listen."

"Excuse me! For me to consider putting you on supervision, I can't in good conscience do it. Now, do I believe you set out to abuse these children? No, I really don't believe that your purpose was to abuse them. But that's what you ended up doing. Not so much physically, but, as Dr. Gamache says very clearly, the kind of humiliation your behavior yields – you don't get it! I don't know how to make it clearer. There's nothing emotionally or psychologically wrong to the extent that you need treatment, that's what Dr. Gamache says. Yet, he makes some recommendations as there's a mental deficit that causes you to act like this. And I believe what he says is true. You have an inability to control your violence and aggressive impulses.

"I watched that videotape again and you indicated you thought you were in control. If that's being in control Mr. Lamar, then you have lots of problems with control. You have a history of alcohol abuse, as far as I'm concerned, having read all these files. If you don't think you have an alcohol problem, again, I think you have a problem seeing exactly what some of your problems are. I'm not putting you on the street in this community quite frankly because I don't have any confidence that you'll listen to what I have to say."

"I will, Your Honor!"

"Well, it's too little, too late. You haven't today and I don't have any confidence that you will! Now, what else did you want to say, you wanted to say something else?"

I could only shake my head.

"No, your Honor.

"I do appreciate the opportunity you've provided us today in court."

"Anything else?" she asked, looking at the prosecutor.

"No said the prosecutor."

"Now, Mr. Lamar, you will be adjudicated and you'll be sentenced to Florida State Prison for a period of five years."

Keitha burst out in tears and walked out the courtroom.

"This will be followed by two years of community control followed by one year of probation with the following special conditions: When you get out, you will attend the Spring for what is the equivalent of the Family Violence Diversion Program. You've been told to do it before and you haven't done it, from what I can tell. I'm telling you that before you may have contact at all with your children, you have to go through the Family Violence Program, do you understand? Had you done that before when you were ordered to do it, perhaps you wouldn't be in this position at this point. You didn't do it then and I'm telling you now, when you get out you have to go through that program. And again, you're not to have any contact, none, until you've completed that program. You are not to have any unsupervised contact with those children until you have also completed a parenting course through the Department Of Children and Family Services; and you're not to have any unsupervised contact with those children until this court, or whoever is sitting here, tells you that it is appropriate for you to do so. You're to be evaluated with regard to any alcohol problem that you may have. I know you think there is no alcohol problem. Dr Gamache thinks there is. From what I read in this prior case histories, I think there's certainly at least the potential of an alcohol problem. So you're to get an evaluation and follow through with any treatment that may be necessary. You're also to be evaluated when you get out to see if there is any other mental health counseling that you need and you're to follow with that treatment. Now, I can only tell you to do these things Mr. Lamar, if you had a history of abiding by prior court orders, you wouldn't be in this position. Even on the facts of this case. So, as far as I'm concerned, I hope you understand. I hope you get it. Now, I hope you take a good look at yourself and really take a good look at who you are, and what you intend by your actions and use better judgment in the future. I can't make you have better judgment, Mr. Lamar, but there are certainly programs available to you and I hope you take advantage of them and that you don't set yourself up to go back to the Florida State Prison. Do you understand that?"

At that moment, I wanted to say, *'No, I don't understand! You say you know what I will do and won't do, that I won't listen to a word you say and yet, you give me five years in prison, and when I get out, I have to do two years of house arrest, followed by one year on probation, attend this program and that program! If you truly feel that I won't follow instructions, then why in the hell are you giving me so many instructions to do?'*

Instead, I just said, "Yes, Your Honor, I understand."

"You're still going to be on supervision and you're going to be on a monitor. We're going to know what you're doing when you get out, Mr. Lamar, so I urge you to do what you need to do. Follow the court order. There are no other conditions."

"The alcohol," the court clerk said.

"The alcohol evaluation, if there is alcohol treatment that's needed, then you're not to drink. It's that simple. Clear?"

I raised my hand.

"Yes?"

"So when I get out, I can't drink no beer or nothing?"

191

"If, in fact, the evaluation shows that you have an alcohol problem, and then I'm telling you NO, you cannot drink! If somebody says there's no problem, then you can drink as long as you don't do it excessively to where it causes you problems."

"So I'm sentenced to five years?"

"Ah huh."

"I want to make it clear to whoever might be sitting on review of this case several years in the future, if it's not this judge, I ask that this court does a law review for good behavior. That this case is not carved in stone! We're not saying that it has to be two years community control followed by one year of probation." said my lawyer.

"That's right," the Judge said.

"If the court hears additional factors that would be beneficial to Mr. Lamar's case, perhaps there can be an early termination of that supervision for him."

"I don't have a problem with that. I want Mr. Lamar to do what he needs to do to get these programs behind him and to do what he needs to do, so he doesn't have other incidents that involve violence with anyone, anything else?" The judge concluded.

"No your Honor, thank you," John said.

"Your Honor, I'm a truck driver. When I get out, I won't be able to drive because of the house arrest with monitor. If you will, could you substitute the house arrest?"

"That's a long time from now," the Judge said, smiling. "I'm not changing it."

I suddenly felt a jerk on my arm. The bailiff's large hand had a full grip around my upper arm as he ordered me to step toward the end to get fingerprinted. I looked back at my family, but they were already gone. I looked back at John as he rounded up his papers. He acted as if he was getting ready to clock out and go home.

The bailiff placed my hand on an ink pad and began fingerprinting.

"I can't believe she just did that," the bailiff muttered.

My heart felt as if it was going to burst. My voice was weak as I asked John from afar to file an appeal. His sudden reply was that my appeal would be shot down because the judge did not go over the guidelines. I felt so helpless and weak. I barely had the strength to walk. I was taken to a holding cell and just sat there, staring down at my shoes. I couldn't swallow how my life had taken this dreadful turn. Five years, five long years of being treated like I was some kind of murderer. I hadn't hurt my children; I kept repeating this to myself and I suddenly began hating the state of Florida and its crooked court system. To me, it was a system that would send a man to prison for disciplining his son when there's no injuries involved and the judge on national TV admits that she felt that I did not set out to harm my son, yet she sentenced me with such harshness. To me, it was clearly a judicial system that allowed a hateful judge to exercise prejudice and unethical judicial practices by bringing up old bogus charges that were not confirmed and allowed to influence the severity of my sentence.

"What about Tangy? You violated probation in California when you didn't comply with the weekend jail sentencing, and you beat your wife. It will be a long time before you get out!"

Her scolding tone kept ringing in my head.

Five long years, followed by a set up to violate and return back to prison was not my comeuppance; I knew I did not deserve this. Wrong or right, there were no genuine concerns on how this five year sentence would affect my children.

At that moment, I could understand how one could go postal.

I knew I couldn't dwell on these negative feelings. I took a deep breath and tried to force out the hate that had compounded inside me. I started recalling a scripture I had read awhile back: *"The Discipline of Jehovah, O' my son do not reject, and do not abhor his reproof, because the one whom Jehovah loves he reproves, even as a father does a son in whom he finds pleasure."*

The power of this scripture began to saturate my mind and an enormous sense of relief came over me. The feeling of hatred began to dissipate. I knew I had to stay strong to keep hope alive. I still held some bit of hope that I wouldn't have to spend five years away from my children.

Jehovah is disciplining me; it isn't bad as it seems everything will be alright, I muttered.

When I returned back at the jail, the inmates had heard my sentence over the radio. I headed for my cell and closed the door. I wasn't in my cell a good fifteen minutes when my cell door slid open by my dorm officer. He informed me that Channel 13 was there again to see me. The black reporter, Jennifer Jones came to mind. She understood my situation, so I had no problem seeing her. Again, I was escorted to the Captain's room. When I entered, I was glad to see that it was indeed Jennifer there to see me. She greeted me with a soft smile and handshake; her cameramen reached out for a handshake as well.

"This is off the camera," Jennifer said to her crew before turning to me. "Mr. Lamar, we were at our studio watching your sentencing. The other crew and I just knew you were going to get probation. Your lawyer seemed to have had everything under control, and when Judge Hawkins said five years in prison, everyone blurted, *what*! Five years, we couldn't believe she would sentence you like that!"

"I know," as I shook my head in disbelief.

"I know this is rough for you, but could you have a short interview with me? It won't take long." When I agreed, she asked me to be seated and she told her cameraman to proceed with the introduction.

"Mr. Lamar," she began. "Today, you were sentenced to five years in prison for disciplining your son. How do you feel about the judge's decision?"

"There are things that I won't say on air. No doubt my sentence was unfair."

"We went to talk with your son today; he said that everything you said about him was true, and that the media and the courts are making it look really bad when it's not. Your son also stated that your wife started this mess and that she was the one who wanted him to get a whipping in the first place."

"Yeah, I know."

"When you get out of prison, what would you say to your son?"

"Let's go fishing, we both love the water."

The reporter gave me a hopeful smile. *I tell you, it took everything I had inside of me not to cry on national television.* I was relieved when the interview quickly ended. It was important to me that I remained strong because had I burst out in tears, that would have made Harriet's day. So I held my head up, shook Jennifer's hand and was escorted back to my cell. After about twenty minutes of laying in my cell in a total daze, I heard something slide underneath my cell door. I looked and saw that it was mail. I rolled off the slab and opened the envelope. It was a certified letter from Children and Family Services.

I began reading and I was outraged to see that it was a letter demanding child support for my son, Toler, and his brothers and sister. Suddenly, a wave of anger and rage took over me.

I can't whoop my child, but you want me to pay child support? How can I pay child support in prison?

I slung the letter to the floor as I paced like a trapped, mad animal.

CHAPTER 16

DAM I SLIPPED!

The next day, I awoke and found that an inmate had slid a newspaper under my door. The subheading read: *Father Nets Time in Jail*.

The article held a six inch by four inch picture of me getting fingerprinted after sentencing. The look on my face was like, *I don't believe this shit*.

I called Sybil. I sadly told her that five years was a long time. I wanted her to just go on with her life. Sybil suddenly burst out into a soft cry, and then the phone went dead. I took a deep breath as I held the receiver to my chest. My phone time had expired on a bad note. I attempted to make another collect call.

Sybil immediately picked up.

"Hello," Sybil answered sobbingly.

"Stop crying. You still want to marry me?"

"Yes," she said, strongly.

"Sybil, do you know what that means? That means you will have to remain faithful for five years."

"I know, I'm not like the other women you've had," she said.

Days followed, I found myself lying face up, staring at the ceiling, pondering endlessly. It had been a week after my sentence, I decided to get my headphones out and listen to the WTMP talk show. That particular weekend, there had been a black democrat by the name of Bob Bilderlin. He was speaking on several dilemmas that people of color have to face in today's society. Racism will always exist, I realized sadly.

That topic was very displeasing to me. I truly felt that the color of one's skin should not be an issue. All people should be treated equally as we are all human. We all eat and shit the same way. While I was listening, a caller called in to talk about my case. The caller asked Bob Bilderlin himself if he would be able to help me get my sentence overturned. Mr. Bilderlin said that he was familiar with my case because of the publicity. He went on to say that he would help and that he would speak about my case that following Saturday on his show. I jumped to my feet with joy! He went as far as to say that he would soon be meeting with the Governor and he would inform him about my case. I was so happy to have caught that discussion. I started researching on how I could contact Bob Bilderlin. Come to find out, the man lived only five blocks from where I lived. At that point, I really was relieved and filled with hope. I called Sybil and had her to take Mr. Bilderlin the videotape of the discipline I had given my boys, in hope that others would see the purpose I was trying to achieve. I also wanted him to see that I had been sentenced way too harshly, especially when the judge clearly stated that she personally didn't believe that it was my intention to cause harm.

About a week later, a white man violently shook his young son to death. He only received probation. The disparity between our two cases made me want to vomit. Here is a man that shook his child to death and got probation, when I only gave my child a good rearing. I got eight years, five in prison. What is wrong with that picture? I recall a quote by Martin Luther King Jr. made in Montgomery, Alabama 1955: *Injustice anywhere is a threat to justice everywhere.*

The following night I called Sybil. She informed me that Bob Bilderlin told her that he would look at the video and for her to get back with him in a couple of days.

A couple of days later, again I called Sybil. She told me that Bob asked her out to dinner to discuss my case. Sybil voice began to rise, she said that

Bob tried to get fresh with her. Sybil said that she got so upset that she demanded back the videotape and left.

I was crushed.

Days passed and I waited to be transported to prison. Sybil started visiting every evening to assure me that she would faithfully wait on my return home. My dad also kept visiting, trying to encourage me that I wouldn't do the whole five year sentence and that I'd end up getting out far sooner.

Hence, you will find out who your true friends are when you go to jail or the hospital. And needless to say, I was at the lowest point in my life. I had many so-called friends, but they couldn't be found or heard from when I needed them. The support of my Dad and Sybil was awesome. I stayed in my cell most of the time and kept myself busy by writing letters and drawing colorful pictures of what I was thinking onto envelopes and mailing them to Sybil. There were times when I'd just pace the floor in a daze, struggling to shake the negative thoughts out of my head.

One evening, while sitting amongst the other inmates, I couldn't help but notice how corrupted the rock cocaine had made many of the men. I knew the drug itself did not discriminate, yet this drug seemed to have a firm grip on African Americans. I had to do a double take when I looked around and saw how many were strung out. It was clear that a large number of strong, handsome brothers were definitely transforming into poorly fed racehorses. The garbage that was spoken from their mouths led me to believe perhaps they were under some sort of curse. I realized that I was living amongst drug infested people, and that I wasn't any better than them. We were all trapped in the system, caged like animals. I began to feel doomed.

I came to a conclusion that I would rather be dead than to become acclimatized to such standards. The more I listened in on the inmates' degrading conversations, the more rueful and depressed I became. I started wondering if I should just go up to my cell, rip my sheet, tie one end on the staircase and the other end around my neck and jump, dangle and kick as I took my last breath. My self-pity and the reality of my situation were getting the best of me.

At some point I said, *to hell with those thoughts.* I knew I was too strong of a man to kill myself, I just wanted to execute the pain and taking my life was not the way. I also realized that the majority of the inmates that I was among were not only fighting addictions, but the taunting of the flesh. The bible speaks of this sinful nature in the book of *Romans 7:14-25.*

A vision of my mother suddenly came to mind and I suddenly recalled the moment that I had struck her. I'll never forget that night. We were still living in Central Park Village Projects. My mother was drunk and staggering about the house, broken-hearted because her man, my little sister's father Eddie Lee, was with another woman. My mother kept yelling and cursing at my sisters like they were whores in the streets. I was only 16, but I thought I was grown.

I got up and told mother, "Go sit your fat ass down somewhere!"

"What? What you say to me," my mother yelled.

She furiously headed for the kitchen and returned with a large butcher knife, rushing toward me. I backed up onto the stairs and the heel of my foot hit the staircase. I lost my balance and mother reached over me and plunged the knife into my left shoulder.

In a defense mode, I knocked her off of me, yelling "Bitch!"

She landed on her back. I pushed the small bookshelf along the wall on top of her. I remember how her eyes were wide, as if she was in shock. Her gay friend, Dan, who had been there the whole time, suddenly got in my face trying to calm me down by saying, "Stop, that's your momma!"

That nasty, low life man was up in my face with his wet hanging lips inches from mine. I stormed out the door, bleeding down the street towards the house of a female friend I knew. She helped me clean my wounds and luckily there wasn't a big need for stitches.

In the quiet of my cell, I exhaled and tried to fluff up the thin pillow. I was then struck by the memory of how I had carried on with my father. Like a tape replaying, I was forced to take a good look at myself. What kind of child was I? What kind of child fights their parents? Guilt joined in on the ride and began eating at me, especially at the fight I had with my mother. When she came at me with that knife, I should have ran out of the door and not returned until she sobered up or at least cooled down. I had let my temper get the best of me. I remembered how I felt the next day when I returned home. I felt like pure shit! I couldn't even look my mother in her eyes. I spoke and she didn't even speak back, only returned a look as if I was a scumbag. She didn't speak to me for days, and my conscious ate me up inside.

That following Sunday after my fight with my mother, I wanted to repent. I didn't own any church clothes and I didn't care; all I wanted was for God to forgive me. I got up and put on my street clothes and walked to the church that was across from the projects. Once I got there, I stood outside of its closed doors; I could hear the preacher yelling. I took a deep breath and opened the double doors. The sun beamed a path up the walkway. The light ran straight down the middle of the church to the pulpit. People on the left and right simultaneously turned their heads toward the open doors and I followed the light between the two aisles down to where the preacher was standing. I dropped to my knees and started praying for forgiveness.

You see, God inspired man to write the Holy Bible to give us instructions on how we should conduct ourselves. In the book of *Proverbs 17: 14* it says that God tells us that "Before a quarrel, take your leave."

What about the command that every child should know? *Exodus 20:12* says, "Honor your father and your mother in order that your days may prove long."

Even after that church visit, I still had a hostile confrontation with my father caused mainly by us drinking alcohol. I should have taken leave when I saw my father drinking too much. At the end of the day, my father was still my father and there should not be an excuse to not honor your parents.

So there I found myself, locked up for giving too harsh of a discipline to my son for being disrespectful. It was time to reap what I had sown. I tossed and turned in bed, trying to fight off my demons. I wished I could fall asleep and never wake again. As I lay there, I wanted to know if I was a good person, a bad person or something in between. That's a question every person should ask themselves. I got up, and slid open my cell door to look down at the inmates.

I turned and slumped into the chair and muttered, "My life is over."

About ten minutes later, from the corner of my eye, I saw the shadow of a man enter my dorm and stood right over me. I looked up and there I saw a strange, white man with stunning blue eyes looking down at me.

"What's up?" I said, not liking how he just walked into my cell, violating my privacy.

"God sent me," he said, softly. His sparkling blue eyes did not shiver, nor blink as he looked down at me.

I sat there speechless for a moment. He went on to say that God loved me and he asked if he could pray for me. The first thing that came to mind was that he was one of those jailhouse preaching psychos. But, there was something about his eyes that persuaded me to say yes. So I did, hoping that he would leave without causing a scene. The man bowed his head and began to pray. Likewise, I bowed mine and hoped like hell he would hurry up and let me be.

The words from this stranger's mouth were words that I couldn't ignore. Suddenly, I began to feel like my skin was crawling. A strong tingle began to move from my toes, up my legs, all the way to my neck. A sore lump began to form at the bottom of my throat. I started to gasp for air as pressure began to build in my neck and face. My heart was pounding and I clinched my face with both hands because it felt as though my face was about to burst. Out of the corner of my eye, I could see that my visitor began to kneel as he continued to pray boldly for deliverance. He proceeded to place his hands on my knee, and when his hand touched me, I felt pressure burst out of my nose with heavy snot flowing out. I cried out for help and tears began flowing uncontrollably down my face. As I tried to catch my breath, this mysterious lump in my throat started slothfully moving up my neck. I was still gasping for air and I noticed that the visitor was crying as he prayed.

I shouted, "I can't breathe! I can't breathe!' Suddenly I caught my breath and when I was able to, I yelled to the visitor, "What was that?"

"The Holy Spirit," the stranger replied, before disappearing.

I must add that after that visit, I felt a hundred pounds lighter and really good. I felt so good that I actually prayed periodically from that point on for the Holy Spirit to not leave me.

"Please don't leave me," I'd pray.

I became more interested in God's word and I began examining the scriptures in the Holy Bible. As I read, my soul became content, especially when I came across what God had to say about discipline.

In the book of *Proverbs 23: 13-14* it states, "Withhold not correction from the child, for if thou beatest him with the rod, he shall not die. Thou shalt beat him with rod, and shalt deliver his soul from hell."

However, the Holy Bible can be hard to read; for a better read and understanding, The New World Translation of the Holy Scriptures reads more clearly so one can comprehend. So, if you are a parent of young children and you're indecisive regarding rearing your child for the simple reason your parents didn't believe in corporal punishment, the book of *Hebrews 12: 7-11* and *Proverbs 13: 24* are must reads.

A few days later, I was still floating on cloud nine with the Holy Spirit. I felt so good and content. It was like I was walking, not on a hard floor, but literally on a cloud. Oh, I felt so good. I decided to call Sybil like usual, only the conversation turned lustful.

I started talking about having sex upon my return and I immediately felt the Holy Spirit leave me. It rushed from the top of my head through my body to my toes, gone in a matter of seconds. I paused, Sybil wanted to hear more, but I was speechless, jolted with the sense that the *Good Spirit* had left me because of lusting. I quickly got off the phone and I exhaled before turning toward my cell. That's when I realized that the floor was hard beneath my feet. My feet felt as if I had been walking for days.

That night, somewhere between the hour of three and four in the morning, like so many nights before, I lay in my one-man cell wide-eyed, trying to drown out the thoughts that led me to this constant sinking feeling born from having been sentenced to five years in prison, two years house arrest followed by one year probation.

All this I received for disciplining my 16-year-old son and his 9-year-old stepbrother who, by influence, had become his older brother's shadow. The thought of my present ominous situation and the outrageously unjust reason behind it felt as though something was continuously squeezing at my heart.

I suffered from extreme pain in my shoulders and joints because of the concrete bed that the Orient Road County Jail provided. I could hear the eerie sounds of food trays clanging down on the metal tables as the kitchen trustees prepared the imitation breakfast.

Many restless and painful nights were spent thinking about the injustice of it all. Knowing that disciplining my boys was my responsibility, as most parents do out of love. I was baffled knowing I never once made a mark on them. Even my wife approved of and encouraged the spanking. Three months later when our marriage fell apart, Harriet, out of vengeance took the matter to the authorities.

The state's attorney had manipulated and twisted the facts, so they got another notch in their conviction record by disregarding the true facts and circumstances. Since I was successfully crushed by the state, I'd stare at the four concrete walls of my cell, sadly overwhelmed.

I knew I had to continue to write and send a message to parents and the ones becoming. So as I rose off my concrete slab with tears flowing down my face, I retrieved my Bible and started to pray for God to give me the knowledge and strength to endure this ordeal along with the ability to write an informative and honest account on what I went through in court, and how I've been labeled a criminal for upholding my responsibility as a parent, disciplining my boys for their rebellious actions so that they might avoid a life of destruction. Yet the most disturbing element of it all is the justice system. I had to ask myself, who is really the parent?

The following day, I was still glued to my seat, writing. Although my writing was bulky and unsure, I had to keep going. Suddenly my thoughts were interrupted when an inmate tapped on my cell door and handed me an article regarding my case. The headline read: *RESPONSIBLE PARENTS SHOULD HAVE THE RIGHT TO DISCIPLINE CHILDREN.* I felt the unfamiliar feeling of pride.

On November 14, 1998, four days after I had been inspired to resume writing, my name was called along with some others, to pack up and prepare to be transported to the Florida State Prison. I'll never forget the feeling of doom as I waited for my turn to have my hands and feet shackled.

Each prisoner was shackled to another, and then in pairs, we walked in unison onto a grayish-blue bus that they called the Blue Bird. It is a bus you would never want to ride.

CHAPTER 17

A WORLD OF ITS OWN

Destination: Lake Butler Correctional Institution. I was en-route to live amongst violent thieves, murderers, rapists, child molesters and other wrongdoers for the next five years. I felt empty and worthless. Yet, the little flicker of light that did remain in my life was Sybil. She was a light that flickered, and I feared would soon flicker out. I believed that there was no woman alive who was going to wait five years for a man without having sex.

I looked up at the man who was shackled onto me; he too stared off into space as if his young Hispanic life was just as over as mine. I looked around the bus, and couldn't help but notice that the majority on the bus were black, all pondering endlessly as if they, too, were doomed. How could one not feel doomed when we were approaching a prison that was surrounded with thick, shiny barbed wire and gun towers? Those towers housed trigger happy officers who were waiting for the chance to gain a reputation.

As we got closer to the entrance of the prison, I immediately put myself in check, preparing to face a world of its own. This was the same self-preparation I done back in 1985 when I was nineteen, my first encounter with the prison system. My charges were leaving the scene of an accident and failure to pay child support. Actually, that prison term was by choice.

I asked to do the rest of my house arrest term in prison because I wanted to escape a growing drug addiction. I only had a year left on house arrest. If I went to prison on a year and a day sentence, I would have been out in two months and two weeks with everything behind me. So I chose to finish up in prison. That was back then and things had drastically changed, although addressing the officers with 'yes sir' and 'no sir' remained the same as it helped prevent unnecessary beat downs.

The blue bird came to a complete stop, then the gates opened and we entered the prison. The bus finally stopped in a huge metal bus garage that was built onto the main building. The bus door slung open and two officers ordered us to exit in the same fashion we got on. One of the three awaiting officers started yelling for all of us to line up alongside the metal wall and bench. *Man, it was daybreak and during that time of year, Jack Frost wasn't playing.* I think it was colder in that metal garage than it was outdoors.

After roll call and getting my property, which was mostly religious books thrown about as if they were trash; and my snacks which were handed down to rude officers to enjoy, I immediately sensed that they wanted me to say something, but I remained quiet.

"I want everyone to line up along the wall and keep your mouths shut!" The officer yelled. The shackles and hand cuffs were taken off.

"Ya'll listen up, strip out of all your clothes, spread your legs, rise up your hands facing me, when I get to you; I want you to open your mouth wide. Do you understand?" the officer yelled.

"Yes sir," we replied.

One officer started screaming in a prisoner's face, wanting to know what his problem was.

"Do you have a problem?" The officer repeated.

"No!" the black prisoner said.

"No what?"

"No sir."

"I didn't think so," the officer growled, as he looked up into the man's face like some drill sergeant.

What really got me was that he started calling all of us punks, and that our momma didn't teach us anything because if she did, we wouldn't be in prison.

"What's your name, boy?" The officer asked as he walked down the line to intimidate us.

However, it wasn't a pretty sight to see a bunch of butt naked black men being chastised by two young, tobacco-spitting, white officers. An ugly sight indeed and it got really ugly when all of us were on the bench, bent over and with our raw butts in the air. The officer wanted the prisoner to cough when he stood behind him so that he could make sure that the prisoner was not trafficking drugs into the prison by carrying it in his rectum. The guard was now approaching me.

Ass muscles, don't fail me now!

It wasn't that I had drugs up my butt, I was just afraid that if I coughed too hard, I might blow out a real stinker.

As you could imagine, the whole inspection was humiliating and embarrassing, but the most embarrassment came when the inspection was over. Still nude, we then had to stand facing the officers with our arms stretched out from our body like a T, legs parted, head cocked back with our mouth open wide. It was embarrassing because it was teeth-chattering cold and Tarzan wasn't swinging.

Luckily, I didn't stay at Lake Butler long and within two weeks I was transferred to Gainesville Drug Treatment Center, a place where the state paid handsomely for each inmate. It was a place where if you successfully completed the nine-month term, thereafter, one would be eligible for work release at a location of his choice. However, if he got kicked out or refused treatment, he would be scarred and wouldn't be eligible for anything. He would be transferred to work as a free laborer in the penal system until his time was up and if he refused to work, he would be taken out of population to serve hard time on lock down. And for whatever reason, years down the line, if the offender returned back to prison, he would still be persecuted for that particular refusal.

I was a little baffled as to why I was selected to go to this place. Later, I learned that, due to the fact that the majority of my arrest record reflected that I had been drinking alcohol before I committed my crime. I was told that was the reason I was placed as a drug offender. I didn't argue the point; hell, I took it as an opportunity to learn something.

Gainesville Drug Treatment Institution looked like a small prison without the gun towers. Mr. Brownlin, the head supervisor who looked like Hitler, was kicking people out of the program mercilessly.

I didn't know if this was true or not, but the rumor was that after an inmate accrued 30 days of enrollment, the institution received a check from the state. From that point on, the inmate would have to walk on pins and needles to complete the program. It seemed that it was all about money because Brownlin was moving people in and out like a production line. His dogmatic foot mostly targeted men of color. I faced a real challenge to successfully complete this program without becoming a snitch, which he used to get information to persecute others.

Weeks followed and still, every morning, I would rise up and look around at all the men snoring lifelessly.

I'm in prison, I would say to myself.

It was a hard pill to swallow and yet I had hoped to win my appeal. That helped keep a smile on my face.

The thought of losing Sybil was becoming more real, to the point where I build up enough nerve to enquire with a prison nurse during my initial check-up. "Can a woman wait five years for a man without having sex?"

The nurse looked as if she was in her early 40s, and she gave me an incredulous look. My eyes did not once quiver as I stared directly into hers. I guess she sensed that I didn't mean any harm and that I just needed to know the answer.

She broke eye contact and replied, "Yes, a woman could wait five years for a man without having sex."

She went on to say that the man needed to maintain good communication with her by means of phone and letters. This was something I wanted to hear, and I started writing and calling Sybil at least two times a week. During this period, I really started loving and appreciating Sybil.

As time passed, I couldn't help but notice how the African American inmates failed to get along. They were always trying to bring one another down and fighting one another. On the other hand, I saw other ethnic groups playing games together and really looking out for one another… especially the Hispanic community. The African Americans were always calling each other *pussy niggas*; envying one another and would demand double on a loan. Even Ray Charles could see that the African American community had no unity. This depressed the hell out of me because I wasn't aware that my ethnicity was so bad off and so selfish. It bothered me to the point where I had to go have a one-on-one with a counselor regarding this issue. My counselor thought it was funny when I told him that I wished I was Japanese and at that time, I was dead-ass serious. I didn't find anything funny! It was just really sad to see my people like this.

After witnessing all the bad that went on inside the prison walls, I was fortunate to abstain from the negativity. Ultimately, I realized I was becoming wiser because the childish things that used to mean a lot to me no longer mattered. I wanted to make my stay worthwhile, so I dug deep into books to self-educate myself and leave the prison wiser and be a better person. In addition, I had learned a significant amount of information on becoming a good writer. I later started coaching a baseball team that played the other dorms on the compound. By no means was this position easy, but it helped me from incarcerating my mind. Within six months in the program, I had accomplished a lot.

One afternoon, a white dude and I got into an argument. In the midst of exchanging words the dude's buddy, who was listening, suddenly threw his cookie that he was eating; it struck me on the jaw and he proceeded to attack me. The confrontation almost got really physical, but it didn't. Still, the three of us were reported. We had to go see Brownlin.

"What's going on with you guys to cause such a disturbance?" Brownlin asked, as the three of us stood before him.

Brownlin immediately set his eyes upon me. I started to explain what happened and the two white dudes followed suit, explaining their side of the story. After everything was said, Brownlin turned to me, telling me that it was what I said to Jim Bob that made Rob jump in and attack me. He went on to say that the two men had been through a lot, and here I come causing more problems for them. He said it as if I should have been ashamed of myself to make Rob to lose his temper. I looked over at Rob and Jim Bob and apologized. Brownlin then told the two men to leave the room, leaving Brownlin, his secretary and myself alone. I was then told that

I would have to be dismissed from the program because I wasn't getting anything out of the program.

"What! What do you mean I'm not getting anything out of the program?" I voiced.

I started calling out all the things that I had accomplished. Brownlin then told his secretary to hand me some papers to sign. It read that I wasn't getting anything out of the program and that I refuse treatment.

"That's a lie!" I said, angrily.

"I'm not going to argue with you… put *refuse to sign* on it," he told the secretary. "I'm going to send you to the dogs!"

Brownlin then swung around in his chair and proceeded to move the cursor around on the monitor.

I just stood there, speechless.

"Leave my office," Brownlin concluded.

"It's best for you to sign," his secretary who was now standing behind me whispered. My eyes flared into hers and back at Brownlin. His back still turned.

"You will only make matters worse for yourself if you don't sign it," the woman coaxed.

I took the paper, but instead of signing my name, I wrote on the dotted line, Didn't Refuse. The secretary didn't notice it, and I left the office.

I was highly upset. Getting kicked out on a refusal was totally unfair. It hurt all of my chances for work release. I was truly working the program and learning some life skills that were no doubt good tools to use to help become a better person. Not to mention, I only had three months to go before completion. However, I was a little more fortunate than the others that had been kicked out. Being that I was a baseball coach for A-Dorm, I was well known on the compound. About ten inmates who didn't want to see me go marched to Brownlin's office to speak on my behalf. This made me feel good, and boy, did I get a quick response. Usually it would take two weeks to see if the accuser would be given a second chance or not. Within two days, I got a response. The following day, I was kicked out and shipped to Gainesville work camp.

It was May of 1999 when I arrived at the Gainesville work camp. Its name spoke for itself because it was all about work. My assignment was to work with the county of Gainesville, cutting and cleaning detention ponds and gutters. Inmates had to get up four in the morning to eat and prepare to load up on the county trucks. We had to work like we were getting paid fifteen dollars an hour, when in reality, we got nothing, not even a barbecue sandwich. I was told by one of the guards that the county paid the correctional institutions over a million dollars a year for prisoners to work.

When I got there, I quickly understood what Brownlin meant when he said that he was sending me to the dogs because I had to work like one. The workers on foot were all black as they cut their way through high brushes that was infested with moccasin snakes with bodies as thick as a navel orange; while the white prisoners zoom around the perimeter on lawn mowers. My biggest complaint was the chaps that the county provided only protected below the knee, a snake that size could bite well above the knee. Therefore, I petitioned to provide full leg chaps for us workers. A couple of weeks later the petition was answered. It stated that they were switching to gas-powered weed eaters with three pronged blades, this would prevent snake attacks. The snakes had no choice but to run or be killed.

It was in my best interest to shut up and accept the change before I got placed on full-time lock down. The charge would've been, refusing to work.

I kept working, but I didn't stop going against Brownlin. I petitioned Tallahassee, asking them to take a look at how he was running things at Gainesville Drug Treatment Center. I informed them how he was kicking inmates out who really needed treatment. I went as far as giving them the names of the men who were treated unfairly.

Weeks passed and I got no response from Tallahassee. Brownlin's foot was still in full swing and the work camp was getting full of weary, black inmates. About ten percent of the workers were white, and their job assignments had them working indoors. Every now and then you would see a Caucasian in the hot fields.

At the work camp, if we weren't working, we were kicked out of the dorm. They'd yell, "Everybody outside!"

The white prisoners, called Housemen, were allowed to stay inside to clean. So the Black and Hispanic workers would lounge under the shade trees, trying to beat the heat.

One day, to our surprise, a large boom truck with white men and chain saws appeared. Before dusk, all the shade trees were cut down. The shaded area immediately turned into a hot desert and that was where we were kicked out into every day.

Indeed, this was nothing more than modern day slavery, but what really troubled me was the reason why I ended up in such a place. I felt that familiar slow burn growing within me at the thought of my wicked wife and that judge, with her political aspiration to serve the state and how it in no way served the interest of my community, nor my children.

Months passed and I finally received my final papers declaring Harriet and I officially divorced. Not long after, Sybil and I started preparing to get married. I was very comfortable with this decision, being that I was marrying my best friend.

When I wrote my father to let him in on the news, he said that he was very pleased with my decision. He also said that he hadn't been feeling well lately. I wrote him back trying to encourage him to see a doctor and exercise. I explained how essential it was to exercise, especially when one was getting up in age.

In response to my letter, he wrote, "If you so smart, than why are you in prison?"

He hit me below the belt, didn't he?

True, I had created a mess of my life, but I wasn't going to lie down and leave prison worse than when I came in. I kept writing and reading books, and started attending the evening programs that the prison provided. This one particular program was designed to help inmates become more prudent and learn how to deal with unwanted emotions. Here, I was able to talk and let out my feelings regarding my children. My beautiful little girl, Tina, had disappeared shortly after my sentence. She was only 14, and no one knew of her whereabouts. I was told that she had started smoking cigarettes and dropped out of school. My daughter was loose in this dog-eat-dog world. I was also told that my son, Toler, was seriously acting out and that my younger sons, Terran and Terrance, looked like they were from Ethiopia and that they looked like they had been thrown away.

Man, I cried so much. Every time I talked about it in group meetings or one-on-one, I would just burst out into tears, stricken with sorrow because I couldn't help them. I went through a ton of sleepless nights and I felt anger building up within me. I was angered to see that HRS had agreed to send me away. I was the only responsible parent my kids had, yet they let my kids go astray. I was so angry that I could have gone postal, shooting the ones responsible. I just thank God that I was able to remain positive. I quit smoking cigarettes and got involved in exercising with weights. In addition to that, I started attending bible study, and that is where I found refreshment to my soul. With tears and all, Jehovah was going to sustain me.

On August 7, 1999, my father was pronounced dead. This was another hard thing for me to accept. I immediately made a request to attend my father's funeral and was granted a twelve hour furlough. Three days before his funeral, I was suddenly denied. I was so upset that I could only lie down on my bunk and think about my father, who I would never see again.

"Raise and shine!" the correctional officer yelled.

I got up, ate and was off to the fields. When we got to our destination, the inmates grabbed their weed whackers and went to work as the one officer looked about. That day was different because it was the day of my father's funeral and working was not on my mind.

The officer was now going into his pockets. He pulled out a can of dip, thumped it a few times and proceeded to reload his bottom lip. As I worked, I watched his every step. He was now walking away from his truck. He kept walking with his focus on someone down the field. I suddenly dashed for his vehicle, jumped in it and burnt rubber out of there.

I was on I–75 southbound. I looked in my rearview mirror and saw nothing but highway. I was pushing at least ninety mph. My father's dead body lying in his casket flashed to mind, and I went even faster. I looked in my rearview mirror and saw that I was now accompanied by a string of flashing cop cars. There was no stopping me; I was going to see my father, one way or another. When I finally reached the funeral, I hook slid into its grounds and jumped out of the truck and raced toward the crowded tent. The string of cops slammed on their brakes, creating a massive dust cloud as they dashed in behind me. I ran toward the casket. I was standing over my father, weeping and telling him how much I loved him and that I would miss him. The cries from family and friends got louder.

"Don't do this, Tolerance!" someone cried, as I reached in the casket and got a good grip onto my father.

The cops came and started trying to tug me away. As they pulled, my father's body began to rise up out of the casket. His head was cocked backed as I tightly held him.

"Turn him loose," demanded the officer.

"Don't do this, Big Toler!" I heard from behind me.

"Turn him loose!"

"You all right", asked the inmate who slept below me.

"Yeah, I was just day dreaming" I replied. I turned over in my bunk and released the tears. The prison officials must had been psychic and felt that I may try to carry out my dream because they changed my custody level so that I wouldn't be eligible to work outside the prison anymore. My new job was to work in the kitchen.

After grieving every night for about a week, I talked to a family member and learned that my father had turned his life around by repenting, getting baptized and living a righteous life before Hepatitis C claimed him. I took a great bit of comfort in hearing that.

Just when I was coming to terms with my father's death, I got more disturbing news. Sybil told me that my stepmother, Vi, had turned on me. Now that my father died, greed raised its ugly head. I learned that Vi had called the police on Sybil for taking my father's suits that I had asked Sybil to get for me. I wanted my father's suits, but for whatever reason, my stepmother didn't want me to have them. She actually called the police to come and take them back. Wow!

Vi must have a man to give them to because she couldn't wear them!

A couple of days later, over the phone, I talked with the wife of my father's friend and she told me that Vi had called her trying to discourage her and her husband from getting a lawyer to help me get out of prison.

"She is against you!" the lady said.

It was like adding salt to my wounds. Vi was a lady who I'd gradually come to love. I had to go lay down for the remainder of that evening. Even today, I feel that my stepmother was the reason I was suddenly denied the right to attend my father's funeral, when all I wanted was his church clothes. There was no doubt that she deserved everything else.

A day or so followed, to everyone's surprise, in walked Brownlin and his crew.

"Everyone in the TV room!" one officer yelled.

All the inmates stopped what they were doing and headed for the TV room.

"You all have the opportunity to return back to the drug treatment center," Brownlin said. "All you need to do is sign this paper."

His secretary waved a form at us. Another one of Brownlin colleagues went on to say that they would have us back in the program in a couple of days after signing. It was obvious that most of the prisoners would rather work for free before they resubmitted themselves back under Brownlin's authority, but there was one dummy that stepped up and signed the paper. Tallahassee must have answered my letter because Brownlin was now looking at everyone and when he spotted me, he started slowly walking toward me.

His eyes glared into mine as he got closer and then, he stopped.

"I know you're hungry, let me feed you," Brownlin said.

"'No, thank you… I'd rather stay here."

If Brownlin's eyes could kill, I would have died right there. Brownlin and his crew marched out to another dorm.

On September 19, 1999 around 9:45 in the morning, my name was called and I was told that I had a visitor. Out the door I went, and there, standing below a row of thick, shiny razor wire was my stepson. To my surprise, he was holding the tail of a beautiful, white wedding gown and on the inside of that gown stood my devoted black woman.

In prison cloths and all, I got happily married to Sybil.

However, after a couple of weeks of taking warm showers, I discovered that my wedding ring was turning green. This ring that I had given to my father was supposed to have been 14K gold. I requested it back when he died and I wanted it to be my wedding band when I married Sybil. Vi had given it to Sybil to give me. This was before the church clothes issue came about.

Why the hell was my finger turning green?

Needless to say, Viola had switched the ring. *Nasty dog*!

In November of 1999, I finally got a letter from the courts. My appeal had been denied, but I refused to lie down.

In December, with the help of family, I submitted a motion that supported an illegal sentence. The argument was to label my case as an incorrect charge. Basically, I had been charged with Aggravated Child Abuse and Malicious Punishment. The legal definition of malice states the intent, without just cause or reason to commit an unlawful act that will result in injury to another or others. According to the definition, committing an unlawful act that will result in injury is not enough to apply the element malicious punishment. I would have had to do it without *cause or reason*, and that would have had to clearly be my intention.

I had disciplined the boys for a good cause and reason. Unfortunately, the form of punishment I used constituted *child abuse*. The element of *malicious punishment* had been added on as an aggravating factor to the charge of child abuse, thereby enhancing the third degree offense of child abuse to a second degree offense of *Aggravated Child Abuse*, which created a more severe sentence.

I think I had a good opportunity, so I filed the necessary forms to file the motion. The process took a long time and a lot of effort, but a year later, the motion was finally answered with a letter in big bold letters, which said *Procedurally Barred*.

"Procedurally barred for what?" I mumbled, disappointedly.

I scanned the letter for a direct answer, but there was none. The sense I got out of this was that the courts wanted me to lie down and ride my sentence out.

I think not!

I submitted another motion that had hardcore evidence showing that my incarceration should had not been any more than twenty two months and that was also shot down.

I then petitioned the courts to show cause as to why I was denied. This took another eight months before the courts responded, and when they did, they make it seem like they never received my argument.

I resubmitted, but I quickly realized how it was all playing out. If you didn't have the money, you didn't have any merit. If you didn't have a paid lawyer to fight for your rights, you didn't have any rights. Right or wrong, the courts could pretty much do what they wanted to do with you.

Hence, if you're not as financially stable as you would like to be, I advise you to create a payment plan toward a particular lawyer, so if you ever need him, he's there for you. You only get what you pay for. If you pay for nothing, you get nothing.

I once had seen an advertisement in a local newspaper of this lawyer who accepted small monthly payments for his services if needed. In these days and times, it is a good thing to have because for some reason or another, you may need an attorney, especially if you've got rebellious kids or a hot-tempered mate.

Every time the court responded to me with some bullshit answer, I'd just submit a motion refuting their claim; it was no longer about getting out, but not giving up.

On June 6, 1999, in the midst of writing this book, I heard over a morning radio station, The Judy Kelbrey Show, announcing that the state of Oklahoma had reinstated a bill regarding parents disciplining their children. I hoped that legislators in other states would come to realize that the law against parents disciplining their own is resulting in parents becoming submissive, which is amplifying our children to become more rebellious.

I came to realize that an enormous number of responsible parents are in trouble for a number of reasons. Some of the reasons are quite apparent, while some are much more subtle. For parents to be aware of these things, they must take important steps, such as getting educated on the surroundings in their community. Parents at times face extremely difficult obstacles when it comes to human services, health and rehabilitative services and various educational establishments. These services themselves can seem like monsters looming in the dark, waiting to pounce. It can be most frightening. Parents of yesterday were given respect; they were looked upon with honor and dignity. Now, unfortunately, things have changed. The Judicial System is unbalanced. A parent may do something that people in high places can't comprehend because they have never been there. Yet, the parent can be placed in a category that he or she doesn't deserve. Now, they must face the liberal special interest groups who say the parent can no longer do their job. In light of that, some cannot, but most do truly know their jobs as parents and do quite well.

Our children, in this world of electronics, have to live and face things that were unheard of twenty five years ago. Again, I must express how important it is to educate yourself on how to properly raise your offspring so that you don't find yourself in my shoes due to ignorance. As parents, one should inquire information regarding the law and its regulations in the state and county in which you reside. Read on certain issues at your leisure. Remember, there is no defense for ignorance. Furthermore, as a parent, involvement in the community is important as well. There are many support groups that you can get involved with that can offer you help. More importantly, pay attention to what your child is being taught because education is much different now-a-days. Our children have to deal with things like outcome-based education, overcrowded schools and a lack of teachers. Our children are suffering when they should not be. We, as parents, have the right to conduct our lives as we see fit. It might not be up to someone else's standards, but for most of us, we try to do the best we can. Our children need us to properly raise them. They need our love and support and our discipline. These are trying times; and it is time to take a stand with ourselves, our lives and the lives of our children.

Children are our future. We, as parents, must guide them to a bright and better one. Falling in love with your mate and not falling in love with your child's upbringing will come back to haunt you. Needless to say, I am the haunted and I regret the decisions that I repeatedly made.

Every day, I read and heard the news about our children. It's depressing to hear the awful things that are committed by some of our children. For instance, there was the Littleton, Colorado school massacre where two teenage kids went on a shooting spree killing fourteen students, one teacher and then, themselves. Or how about the 6-year-old girl who was shot to death by a 6-year-old boy at Buell Elementary in Mount Morris Township, Michigan? As the teacher dialed 911 on her cell phone, the boy who fired the shot slipped out of the classroom and ducked into the boys' bathroom and stuffed the gun in a waste can. This boy was not even in his teens yet and he had already learned this horrible behavior.

I'm quite sure this 6-year-old youngster didn't hang out on the street corner to pick up such behavior. His peers are of his age, and if they beheld such a violent mentality, then where did his peers learn such behavior?

Would it be safe to say that there's a good chance that the boy didn't learn this violent behavior from his peers and that his bad association was not of flesh? In Webster's New World Dictionary, the word *associate* under the third category means: to connect in the mind.

Unfortunately, we have a bigger challenge before us because it's not always about what type of child your child is associating with, but what *thing* your child is associating with.

Reader, do you see where I'm heading?

Sad to say, there is another issue that we parents continue to ignore, and that is what our children watch on television. The violence on many television programs can soil our children's young minds. It can put their minds in a mode that is reflected before them. For example, the 13-year-old boy out of Miami who admitted that he accidentally killed a 6-year-old girl while imitating a pro wrestler. The little girl was literally beaten to death. Now, should the boy get life in prison? I say no because I'm aware of the damage that television can influence, and I take my hat off to the parents who allow their siblings to watch only Family, Disney and Educational channels.

Parents, it doesn't matter if you want to accept this or not, but television, vulgar rap music and violent video games are things that play a big part in why our children do some of the awful things that they do. I'm a living witness who actually heard young prisoners admit during a general conversation, that the rap music is what amped them to rob and shoot because that was what the song was all about.

Look, I don't want to make anyone mad here, but if you're not taking a stand to govern the things your children watch on television and the games and music that they entertain themselves with, then you are contributing bad influences on your child. We, as parents, need to realize this and not support such entertainment.

On June 8, 1999 USA Today stated that the Republican's House Speaker, Dennis Haistert, and Judiciary Committee Chairman Henry Hyde, began to work on a youth crime bill in hopes of decreasing the lawlessness that is being committed by our young ones. It's evident that the youth crime rate is climbing and it's going to continue to climb until we realize that a better society for us to live in starts at home.

Here's the twist: in Florida, we are not allowed to give our children a good ass whipping. If a parent uses a belt or switch on their child, the parent may lose their freedom. God forbid if your child is rebellious and knows of this law. However, the Florida law does allow the parent to spank on their buttocks with open hand until the hand stings, which is an indication to stop. There are other states that don't want parents to give an effective discipline. Just to name one, Massachusetts.

I read an article about a Boston minister and the headline read: *Minister Beats Rap after Spanking His Son*. The minister said that he had disciplined his 12-year-old son with the end of a leather strap. The Department of Social Services filed an abuse finding, but later offered to drop the charge if he agreed not to spank the boy again.

How would the boy now respond after seeing that his father would get punished if he tried to chastise him?

This law has indeed caused a conundrum with families of all nationalities because some kids need a good rearing, whereas with some you don't have to lift a finger to. Needless to say, that wasn't my case, I took a stand that put me under a ban, but the question still remained: Where Does The Parent Stand?

We stand in a country that was founded and based on Biblical principles, and through the history of this country, its leaders have continuously found ways to circumvent and compromise the beliefs, views and purpose of this country's pioneers.

We stand before people, who can be considered, by today's standards, as modern day Pharisees, who are scholars of the law and because of their learning have been given positions of authority, prestige and honor. Because of pride and fear that they'll fall from glory, they have chosen to ignore the underlying issues and true purposes of these laws for the sole purpose of justifying their existence.

We stand before some collective and individual judicial bodies, which have been blinded by their greed and driven by their own political aspirations.

We stand before certain Judges and lawyers who are atheists and contentious people, whose love flows abundantly when they are only thinking of themselves or their bank accounts.

We stand before legislatures who would pass a bill making it legal for a parent to kill a child by way of abortion, and then this same legislative body adopts laws that send parents to prison for giving their child a good ass whipping when needed.

We stand before people like Judy Hawkins, who swore an oath to uphold the Constitution of the United States, a constitution that's based on Biblical principles and yet, her lifestyle, based on her sexual orientation, is an abomination to such principles and its Creator.

We stand before a system whose leaders are so arrogant that they can't see that they commit moral robbery, when in their own minds they've established equality between themselves and God by setting themselves up as a Divine Authority.

We stand before a nation that screams freedom from coast to coast, and yet within the confines of its territories, it establishes a system that forces its beliefs and values upon God fearing citizens, and strips mothers and fathers of essential parental rights. A nation that has to sit and watch the President prepare to recruit and send our children off to die by means of war, when none of the soldiers are his own.

We stand before a nation in which the media reminds us that the scribes of Biblical days, whose purpose was to keep records of laws and teachings of the prophets, were subverted by their own lust and sought to be recognized in their work. Just like the days of old, the media, our modern day scribes, are destroying the lives of American citizens, not for the sake of truth or to keep the public informed, but for individual or network popularity. These are people who will mock an NFL player like

Tim Tebow, by using God's name in vain and causing controversy and mockery just to ramp up ratings and their overwhelming desire to be number one at any cost.

We stand in the shadows of our children, who have all the power in our household, thanks to new legislation and recently enacted laws.

We stand to lose our children if they commit certain crimes and the court will certify them over as adults and send them to prison for life, or even death. Yet a parent better not dare raise a strap at them.

We stand in the midst of a nation that has stripped us of all parental discretion, a nation that has adopted a system that determines when the children that we have the responsibility to raise and support, can be punished as an adult. Parents have no say in this decision, although we know our children best.

We stand on confused and unstable legs, knowing that at any time, our children can snatch the rug right out from under us with one word to authorities.

We stand bowed before our children, not because we are weak or ineffective parents, but because the judicial system has its bureaucratic foot on our parental necks, severely limiting our ability to be productive and aggressive parents.

We stand out of the way while our children exercise their judicial power to control us and manipulate us into being obedient and submissive parents.

We stand before a nation that voted for Mr. Barack Obama, an African American, to become President of the United States, then suddenly, Republicans and other hateful groups come out the woodwork like never before to oppose and denounced everything President Obama stood for, turning this great nation into a political circus and refusing to come to an agreement because of the color of his skin, not because of increased taxes.

This country is considered one of the world's superpowers, and in spite of my disagreement with many of these country policies, I still love this nation, and I'm proud to be one of its citizens.

I point out what's wrong because it's my country, I love people, and it's my love that leads me to write. It was my love for my sons that led me to do what I felt was needed that day that I disciplined them. It seems to me that if this country was founded on Biblical principles regarding how to discipline our children, then the laws enacted in this country would have to conform to such fundamentals as our forefathers intended. Instead, we enact laws that conflict with God's Law's.

What troubles me most of all is that the principles established by this country's founders may no longer be applicable in today's society. With all the scholars and experts in sociology, ministers of the gospels, and historians with all the knowledge and better understanding we have in this country today, why can't we see that the further we get away from the intentions and teachings of our forefathers, the further our children get away from being submissive and obedient to their parents?

I remember reading that this country's pioneers established that there should be a separation of church and state. But our leaders of today – the politicians, legislatures, judges – have distorted, minimized, compromised and even dismissed those Biblical principles that were so dear to our forefathers, until they have completely rearranged that whole separation thing that was so important at the beginning of this nation's life. Unfortunately, there is still a separation, but only now the state separates the church.

Christ established the church, so the principles set forth to govern this country was born of Christ. This is a perfect example of what the prophet, Isaiah, was alluding to in this excerpt of *Isaiah: 9:6* "For unto us a child is born, unto us a son is given, and the Government shall be upon his shoulder."

I believe the youth of this nation have embarked upon a very destructive path. Our society as a whole, with its insidious rules and double standards, are on a never-ending quest for that ever elusive thing we call, freedom.

AFTERWORD

In December of 2001, at age thirty-six, I was released to my family. My oldest son Lil Toler was in jail and on his way to prison. I intervened and was able to get his sentence reduced to House Arrest. Tangy had a baby boy she named Kelvin, the spitting image of her. Later I learned that Kelvin was no doubt my son. I proudly visited her and my son. Unfortunately, I started driving over the road. Swallowed up by wants and needs, my visitation to keep a good relationship with my children again weakened. To make a long story short, somehow or another, all my children from the oldest to my youngest, was off the chain. They had no direction as to where they were headed. Eventually, I had my two oldest children come and live with me and my wife Sybil as I took the road. That is when I discovered that the word *disrespect* was an understatement. My beloved ones were like mobsters. I tried to reason with them, but their minds were already poisoned. I was crushed to see the state my kids were in. I had to dismiss them from my home. Things weren't going as I had planned. By my choice, Sybil and I later separated. A few years passed, and I then divorced Sybil for a younger woman.

On December 14th, 2010 I married a thirty-six year old woman by the name of Tonita Williams, the woman I mentioned earlier on the acknowledgment page.

Nevertheless, let's touch on a few things.

Ladies, why is it when an absent dad decides to show his face again, the mother and the teen approach dad as if all they want is to see what they could get out of him. Damn him as a person! To me, that is wrong. That type of approach makes fathers want to leave and never return.

I firmly believe that one of the reasons the statistics for deadbeat dads is so high is because of you women who are associated with them. *Yeah I said it!*

You fathers, I know how it is: damned if we do, damned if we don't. But still, the statistics regarding fatherless homes in this country don't lie. Fathers must take a stand and get with their children before they become adults, if not it may be too late. Whatever the reason was that made you inactive in your youngster's life, get over it, return and try to foster a good relationship.

If your child is in his or her teens, do not allow them to put a guilt trip on you and make you become submissive. If you allow guilt to cloud your judgments, your child will sense that and will try to navigate your relationship. Your child may become mouthy toward you. Your child may become manipulative and always have their hands out wanting money. Take a stand and tell your child that you are aware of the decisions that caused you to go away. Ask him or her for forgiveness, and then forgive yourself. You are the father, not some man there to give out money. Softly explain that money can't buy love and that it takes two to hold a good relationship. However, it's also important to get your child to see that they can pick up a phone and call to say hello. If you end conversations with *I love you*, the child should feel comfortable enough to reciprocate. Simple acts like this can do wonders. Give it your all to express to them that communication is very important. Furthermore, if a child shows interest in his or her absentee parent, there is a far greater chance for the two to develop a good ongoing relationship. Money, quality time, etc… will follow.

If you are an absent father, *FIND YOUR CHILDREN! THEY NEED YOU!*

The United Nations Children's Fund says fifty percent of the white children born in the United States since 1980 will spend part of their childhood raised by single parents. For black children, the percentage is about eighty percent.

This crisis of fatherless children is a nationwide problem. I believe that one of the largest factors in the creation of dysfunctional families is the lack of a fatherly figure in a child's life. Furthermore, we as fathers are responsible for our children, whether we remain involved with the mother or not. Our children need us. It is not the responsibility of the DCF (Department Of Children And Families), CPS (Child Protective Services) or any other sources to raise and help support our children; it is our own. Therefore, if the mother of your children makes you feel angry, unappreciated or unaccepted, please don't give up! Seek and hold a good relationship with your children.

To be a father, you must first be a man, and parts of our fatherly responsibilities consist of passing the lessons of manhood that we have learned onto our sons. We need to teach them what it means to be a man and you can't do that unless you are already one. Don't let relationship issues drive you away from your children. If you do, it will haunt you in the long run. Trust me, I have five boys and two girls, I am a living testimony.

If you and your spouse decide to go your separate ways and there are babies or small children involved, you must not allow yourself to become selfish and not help financially when you can afford to help. On the other hand, if a parent is truly trying to find a job and is in a financial rut, spending quality time is priceless. Yeah, I know that doesn't pay the bills or buy new shoes, but if you're broke, what else can you do? You cannot squeeze blood out of a turnip!

As years passed and times got harder, I didn't let my kids have their way and I stood up to them, they then cursed me out as if I was nothing. I was called names I had never been called. They wanted to fight and curse out their mother. My second oldest son told his own mother to suck his dick. It should be a crime to be so disrespectful towards parents. I hated the state that my kids were in and it seemed hopeless to continue to hold a relationship. It was obvious they didn't give a hoot about me. They were in their twenties and they didn't have any respect for me nor anyone else. It bothered me, but they were grown, and like I said earlier, if you stay away and they become adults, it might be too late for a relationship. For me, it was time to let them go before I caught a charge or be put to death by one of them.

Yeah, that's how bad it had got. Hell, my second to youngest son Kelvin, his teacher called complaining about him disrupting her class and cursing her out, and for me to go get him, and I did, followed by lunch and a long talk. I learned that he also gave his mother pure hell. His mother had to call the police on him more than once due to him cursing her out and raising hell in her house about her crack head lover; then he would straight up take and smoke her cigarettes in her face. My son's excuse was that he was high off of marijuana. He was only fourteen.

Who in the hell had been raising this boy, thugs?

I called Kelvin early the following morning to ask him to spend the day with me. He told me that he was on his way to his girlfriend's house, to call him around six that evening. I was like damn!

Our children are growing up too fast. It's jarring to see how disrespectful they have become. It's safe to say teens today can be extremely dangerous.

This is why a lot of youngsters don't see age forty five. Many die young because God tells us, "The child who disrespects their parents, their days will be cut short." - *Exodus 20:12.*

"Jehovah God's premonition tells us that there will be days like this." – *2 Timothy 3: 1-3.*

"Jehovah also encourages us in *Ephesians 6: 1-3.*"

I felt like something was missing from my life.

God inspired me to write this book in 1996 and to publish it in my late 40's. That would put me around the year 2014.

On January 14, 2011 a month after getting married, my estranged wife gave birth to a beautiful baby boy whom I named Tolerance. Living in this day and time, Tonita and I needed to have some tolerance between us. I'm proud because I was given another chance to be a better father by applying what I have learned. I pray that I am able to develop a respectful child who loves me. I can tolerate that.

On Sunday February 16, 2014 exactly at 11:49am my cell phone rang. An investigator was on the line to inform me of some shocking news that my son Kelvin, at age sixteen, had been locked up for over a year on a robbery charge. His release date from prison would be February 17th the following day. Sadly, his mother was back on drugs and nowhere to be found. I was asked if I could have him released into my custody and see after him.

"Absolutely!"

With open arms.

All of you out there, whatever your dreams are, whatever is in your heart to achieve, and whatever you need to overcome, don't ever give up because you don't know what God has in store for you.

I hope you enjoyed reading my book, and I hope that you picked up on a few pointers that may help you do things differently and make better decisions in your life.

Remember, *forgive* the ones who have offended you.

God Bless.

If you would like to comment about this book, go to tolerlamar@gmail.com

Printed in the United States
By Bookmasters